MW01170749

Why Collectivism Matters

A critique of Collectivism's effects on the African Continent

By Tsu Shipalana

Contents

Preface

'Collectivism matters in the same way crime matters'

Why I wrote this book

One morning I was winding down my evening scrolling through the news channels when I saw a banner at the bottom of my TV screen reading; "Breaking News - Zimbabwean President Emmerson Mnangagwa orders immediate release of Tendai Biti"

Now whether charges brought up against Biti were valid or not was of no concern to me, what struck me was the notion that a president of a nation could simply order a release of a citizen without any due process. I am quite familiar with presidential pardons and granting of amnesties, but I understand that these tend to follow a preconceived and constituted judicial process. This was just another signal that even though some African countries celebrated the ousting of former president Robert Mugabe; as Africans we continue to elect presidents that possess an authoritarian streak in the way they govern. I.e. Biti's case is a judicial matter and true democracies separate the presidency and their judicial system.

Another concern was the fact that voices that objected to the manner in which President Mnangagwa intervened in this matter were in the minority. In Africa, we tend to look at presidents the same way imperial subjects view their king. My thoughts continued down this rabbit hole as I asked myself the following question; why was it the case?

Preface

Trying to answer this question was the catalyst of my journey into African History, African people and Africa in general. My quest to answer this question eventually led to the authoring of this book.

In retrospect, the Tendai Biti issue was of little value in the grander scheme of things, I did not even bother to find out how the matter was concluded. Though insignificant, I mentioned it because it was that little piece of news that triggered my journey that led to this book.

Sometimes in life, it's the insignificant things that tend to trigger a domino effect that eventually leads to a collapse of something bigger, or should I say, something significant. For example, most agree that Rosa Parks' refusal to give up a seat for a white person would have been insignificant if the bus driver just left her alone, but the heavy handedness of the Montgomery law enforcement triggered the mass Montgomery Bus Boycott that was instrumental in the American Civil Rights Movement. One can also mention the South African June 16th protests (1976), where the boorish Apartheid government needlessly opened gunfire on students who were simply asking not to be taught physics and mathematics in Afrikaans. The callousness of the government's response jolted the world (and those within South Africa) into realising the government's brutality and indefensibility. This of course led to the eventual collapse of the Apartheid system. So in a sense, the Tendai Biti news was of little significance to me but was enough to lead me down a journey of immense discovery, thinking and ultimately writing a book. On a quest to answer my "why", the following questions came to mind;

Preface

i. Why Africa keeps electing presidents that don't want to "step down"

ii. Why Africa keeps electing presidents with authoritarian streaks

iii. Why the general ubiquitous poor governance when compared to the rest of the world

I delved into book stores, scouring many book shelves in an effort to answer this burning ultimate WHY question. I should note that at this point, I had yet to decide to write a book. Whenever I had a question or was interested in any topic, I always looked for the one book that would answer some (if not all) of my questions or a book that discussed the topic I was interested in with detail.

I remember a time when I wanted to understand the South African Labour law system for work reasons; I simply bought a book that turned out to be quite useful. I was looking for the same book with regards to my "why". I found many books on Africa, books that depicted our history beautifully, interesting biographies of African prominent figures, economies and African societies. Reading all this literature necessitated reading about philosophies such as uBuntu, various economic theories, classes and ideologies like Marxism, Communism, Capitalism and World History in general. The effort to find out the reason for Africa's current state took me through all these journeys.

In this quest, one thing became very clear to me, although I found some of the answers to my question; the answers did not lie in one singular book. I found my answer through my personal experiences, observations as well as the amalgamation of information attained from various books. It appeared as if the one book I was searching for did not exist, or to show some bit of humility; let me rather say that the book was not easy to find. It was this moment that I thought to myself; "If this one book is so 'hard to find', why don't I just write the book myself". Write a book that bridges the gaps between all these journeys and answer the questions I was confronted with. It is important that when one writes a book, one ensures that the book should have something new to say or in this case, have something new to contribute to the pool of African literature. If I had discovered that singular book, I would have simply added that single book to my long list of "Must reads". I beg the reader to not take this statement as a criticism to the current African literature in circulation; those books contribute a lot to African literature in their own way. The aim is that this book should be able to take the reader from where I was then to where I am today.

In essence, I write the book for my past self. I knew that since there's very little that is unique about me, if the book is informative and engaging to the past me, it will be quite informative and engaging to many like me.

So where was I then, who was this 'past me'? The benefit of being a man of average intelligence is that one is keenly aware of the fact that what one does not know, truly speaking, a lot of people don't know either. Back then, I knew Karl Marx but could not define Marxism and the only metric I had for a politician was corruption and the promises he or she made; I could not even define the term ideology. I knew Hitler was a very bad person and Nazism was a virulent political system but could not name one Nazi other than Adolf Hitler himself. I knew 6 million Jews died in the holocaust during WWII but could not quantify deaths caused by communism. I could not explain the downsides of Socialism or why the USSR failed. I believed that our presidents should emulate leaders like Fidel Castro because Cuba had good doctors and everybody could read (to this day I own a cap with the iconic face of Che Guevara on the forehead - yes that picture). I knew the likes of Kwame Nkrumah, Mobido Keita, Sékou Touré and Julius Nyerere but could not understand why the two were eventually ousted from power by popular demand; a fact most Africans would rather forget. I attributed all of Africa's poverty to the lecherous greed of politicians. Even after all this, my general knowledge of Africa was not below average, like I said before, what I did not know; many people did not know either.

I sincerely believe that we have a knowledge (nevermind wisdom) problem and this lack of knowledge has paved the way for various mountebanks walking amongst us to spread falsehoods in the form of revised history, failed practices and pure sophistry. One major benefit of knowledge is that it equips one with the tools and information required to detect lies. With this book, the reader who possesses the same bit of knowledge and awareness I had then should be more informed and possess a more *nous* understanding of their surrounding and the African political environment once they've finished reading this book. I also hope those already in possession of a higher understanding and nous knowledge appreciate my contribution to the ways in which we can help my beloved African continent reach its full potential.

Chapter 1: Introduction

When one thinks of Africa, one cannot help but confront its governmental failures post-colonialism, its lack of progress, and the current levels of poverty. I don't think you will find many Africans that will deny that when it comes to socio-economic development, we're just not where we should be. Africa has been freed from the grips of imperialism (colonial rule) for over 40 years but has not witnessed much economic and social progress when compared to its Eastern European, Asian and South American counterparts that had experienced similar exploitation (in the negative form) during colonial rule. Countries like Chad, Equatorial Guinea, Somalia, Mozambique and Congo witnessed a reversal in fortunes at one particular time post-independence.

Africans were very much aware of the challenges they faced once their countries attained independence; this sentiment was so widespread that in 1979, The Organisation of African Unity published the *Lagos Plan of Action for the Economic Development of Africa 1980-2000* (The Lagos Plan of Action). This document aimed to redress these challenges and identified Africa's dependence on Western foreign aid as one of the hurdles each country would have to scale to tackle the challenges they faced. As stated in its preamble (introduction);

> *Africa is unable to point to any significant growth rate, or satisfactory index of general well-being, in the past 20 years. Faced with this situation, and determined to undertake measures for the basic restructuring of the economic base of*

1

Introduction

*our continent, we resolved to adopt a far-reaching regional
approach based primarily on collective self-reliance[1].*

The Lagos Plan of Action outlines the challenges the continent
was experiencing in 1980. Amongst other things, the document
laments the continent's lack of growth over the preceding 20
years;

*We view, with distress, that our continent remains the least
developed of all the continents: the total Gross Domestic
Production of our countries being only 2.7 percent of the
world's per capita income and averaging US$ 166[2]*

It goes on to lament the structural weaknesses that adversely
affect food production, basic response to floods, pandemics, and
various other natural disasters.

In 1981, the World Bank also published its independent
document titled The *Accelerated Development in Sub-Saharan
Africa: A Plan for Action* (colloquially known as *The Berg
Report*). This report also sought to study the challenges facing
developing Sub-Saharan Africa and it too recommended policies
that would aim to redress those challenges. Though both reports
were in concurrence with the prevailing state of affairs, this
report differed from the Lagos Plan in the sense that it
emphasized the need to *open up* the economy in order to
stimulate economic growth. The Berg Report deplored the
prevalence of state intervention, price controls and various
forms of import restrictions.

---

[1] https://web.archive.org/web/20070106003042/http://uneca.org/itca/ariportal/docs/lagos_plan.PDF -
page 4
[2] https://web.archive.org/web/20070106003042/http://uneca.org/itca/ariportal/docs/lagos_plan.PDF
page 5

Introduction

These two reports alone serve as actual proof of Africa's awareness of the challenges it faced post-liberation; regrettably, these reports also highlight that very little progress has been made since 1980 as many of the observations in these reports are still valid today. For instance, if one looks at the 2021 Fragile States Index (FSI) produced by The Fund for Peace (FFP); one sees that 15 of the 20 lowest-performing countries are in the African continent (Central African Republic, Chad, Sudan, Zimbabwe, Ethiopia, Nigeria, Guinea, Cameroon, Burundi, Eritrea, Libya, and Mali[3]). The FFP looks at factors such as[4];

> *i) The Security Apparatus - Threats to the state such as terrorism, coups, mutinies and rebel movements*
> *ii) Factionalized Elites – the fragmentation of state institutions along ethnic, class, clan, racial or religious lines*
> *iii) Group Grievance – Strong divisions between different groups as a result of particular characteristic(s), current or historic events.*
> *iv.) The Economy - Economic stagnation or decline (Based on GDP, unemployment, inflation, poverty and foreign debt)*
> *v) Economic Inequality - Disparities in standards of living and socio-economic progress amongst various groups*
> *vi.) Human Flight and Brain Drain - The loss of skilled workforce as a result of emigration for political or economic reasons*
> *vii) State Legitimacy - Confidence the population has in the government*
> *viii) Public Services - Presence of government services such as policing, sanitation, tax collection, availability of health care facilities, etc.)*

---

[3] https://fragilestatesindex.org/global-data/
[4] https://fragilestatesindex.org/methodology/

Introduction

ix) Human Rights - Protection of fundamental human rights (free press, an independent judiciary, free and effective opposition, right to trial etc.)
x) Demographic Pressures - Food supply, the proneness of droughts or epidemics
xi) Refugees and Internally Displaced Persons - Inflow of refugees seeking asylum or the number of people forced to flee the country as a result of well-perceived imminent danger
xii) External Intervention.

This report clarifies that some of the factors that count against a country lay beyond the country's control; factors like the inflow of asylum seekers or the challenges posed by geographical landscapes. However, the report also supports the widely held sentiment of many Africans who are increasingly becoming disillusioned by the continent's insufficient development. You might have to visit some of these nations to fully comprehend the veracity of this statement. The poverty ranges from poverty in the form of living in dilapidated governmental housing to poverty in the form of mud huts or houses built from corrugated zinc. In 2017 for instance, the infrastructure was so dilapidated that the Zimbabwean government declared a State of Disaster for all roads in the country to expedite the release of funds for maintenance and repair works[5].

The lack of adequate healthcare facilities necessary to sustain and prolong life is still a problem. In 2018, the World Bank statistics showed that the average life expectancy of Sub-Saharan Africa is 61, compared to 75 years for the average Latin American & the Caribbean man[6] (the Australian life expectancy is 83, 81 in the United Kingdom and 69 in India). There are

---

[5] Zimbabwean roads - https://allafrica.com/stories/202102100704.html
https://www.bbc.com/news/av/world-africa-39116532
[6] https://data.worldbank.org/indicator/SP.DYN.LE00.IN?locations=ZG

cases where a 150km radius area is serviced by one poorly staffed hospital (one doctor with little equipment). The St Joseph's hospital in Uganda serves the whole surrounding villages and some South Sudanese nationals.

Africa suffers from poor infrastructure, be it schools as some remain unsheltered, telecommunications, internet connectivity, lack of running water and sanitation or vaccines that would have eradicated diseases that have been eradicated in most 1st world countries. As of 2017, Africa is yet to be declared polio-free unlike other continents with the exception of Afghanistan and Pakistan. The Ebola virus is another one that periodically wreaks havoc whenever it rears its head; the Congo region is one particular example.

Same story
Africa has always had a governance problem, and when one looks at our history; one quickly realizes that most leaders we've elected in the past 60 years have turned out to be despots, military dictators or outright corrupt bandits that stripped their countries off their resources for personal gain.

My fellow African remembers his disappointment as he witnessed the once promising government of Ahmed Sekou Toure from Guinea degenerate into a repressive dictatorship that led to the Mamadou Boiro concentration camp.

During President Ahmed Sékou Touré's reign, Camp Boiro became a dreaded symbol of his authoritarianism. Those perceived to be Touré's opponents were interned in this camp, a concentration camp where political prisoners were beaten, tortured, and starved to death. It is estimated that over 5 000 people were thrown into this camp[7], the list of prisoners includes people like Achkar Marof (famous actor and former Guinean ambassador to the United Nations), Diawadou Barry (Minister of Economy & Finance), Fodéba Keïta (dancer, musician, writer, and the former Minister of Defence, who as irony would have it, helped construct the camp) Mouctar Diallo and Namory Keïta who were starved to death during their stay in the camp[8].

From the inception of its independent rule, the African continent has been plagued by collectivism. Like the USSR, countries such as Algeria, Angola, Djibouti, Equatorial Guinea, Egypt Eritrea, Ghana, Guinea, Guinea-Bissau, Libya, Madagascar, Mali, Mauritania, São Tomé and Príncipe, Senegal, Seychelles, Sierra Leone, Sudan, Tanzania, Tanganyika, Uganda, Zambia, Zanzibar, Rwanda, Republic of Côte d'Ivoire and DRC all at one point or another, operated as one party states under a centrally planned government.

To this day we still see countries that have remained *de-facto* one-party states with current opposition parties serving as nothing more than ornaments meant to shield off any international criticism of being one-party states. In theory, these countries (such as Burundi, Cameroon, Chad, Republic of the Congo, Djibouti, Equatorial Guinea, Ethiopia, Namibia, Rwanda, South Sudan, Uganda, Western Sahara and Zimbabwe) are multiparty states in the sense that other parties exist; however, any adulation of their "democracies" may be regarded as mere puffery as the opposition has little hope of winning elections nevermind campaigning freely.

---

[7] Human Rights Watch - GUINEA Dying for Change Brutality and Repression by Guinean Security Forces in Response to a Nationwide Strike Vol 19
[8] Gomez, Alsény René - La Guinée peut-elle être change (Can Guinea be changed?)

Introduction

Dr Kwame Nkrumah was another leader that showed great promise once he took office as the first Prime Minister of Ghana, a country that was then regarded as the richest nation in Africa. But following the implementation of a string of socialist policies, he turned the golden jewel of Africa, the Gold Coast, into an oppressive authoritarian state. In 1963 for example, at the zenith of his rule, he unconstitutionally removed Chief Justice Kobina Arku Korsah for having failed to convict 3 of the 5 political opponents in a recent treason trial.

The trial was held following the August 1st, 1962 attack on Nkrumah's life in the Eastern town of Kulungugu; in what would be known as the Kulungugu Bomb attack. The Ghanaian leader was travelling from a diplomatic meeting with the Upper Volta (Burkina Faso) president Maurice Yaméogo when bad roads culminated by extreme rainy conditions forced his convoy into a pit stop in the village of Kulungugu in the Bawku District North-East of Ghana. As the president was greeting school children who had been eagerly anticipating his convoy, a lone figure of a school child immerged from the crowd and approached the leader holding a bouquet of flowers. But as the child came closer, members of the security force (Captain Samuel Buckman in particular) noticed that the ticking sounds he kept hearing grew louder as the child came closer and instinctively tackled Kwame Nkrumah to the ground; timeously saving the leader and those around from instant death[9].

The worst thing one can do to one's fellow countrymen is to attempt to kill a despotic leader and fail; for this subjects

---

[9] Johnson, Paul - History of the Modern World page 512 (Johnson)
https://www.eaumf.org/ejm-blog/2017/8/1/august-1st-1962-nkrumah-is-injured-by-an-attempt-on-his-life-from-a-bomb-in-kulungugu

Introduction

everybody within that country to a rage and paranoia that knows no bounds.

This attempt on the leader's life was the perfect *Reichstag fire*[10] event that Nkrumah would use as a pretext for curbing the people's civil liberties and the purging of political opponents.

Following the removal of Chief Justice Kobina Arku Korsah, President Nkrumah appointed a biddable panel of judges that retried and convicted all of the accused. Adding to the destruction of the respect for the judiciary and rule of law, Ghana's economy was left in a poorer state than it was in the pre-colonial era due to confiscatory socialist policies that were in place; leading to suffering and unrest amongst the population. Such mass disillusionment among locals eventually led to a coup d'état in February 1966, that drove the leader into exile in Guinea.

In Africa, the Coup d'état became a very common way of forcing a change of leadership amid deteriorating living standards (some were mere power grabs). By the end of 2018, Africa had undergone 113 coup d'états[11]. The lack of development compared to other nations around the world confirms the fact that the African continent suffers from a cancerous poor form of governance. Government

---

[10] *The Reichstag fire was the 27 February 1933 arson attack on the Reichstag building, home of the German parliament in Berlin. Hitler's government attributed the fire to communist agitators. The Nazi Party used the fire as a pretext to claim that communists were plotting against the German government, which made the fire pivotal in the establishment of Nazi Germany

[11] Coup d'etats in Africa: The Emergence, Prevalence and Eradication - Valery Besong
https://journals.sagepub.com/doi/10.1177/07388942209348821

maladministration has resulted in little development and
persistent high levels of poverty.

False attributes to African poverty

The question remains, what's the cause of all this? What has
happened in Africa for her to experience such misfortunes? Now
before I attempt to answer this question I feel it necessary to
take a moment to give credit to the craftiness of the politician
for his ability to distort and deflect any criticism of African
governance; the politician's ability to intentionally contort all
forms of criticism into racism is one of his greatest attributes. I
am referring to the constant labelling of all critics as racists or
sell-outs motivated by a (self) hatred of black governance in
general; a phenomenon many citizens are all too familiar with.
Each criticism is labelled as racist attacks by adversaries that
wish to recolonize Africa through sabotage, trickery, and pure
sophistry.

The politician and their apologists have attributed the high
levels of poverty to a lack of education during the colonial
years; poor infrastructure, poor structural development,
economic sanctions, civil wars, and the corruption and greed of
the ruling elite.

It's Education!

From the podiums they shout; it's Education!
Even if one managed to successfully (and rightfully) pin the
blame on the feet of the colonizers, we should also acknowledge
that one simply has to educate one generation to overcome the
insufficiencies of the past. Post-liberation governments had
ample time to open up the educational spaces to the poor
uneducated masses. The current poor education system is the

result of poor governance and a lack of structural development toward educational institutions (like school buildings). It is a secondary effect that cannot be used as an attribute to the root causes of poverty. A good government has good schools.

When one speaks of education, it is easy to forget that there are many types of education, we normally think of learning mathematics, science, and improving basic literacy but disregard many other forms of education. Although this kind of education is one we should cherish, it's also worth noting that this kind of education does not necessarily lead to wealth creation. A nation needs artisanal skilled individuals. Although teachers form an integral part of society, one cannot build a nation from only breeding school teachers - Zimbabwe bears testament to this. Wealth is generated from production, the production that stems from the business acumen and entrepreneurial education that *Rich Dad Poor Dad* author Robert Kiyosaki often rails about in all his writings. The exercise of this kind of education is largely dependent on the openness of the market and is often worthless without liberty. Cuba has a high literacy rate just like most African countries today have high literacy rates; but has not seen much economic progress due to its implementation of policies that just don't lead to wealth generation (However, one must commend Cubans for prolonging the life of the 1950's Buick, albeit not by choice).

To become rich living in Cuba, Swaziland or Angola is very difficult. For instance, Cuba*[12] for one, did not allow most

---

[12] *In 2019, Cuba passed a constitution that paved the way for private ownership of property
https://scholarlycommons.law.case.edu/jil/vol52/iss1/28/
https://www.gacetaoficial.gob.cu/es/constitucion-de-la-republica-de-cuba-proclamada-el-10-de-abril-de-2019
https://horizontecubano.law.columbia.edu/news/constitutional-regulation-private-property

forms of ownership (until 2019); Swaziland is an autocracy and most other countries are plagued with corruption that one cannot get ahead without clandestine connections to some government bureaucrat. In these environments, education just does not take you far. For many years, India produced many learned citizens, but the caste system, for example, put a cap on many wishing to get ahead through education. Many Indians looking to climb up the socio-economic ladder or those who wished to marry across the caste lines were forced to migrate. The African should know this because the African is inherently entrepreneurial but is shackled by an inconducive socio-economic environment.

Secondly, we've got countries that inherited poor educational structures but still saw huge economic progress. Typical examples would be countries like China, Thailand, UAE, Vietnam, Botswana and India which have proven that the inheritance of poor educational infrastructure (and an uneducated populace) should not be an unwavering perpetual hindrance to socio-economic progress. These nations experienced rapid growth from the '40s and '50s onwards. These countries have proven that once good governance is in place, the society can build structures and implement policies that make it possible to improve the education system and improve literacy rates. Zimbabwe had a good education system but bad governance meant that the country could not provide its citizens with an environment conducive to economic growth. Education (or a lack of it) is not the cause of our current plight, it is a result. One must reject the notion that a poor education system is the cause of our current predicament.

Structural Development

The inheritance of poor structural development is another excuse that is thrown around. This is another claim I chose not to dispute because even if it were true, this excuse fails to cut the mustard. After all, one has to accept that poor infrastructure is the starting point of any developing nation. It cannot be the cause for the lack of economic and social progress; the above examples of China, Thailand, UAE, Vietnam, and Botswana belie the notion that the inheritance of good infrastructure is a prerequisite to socio-economic progress. Remember, we are lamenting the lack of development, not the absence of a First World society in Africa (even the staunchest of critics or optimists will admit that that's a bridge too far).

The United States rose from a backward colony of the British Empire to a world power regardless of its poor structural development at the time of independence. Germany was utterly destroyed - twice -after the World Wars but managed to rise from its ashes to become one of the leading European economies today. Once again, good governments are able to build up a nation from ruins; bad governments take ready-built nations into ruins.

Sanctions

To blame sanctions for lack of economic progress is like a prisoner blaming his imprisonment for a lack of his economic progress, both men might be correct in their assessment, however, we clearly see that there is something they are not telling us; that is, why they were in that position in the first place.

Introduction

Sanctions were generally imposed on countries due to poor governance and human rights violations, they were implemented as punitive measures for atrocities committed against citizens i.e. Zimbabwe, Uganda, Congo and South Africa. This is also a secondary effect just like in the case of education.

We've seen quite a few African nations that have never experienced economic sanctions but still failed to achieve any economic progress, we've also witnessed instances where nations *recalcitrantly* maintained their *modus operandi* proving that the imposed sanctions failed in their intended purpose. Rhodesia, the Apartheid South African government and Iran are classic examples of governments that resisted the effects of economic sanctions. Apartheid South Africa had one of the strongest economies in Africa despite world *condemnation* coupled with UN economic sanctions. In fact, we see how these two nations managed to take great leaps forward in socio-economic progress as a result of international isolation. The arms embargo imposed on the Apartheid government had the unintended consequence of forcing the government into developing an arms manufacturing industry that produced the strongest military force (and military exporter) in Africa and subsequently achieved nuclear capabilities. As former Apartheid president FW De Klerk stated in his autobiography;

> *For the most part, South Africa succeeded in circumventing sanctions, either through import substitution or the adoption of sophisticated sanction-busting strategies. In many respects the sanctions appeared to achieve the opposite effect of the intention, as is so often the case when governments interfere with economic processes for ideological purposes: the arms embargo led to South Africa establishing its own highly sophisticated armament industry, to the point where armaments*

became a major export; the oil embargo led to South Africa
establishing the world's largest and most effective oil [industry]
from coal industry which provided the base for the expansion of
the country's entire chemical sector[13]

Some will protest that the intrinsic effeteness of the sanctions against the apartheid government was the reason why that government managed to circumvent sanctions (through various strategies to remain well connected to the outside economic world), but their ability to circumvent sanctions only serves to prove that sanctions don't always serve as a deterrent. However, I don't believe anyone prefers sanctions imposed on their country unless it's for political reasons of course.

Nonetheless, only bad governments experience worldwide imposed sanctions, sanctions are not the cause of bad governance - a bad government self-inflicts sanctions in the same way that it self-inflicts poverty (or the criminal that self-inflicts his imprisonment).

Civil War, surely!
I cannot dispute that some African nations have also been negatively impacted by war; there is merit to the claim that countries are poorer today as a result of internal conflict. Countries like Lebanon, Syria, Congo, Somalia, Iraq and Sudan etc. have gone through a total collapse of everyday normal life due to fighting and violence brought by civil wars. One also accepts that countries that bring civil wars to an end generally get back to similar levels of experienced before the civil unrest prosperity (countries such as India, Ethiopia, and Yugoslavian territories surpass it). Japan was reconstructed within 7 years

---

[13] de Klerk FW, The Last Trek, page 70

after the atomic bombs were dropped over the Japanese cities of Hiroshima and Nagasaki. Civil war is indeed destructive, but several countries have proven that it is not a death nail; Angola and Nigeria are countries that give testament to this claim.

Let's discuss Corruption

Then we come to corruption, a devil that has plagued governance beyond Ancient Greece to the almighty Roman Empire; corruption and greed are the most commonly cited reasons for why we are where we are today. Although there's a lot of validity to this, we need to remember that these are human flaws prevalent in all human beings in all societies, but why do they seem to affect us (Africa) differently? Even prosperous countries are governed by the very same human species that governs Africa; their prosperous society is plagued by as many avaricious politicians as societies in developing nations. Yet we continue to see huge disparities in wealth when comparing both societies, these first-world countries still managed to achieve better development and attain higher standards of living compared to African societies.

One factor that explains this disparity is that these countries manage to throttle the actions of their corrupt leaders by limiting the overall authority politicians have in government. Corruption destroys a country when immense power is bestowed on its leaders, the leaders are able to shield themselves from scrutiny ensuring that their corruption remains covered and as a result, unpunished.

It is not that these nations are governed by better men (and women), but that their system does not make stealing money easy; If the system depends on man's nature and goodwill, the system is destined to fail because, like all systems at one point or another, eventually come under the tutelage of bad-natured individuals who end up destroying the system from within. Africa experiences the same challenges experienced in other countries worldwide but seems to be worse off in general. Despite having one or two countries in the continent having a footprint on the economic world stage, sadly these countries proved to be the exception rather than the general trend.

Africa's current levels of poverty are not due to poor education, sanctions, civil wars, corruption, greed, poor infrastructure or structural development. Africa is poor today because Africa has a wealth-generating problem. It is not that Africans do not know how to generate wealth in their personal capacity, but that at a macroscopic level, we implement (elect) government structures that do not stimulate wealth generation; in fact, we implement governmental structures and policies that often become impediments to wealth generation. It is not a problem that is endemic to Africa; history regales us with many tales of great societies like the Roman Empire, Ottoman Empires, Israel, China, England, and Greece that at one point had the very same wealth-generating problem we experienced in recent years. In essence, we do not elect leaders that know how to build a government that is best suited for economic growth.

Enough with the Africa-Bashing

But enough of the Africa-bashing narrative, as I stated before, although the current state of the continent warrants severe criticism, this book will not be another work that seeks to outline the poverty and ailments of this beautiful continent. This will not be another *Africa-do-better* rant that excoriates the African in his capacity; Readers can open a copy of Chika

Onyeani's *Capitalist Nigger* for such entertainment. Once again, that path has been thoroughly explored through the many volumes of books that address poverty. Africans are as gifted in talent and intellect as peoples of other continents, yet we cannot seem to get governance right[14].

I was interested in exploring our modern history and the fundamental steps we've taken to get to where we are today. As an African myself, I felt that it was quite important to ensure that I view the matter objectively, and to remove any forms of emotionalism for my observations to maintain some sense of truthfulness and rationality.

We generally get defensive when confronted with the failings of African governments, especially when the reproach happens to come from those foreign to the continent, (the *'Blair keep your England, and let me keep my Zimbabwe'* quote by Robert Mugabe comes to mind).

Another reason for our chagrin is that some of these critics happen to be the very same individuals who were critical of Africa's decolonization from the very begining, arguing that Africans were not ready to govern themselves. Individuals with valid and constructive criticism are lumped into the same group as these eternal naysayers who've always been rooting for Africa to fail even before she had attained her independence. In

---

[14] To quote the Lagos Action of Plan once more;
In assessing those problems, we are convinced that Africa's underdevelopment is not inevitable. Indeed, it is a paradox when one bears in mind the immense human and natural resources of the continent. In addition to its reservoir of human resources, our continent has 97 percent of world reserves of chrome, 85 percent of world reserves of platinum, 64 percent of world reserves of manganese, 25 percent of world reserves of uranium, and 13 percent of world reserves of copper, without mentioning bauxite, nickel and lead; 20 percent of world hydro-electrical potential, 20 percent of traded oil in the world (if we exclude the United States and the USSR); 70 percent of world cocoa production; one-third of world coffee production, 50 percent of palm produce, to mention just a few - Lagos Plan of Action – Point number 5 -

fact, they will probably argue that Africa's current failures appear to have substantiated their views; however, countries like Egypt, India and Botswana which were also at the receiving end of similar gloomy deprecating sentiments belie this notion. To lament Africa's poor socio-economic development is not an advocacy toward a return to colonialism; notwithstanding the fact that Africans have a right to govern themselves.

No matter how disillusioned we may be by our current circumstances, you will struggle to find Africans willing to take up the option of returning to the colonial days. Unfortunately, our defensiveness works to the benefit of our failing leaders as well. Those constantly cheering for the demise of black rule raise the African's defensive shield, which renders most Africans inclined to perceive any constructive criticism as foreign attacks by the very same cheerleaders angling and wishing for their failure. The black South Africans that were critical of the Zuma government (and ANC) were admonished and often derided as *Clever blacks*. In the words of British political writer Guy Arnold;

> *Several African leaders found little difficulty in making the transition from popular nationalists fighting the colonial oppressors into one-party rule dictator who believed himself to be above the law and would indeed be all powerful until his turn came to be overthrown in a coup. The fact that such behaviour was all too apparent gave much satisfaction to reactionaries in the former metropolitan powers who had argued that their colonies were not ready for independence and the fact of their satisfaction led many Africans to support their*

tyrants since they could not bring themselves to agree with their former colonial masters[15].

Our antagonism toward any criticism allowed the inherent collectivist mindset to prosper. This was because everyone understood - analogous to a bundle of sticks - that a collectivised army is in a stronger position to defend *against attacks* than a fragmented one. Unfortunately, the collectivist mindset is better in times of war, but not very much so in peace times.

Africa is diverse in languages, religions, traditional and cultural practices but quite uniform in one arena; we generally harbour a collectivist mindset and cherish collectivism as a whole. The collective mindset seeps into our political thinking, whether in the form of Marxism, theocracies, Pan-Africanism or Fascism; our ideologies come in many variants but they all share one commonality, they impose the tyranny of the collective over the individual.

I have always been frustrated by Africa's undying commitment to Collectivism because I believe that it is this commitment that prevents Africa from coming even close to winning its fight against poverty.

Prosperous nations continue to prove that a successful economy is one that is individual-centric, the free market system has won the economic debate; it aims not to impose the collective will of the society over the individual. This is a concept we grasp to its fullest in a judicial system, but fail to transfer that same understanding to the socio-economic sphere. In our courts,

---

[15] Arnold G, Africa A Modern History, page 235

people are prosecuted individually and each case is arbitrated individually in order to reach a just outcome.

In Africa, this collectivist mindset has continued to hinder our economic progress in the same way collectivism hindered economic progress wherever it has been implemented historically. This collective mindset breeds Collectivism.

When one mentions "Collectivism", one may think of Marxism, the ideology popularized by Karl Marx. However, the carapace of collectivism covers ideologies much broader than Marxism and Communism. The South African Nationalist Party (NP) was vehemently anti-communist but was besotted with their racial "superiority", thus extremely tribal and subsequently, collectivist in their thinking. The Collective Will passed laws like the Immorality Act and Mixed Marriages Act that prohibited inter-racial marriages and sexual relations of the individual. All Afrikaners were expected to postulate and follow the mythical belief of *God's chosen people* (Calvinists); resulting in the labelling of any individual straying from this basic 'truth' as race traitors or worse, enemies of the race

We have a lot of collectivists that might not believe that they are Marxists, but do in fact unknowingly behave in a manner advocated by the works of Karl Marx, Freidrich Engels, Ludwig Feuerbach, Jean-Jacques Rousseau, Lenin and various leaders and philosophers that were leading advocates of such societies. Hence we have the strains in the form of Socialism, Fascism, Nazism, Maoism, Leninism, Stalinism, Jacobinism (preceded Marx) and *villagization*; these strains might have their own agitators but what they all have in common is that they put the collective, the state, above any human right or the individual.

A window Into the Future

The battle for the last 200 years has always been ideological, history has taught us that the ideology a leader subscribes to shapes their whole leadership; from ideology, one can predict the leader's actions, the consequences of their actions and the environment in which his policies will create.

In Africa, I believe that we don't pay enough attention to ideology; the average person cannot even explain the term ideology even though it is the biggest window available to look into the future. Our ignorance of ideology, in general, leads to the tendency of overlooking our leader's ideology as well, both aspiring and incumbent. The Germans who tend to always have that singular word intended to describe broad concepts popularized the term *Weltanschauung*, meaning 'world view'; they popularized the meaning of the word and more importantly, the importance of the concept of *Weltanschauung*. The concept of *Weltanschauung* goes deeper than just 'world view' because a person's *Weltanschauung* encompasses his or her philosophical, tribal, cultural, economic ethics and moral beliefs; it encompasses one's past experiences and a person's overall mindset.

By overlooking ideology, we overlook the politician's worldview and subsequently, we fail to perceive and anticipate their future actions; that is, their future diktats, policies and the consequences of their suggested policies. Imagine if you were to learn that the current political candidate you support also happens to genuinely believe that Albinos don't die but like Enoch from the Bible, just get up one morning and 'leave for good'. Do you think that bit of seemingly innocuous piece of data would add any weight to your decision-making process? I think it should.

Our presidential choices are based on rhetoric and not their *Weltanschauung*. As a result, we end up electing leaders with beliefs that do not bring the country any economic growth. We elect leaders with the Weltanschauung that makes them react in inconducive manners to social challenges regardless of their intentions.

One might ask the question, "How do I know a politician's worldview since most don't even show their true colours until it is too late". Well, a worldview is not something one can hide because one's *Weltanschauung* reveals itself through one's speeches and quite vividly, in their writing (i.e. Hitler's worldview is fully displayed in his 2 volume diatribe *Mein Kampf*). This is the reason why in the USA, certain sections of the public start digging for one's doctoral thesis once they learned that an individual is planning to run for the presidential office. I believe that once we start paying attention to our leaders' worldview, we will be able to see our leaders for who they truly are which will as a result place us in a better position to extricate the African from the scourge of collectivism.

In South Africa, many South Africans support the African National Congress (ANC)[16], Economic Freedom Fighters (EFF) or South African Communist Party (SACP) but are not familiar with Karl Marx's writings nevermind the communist symbol (the hammer and sickle - ☭). It is quite difficult to fight a societal ailment if you are not equipped to diagnose it - nevermind knowing if it afflicts you in the first place.

---

[16] I genuinely don't believe that the African National Congress is a Communist/socialist organisation

Introduction

Since a lot of collectivists practice (and are of a mindset of) a doctrine popularized by Karl Marx, communists are sometimes referred to as Marxists. It is axiomatic that Stalin was a Marxist even though he is attributed as the father of Stalinism. It is quite interesting and worth noting that all Marxists that collapse their economies after implementing the very same policies advocated by Karl Marx policies are maligned by fellow Marxists in the history books, their ways of governance are partitioned into new ideological strains for the purpose of disassociating the Marxist creed from the failures of these practitioners, hence we've got Maoism, Stalinism, Leninism etc. They "were not true Marxists" because they failed.

Collectivists govern most countries with high levels of poverty. The tragic thing is that even though most African countries are governed by Marxists, the majority of the governed people do not even know what Marxism is. Ideologies are not taught in our primary and secondary schools, we learn that Hitler killed six million Jews but not what constitutes Nazism or a Nazi (some people believe that a Nazi is a politician we do not like), we learn about communists but not the history and effects of communism.

The Others
Theocratic collectivists that tend to keep their economies afloat are not following the centralised doctrine that prescribes control over the market and production, and thus pose a lesser economical threat to a country's developmental progress. Iran and Saud Arabia may be regarded as theocracies but have not collapsed their economies through redistributive policies.

Introduction

Special economic zones like Hong Kong lay credence to the fact that collectivist governments can thrive economically whenever they steer clear of economic central planning and the takeover of production; this is, of course, a sad truth because authoritative governments can survive for a longer period as the denizens live with little liberty.

Marxism/communism was thought to have been defeated in 1989 as the world witnessed the disintegration of the USSR, the fall of the Berlin wall and protests at Tiananmen Square, but its remnants still live on to this day. The United States went through a wave of a socialism onslaught, with the resurfacing of the democratic socialism movement, precipitated by its most famous proponent Senator and presidential candidate Bernie Sanders, preaching and advocating for a "Green New Deal". If implemented, this Green New Deal policy would usher in efforts to redistribute wealth, from the hands of the wealthy to the poorer masses, destroy modern transportation and reverse all technological advancement in the name of combating climate change and eradicating poverty.

The British people have also witnessed a rise of the far left - Jeremy Corbyn, into the leadership of the United Kingdom's opposition party; as did South Africa, with the rise of the Economic Freedom Fighters party. The fight against Collectivism is now more important than it has been within the last 30 years because we are seeing the re-emergence of a very destructive force gaining momentum, threatening to reverse and destroy any progress we have made.

This book is my contribution to the fight, it is my effort to spread the message on the destructiveness of collectivism and my plea to Africans, as to why our main focus should be to bring an end to collectivist ideologies prevailing in African minds, in order to build stronger economies that will afford us a better life, better access to First-class healthcare, education and a higher standard of living.

Brothers in Arms

Although most African countries have dialled back their adoption of socialism after witnessing the fruitlessness of the economic pursuit, there persists a collectivist approach to tackling social ailments. One realizes that Marxism is imbedded in post-colonial Africa's DNA and mindset. Africans see Collectivism as a better way of governing compared to capitalism (the free market system). The predilection to this collectivist world is aided by the fact that Marxism and Africa were brothers in arms in the fight against colonization.

In Africa's fight for Liberation, the communist became her dearest friend. The communist was not just against African colonialism, he actively fought against it and the African's battle for liberation became his own. Years spent at the trenches during numerous battles solidified this bond and understanding the history of this bond will lead one to not underestimate the challenges that lay ahead when advocating against collectivism in Africa. Uprooting this mindset out of Africa is the only way she can rid herself of an ailment the rest of the world has taken big strides in eradicating, the scourge of poverty.

It is important to remember that a mindset is malleable; what would be the point of this book if it wasn't, I for one have also come across Africans in my personal life that are not of this mindset. One's acceptance of an idea is largely dependent on their openness to other ideas rather than the idea itself, and since

Introduction

I am of the view that a lot of us are indeed of a pensive disposition, I find it worthwhile in making this argument.

A big challenge in advocating for Africa to turn away from collectivism is that you are asking Africa to abandon her brother in arms, a comrade in the form of the International Brigade (George Orwell and Ernst Hemingway notably) such as that seen in the Spanish Civil War that made personal sacrifices just so they could come to her aid when she was defenceless and suffering from mass exploitation by the European powers. This book also aims to study this relationship and document my reasons as to why I believe Africa needs to prioritize its well-being and economic progress ahead of its loyalty and commitment to collectivism. I aim to convince the reader using pure reasoning as to why collectivism is immoral and why we cannot reach high levels of prosperity with this baggage in tow.

Chapter 2: Short History of Collectivism
(Readers familiarised with Collectivism-Marxism may skip to chapter 3)

One of the main forms of collectivism that warrant further analysis is that of Communism as it is the most systemized, prevalent and well-documented of all.

What's the Difference?
People use the terms Communism and Socialism interchangeably, leaving many confused with the belief that these are two different strains of Ideologies. Communism is the end state of affairs; it is an envisioned society in a state where all men are equal. Socialism is the vehicle that takes us to communism; it is the transitional process in which a society's means and factors of production are transferred from private hands to communal ownership. In essence, the ownership of labour, capital, raw materials and profit is taken from private hands into the hands of a central authority. As Ludwig von Mises wrote;

> *Socialism aims to transfer the means of production from private ownership to the ownership of organized society, to the State. The socialistic State owns all material factors of production and thus directs it[17].*

To date, no country has achieved communism; but this mere fact does little to deter those trying to direct us toward this social order, with the USSR having gone the furthest in this experiment. We may also note that socialists are commonly called communists in practice even if they are not in a state of communism. But we label them in the same way we label

---

[17] Mises, Ludwig von - Socialism page 56

anarchists and paedophiles because once an individual advocates for a certain ideal; they do not have to accomplish their goals to own that title. Fortunately, the law does not apply this criterion (one is not considered a murderer for advocating for murder). That's why I find the labelling of socialists as communists inconsequential as both are advocating for the same ends; the socially collectivized society ordered around the vision of a single central planning authority. Even Mikhail Bakunin, the Russian socialist and founder of collectivist anarchism happened to share this sentiment and went on to express it in his famous essay titled *The Paris Commune and the Idea of the State*;

It is at this point that a fundamental division arises between the socialists and revolutionary collectivists on the one hand and the authoritarian communists who support the absolute power of the State on the other. Their ultimate aim is identical. Both equally desire to create a new social order based first on the organization of collective labor, inevitably imposed upon each and all by the natural force of events, under conditions equal for all, and second, upon the collective ownership of the tools of production.

A socialist that disavows communism is either dishonest or ignorant, with the latter sadly being in the majority. The USSR-Bolsheviks were often called communists even though they regarded themselves as socialists – the Union of Soviet Socialist Republics. The means through which a society is taken from the current state (inequality) to the egalitarian state is through Socialism, it is through redistributive measures that it can take from the haves to the have-nots. Socialism is understood to be economic because it deals mostly with money and resource allocation (elements of production), this is despite the fact that

'Socialist' regimes also pass laws that have nothing to do with production; laws that only serve the purpose of giving more power to the government over the citizen. The restriction of movement is a typical example, most "communist" countries restricted travel because they fundamentally understand that you have to lock people in - in order to subject them to such a society.

Theoretically, socialism can exist without communism, albeit temporarily; but communism cannot exist without socialism. A socialist that does not wish to follow the teachings of Karl Marx would have to relinquish the prerequisite element of coercion and central planning; however, without these two things - it is quite evident that a socialist society would be difficult to sustain as the top earners would simply opt-out. The Israel Kibbutzim (now privatized) serves as an example of a society that practices a socialist economic system free of coercion and those within the community were free to leave the community whenever they wanted[18]. As the outside world transformed, it struggled to keep the human capital (people) it produced as kids that graduated from higher education often opted to leave the system in pursuit of greener pastures in modern free economies. Socialism is an absolute system in the sense that all its members have to participate (some unwillingly) for it to achieve what it aims to achieve. This is the inherent coercion that makes me believe that whenever some charismatic politicians talk of socialism, democratic socialism or villagization; they are making reference to a socialism in-line with the teachings of Karl Marx. This assertion is evidenced by numerous examples of politicians in favour of the socialist economic structure but remain oblivious to the fact that this leads to communism.

---

[18] Ran Abramitzky's Mystery of the Kibbutz into daily life within this society

A brief look at the history of communism will clarify any misunderstanding or conflation one might have concerning these concepts. Socialists of the 19th century did not suffer from this confusion as many "Socialist Parties across" Europe canonized Karl Marx and Freidrich Engel's *The Communist Manifesto* (such as the German Social Democratic Party). One better understands the ideology by reading the 10 creeds of The Communist Manifesto;

1. Abolition of property in land and application of all rents of land to public purposes.

2. A heavy progressive or graduated income tax.

3. Abolition of all rights of inheritance.

4. Confiscation of the property of all emigrants and rebels.

5. Centralisation of credit in the hands of the state, by means of a national bank with State capital and an exclusive monopoly.

6. Centralisation of the means of communication and transport in the hands of the State.

7. Extension of factories and instruments of production owned by the State; the bringing into cultivation of waste-lands, and the improvement of the soil generally in accordance with a common plan.

8. Equal liability of all to work. Establishment of industrial armies, especially for agriculture.

9. Combination of agriculture with manufacturing industries; gradual abolition of all the distinction between town and country by a more equable distribution of the 27 Chapter II: Proletarians and Communists populace over the country.

10. Free education for all children in public schools. Abolition of children's factory labour in its present form. Combination of education with industrial production[19]

---

[19] Marx, Engels – Communist Manifesto page 243 Penguin Classics

Communism, though linked to Karl Marx and Freidrich Engels, precedes them by hundreds of years. Modern followers of communism subscribe to the theory that the proletariat (peasants and the working class) are bound to follow a certain sequence that will ultimately lead them to an earthly paradise. This is the same deterministic view of human history as outlined in Progressivism which asserts that human history is simply a tale of unchaining human beings from a state of bondage to ultimate freedom; freedom in the form of financial freedom to freedom from suffering in general. They assert that a society must be proactively moved - often through central command - along this predetermined course of history and that that progression simply cannot be left to the free market. The progressive sequence is ignited by the peasants (workers) preferably under the leadership of a Marxist, overthrowing a bourgeoisie (owners and employers) to embark on the path to paradise. The progressives subscribe to the same notion of paradise but believe that the path must be embarked upon proactively rather than waiting for the spontaneous proletariat's (working class) revolution that Marx predicted.

The Utopia

What is this Utopia?

- Well, it is a perfect democracy with plenty of food and material wealth for all, absent of necessity – **Liberty**.
- Working in unison towards a common goal - **Fraternity**.
- The pursuit of equal opportunity and outcome - **Equality**.

This whole society under the tutelage of an anointed expert who would carry out the central plan to ensure the whole sequence is followed through. Communism is a system in which all people live cooperatively and hold all property in common. In essence, it's the abolition of the private ownership of property[20].

Tracing the origins of communism poses a few challenges because communism is an ideology that organically rises from human nature. The old social order was a closed society which made it quite difficult to move up the established social classes as the majority of the population was prohibited from holding certain social ranks as a result of their gender, race and/or tribe. This prevention of social movement through the social rankings as well as the effects of serfdom were such a hindrance to the property-less members of society that it is not surprising that some members started expressing sentiments that aimed to abolish the private ownership of property completely.

Tracing the origins of communism is indeed difficult; however, the task becomes a bit easier when one tries to trace its origins as an organized movement; an organized movement in the sense that there is a coordinated effort by a particular group working towards a certain goal. And a good place to start is in the world of literature, the birthplace of all good and evil movements.

David Priestland's *The Red Flag* is one of the books I highly recommend to any reader wishing to gain a comprehensive history lesson on communism. In this book, he alludes to The Prometheus trilogy by the ancient Greek author of the Greek tragedy Aeschylus (meaning foresight) and he goes on to explain why this play served as a great source of inspiration for communism. This play is based on the myth of Prometheus, an old titan god who stole fire from Zeus and other powerful

---

[20] Marx - With the appropriation of the total productive forces through united individuals, private property comes to an end. Quote from The German Ideology Essay

Olympian gods for the purpose of gifting it to mankind. This gift brought knowledge and progress to mankind. However, this treachery and sheer insubordination incurs the wrath of Zeus, who in turn condemns Prometheus to severe punishment by binding him to a rock on a mountaintop; which left him exposed to various sorts of natural elements such as extreme weather and a very cunning eagle that paid him daily visits to feast on his liver. But this daily torment and absolute state of perdition failed to affect Prometheus' fortitude, as he *recalcitrantly* vowed to continue his resistance against Zeus for the benefit of mankind. Any play or set of events that show all kinds of contempt for authority served as a great inspiration to liberation communists. And it is no surprise that Karl Marx was born off this streak of communism[21].

One historical figure worth noting is Sir Thomas More; he was an English lawyer, statesman, author, and noted Renaissance humanist who was one of the early writers that spoke of common ownership of land and the Utopian society as early as the 16th century. Saint Thomas More, as he was posthumously canonized by the catholic church, actually wrote a book named Utopia, or more accurately *"Libellus vere aureus, nec minus salutaris quam festivus, de optimo rei publicae statu deque nova insula Utopia"*, which *may be translated as "a Truly golden account on the best state of a Republic and of a new island of Utopia"*. In this work, first published in 1516, he told a story of a fictional man who stumbled on an island called Utopia. Utopia, meaning "no place" in Greek and synonymous with "happy place" in today's world, is an idyllic island that consists of a community that venerates egalitarianism. More writes of a man that stumbles on a hidden society free of need and toil as a

---

[21] Marx also mentioned this play in the *Critique of Hegel's Philosophy of Right* essay

result of having abolished the private ownership of property. Everything is provisioned for; everything is produced and consumed communally. On this island, the man encounters houses that....

> *"are large, but enclosed with buildings, that on all hands face the streets, so that every house has both a door to the street and a back door to the garden. Their doors have all two leaves, which, as they are easily opened, so they shut of their own accord; and, there being no property among them, every man may freely enter into any house whatsoever. At every ten years' end they shift their houses by lots[22]."*

This island implemented the same salary caps, wealth tax and pacifist policies some modern-day collectivists advocate for today. The book contains the *same ol'* reproaching of the prevailing state of affairs as a great "conspiracy of the rich" and the *same ol* vilification of landlords as greedy useless parasites. Interestingly, one also picks up the common trait of refusing to come to terms with the worldly existence of Need.

The Diggers

Thomas More's writing precipitated a new wave of writing and thinking. One of the many figures emboldened by the works of Thomas More was the likes of Gerard Winstanley. After going through bankruptcy which resulted from the outbreak of the English Civil War, he banded with contemporaries in a similar situation and became the voice of the common people (including the landless poor). He became the spokesperson of a group commonly referred to as 'THE DIGGERS', a sobriquet bestowed on them due to their belief in the common ownership of land and the notion that;

---

[22] Thomas, More - Utopia page 39 Of Their Towns, Particularly of Amaurot

" the land should be available to every person to dig and sow, so that everyone, rich or poor, could live, grow and eat by the sweat of their own brows, as according to them "The earth was made to be a common treasury for all[23]."

The Diggers gained notoriety when they took over (occupied) common land which was not in use or which they believed belonged to no one; to farm the land to allow everyone who worked the land to eat. This is how they earned the name "The Diggers", after following a modus operandi South Africa's Economic Freedom Fighters can only dream about and would readily follow if only the laws permitted it.

They were sometimes called the "True Levellers" because the Diggers were an offshoot of a larger group called the Levellers. The Levellers were an anti-establishment political movement that advocated for the separation of church and state. However, The Diggers believed that the Levellers didn't go far enough in their postulations in addressing the inequalities of their society. For instance, the Levellers did not advocate for the abolishment of private ownership or the monarchy while The Diggers advocated for absolute communal ownership of Land. They believed that the shared ownership of land is as much a human right as is the right to life itself. Winstanley wrote *"that the earth was made to be a common treasury of livelihood for all, without respect of persons, and was not made to be bought and sold...[and] none ought to be lords and landlords over another, but the earth is free for every son and daughter of mankind, to live free upon[24]".*

---

[23] GH Sabine – A History Of Political Theory page 478 and page 487 3rd edition
https://wigandiggersfestival.org/about/
https://www.marxists.org/reference/archive/winstanley/1649/levellers-standard.htm
[24] https://www.culturematters.org.uk/index.php/culture/theory/item/2978-a-common-treasury-for-all-gerrard-winstanley-and-the-diggers

For a little while, it seemed as if the neighbouring communities and rich landowners were warming up to this growing trend until the leaders started sending soldiers to drive these occupiers off the lands. Although the beatings from government soldiers, destruction of crops and other investments eventually brought this movement to an end, Winstanley's collectivist teachings survived long enough to get picked up by the following generations.

The Social Contract

Although the communist presence within the English political sphere was ephemeral, such voices would have long-lasting effects once they were picked up across the English Channel. Jean-Jacques Rousseau, a Swiss philosopher, writer and composer became the bacillus that seeped into French society; the minds and souls of the peasants who were increasingly growing weary of King Louis XV's extravagance, military expeditions and humiliating defeat at the hands of the Prussians and Great Britain in the Seven Years War. As William Doyle summarised;

> *"At sea, the British destroyed both the Atlantic and Mediterranean fleets, drove French power out of India and North America, and all but strangled the trade of the French Caribbean*[25]*".*

Rousseau's biggest contribution to communism was his rejection of natural (objective) law. He rejected the notion that all human beings possess indefeasible inalienable rights that ought to be observed by the state. As George H Sabine so

---

[25] Doyle, William - The French Revolution page 20

eloquently explained, *'he took from Plato the presumption, implicit in all the philosophy of the city-state, that the community is itself the chief moralizing agency and therefore represents the highest moral value[26].'* He believed that man is only bound by the laws derived from well-established organic community norms.

In the Social Contract, first published in 1762, he explained why man is obligated to serve the collective. He argued that since man gains his liberties and morals from the community, he is thus indebted to the community; that since man enjoys the liberties bestowed on him by society, he may be subjugated by the community in return. That is the deal man accepted by enjoying such liberties, THAT IS THE SOCIAL CONTRACT. In essence, the community decides what is moral and immoral.

The State is portrayed as a living organism with its own goals and aspirations; the members of the state are subordinate to those aspirations. The state is thus handed the authority to *move and dispose of each part as may be most advantageous to the whole.* What could go wrong?

Ultimately, the book wished to address the existence of inequality. In The Social Contract, just like Thomas More's, he envisioned a Utopia where people as a whole would meet in assemblies, renounce their individualism and vow to always act in accordance with the general will of the people. He believed that in such a society, such actions would result in the abolition of inequality and privilege while promoting self-sacrifice for the good of society. Rousseau was one of the early philosophers that brought up an ideology that would not just impact the political

---

[26] GH Sabine – A History Of Political Theory page 581 a

structure of that time, but a system that would govern a person's whole life; socially, politically and culturally – what we call totalitarianism. This is the model that communism followed throughout its whole history of governing.

> "the social pact establishes so great a degree of equality between citizens that they all commit themselves to the same conditions and ought all to enjoy the same rights. Thus by the nature of the pact every act of sovereignty, that is to say every authentic act of the general will, creates an obligation or a benefit for all the citizens equally, so that the sovereign authority has jurisdiction exclusively over the body of the nation, without giving special treatment to any of its members[27]"

Like modern-day collectivists, Rousseau was not open to dissenting opinions, often leading to great fallouts with all close to him, from the likes of Denis Diderot to David Hume. In *Intellectuals*, English author and historian, Paul Johnson laid bare the cantankerous, disputatious and narcissistic nature of Jean-Jacques Rousseau's character. His one-time 'friend', English philosopher David Hume described Rousseau as simply *a monster who saw himself as the most important being in the universe*. Another 'former friend' and French philosopher Denis Diderot was equally as unforgiving in his summation of the man, describing him as *deceitful, vain as Satan, ungrateful, cruel, hypocritical and full of Malice[28]*.

One would readily accept that such criticisms may have been the result of 'sour grapes' or unrelated slights these men may have suffered at the hands of the maestro, however, the choices

---

[27] Rousseau, Jean-Jacques – The social contract Chapter 6
[28] Johnson, Paul - Intellectuals page 26

Rousseau made in his personal life only served to buttress these assessments. Rousseau had 5 children with an illiterate servant, Theresa Levasseur, of whom he never married, and had all children she bore him *given up for adoption* by abandoning them at the door of the local hospital. He is always quoted lamenting the fact that he was never brave enough to raise a family of his own[29]. Regardless of his shortfalls in character, his works would go on to outlive his generation and many generations to come. His works influenced philosophers like Emmanuel Kant and quite significantly, Maximillian Robespierre, a French lawyer who went on to become one of the great radical agitators to the French aristocracy.

The French Revolution

The works of Rousseau coupled with economic struggles enhanced the French population's appetite for a democratic government. The revolutionary spirit managed to organize itself into a genuine political movement that predicated a seismic event that sent shockwaves across European society. In 1789, the Estates General was convened for the first time since 1614. The Estates-General was the French king's consultative assembly of the different estates (classes) within the French kingdom[30]. It was always comprised of 3 branches called estates; the First Estate (which was the clergy), the Second (nobility) and the Third Estate (The common folk).

The First and Second Estates represented less than 10% of the population; but despite the disparity in representation, each

---

[29] Ibid
[30] https://www.britannica.com/topic/Estates-General
Jean-Jacques Rousseau The Social Contract (Christopher Betts) Translation Explanation note #28

estate had an equal vote in political matters. The problem with this unequal representation did not lie in its composition, but in the fact that the smaller group was easily subjected to tyranny by majority vote. The First and Second Estates often took advantage of this by passing laws that benefitted their classes directly, and often to the detriment of the Third Estate. The Third Estate could not prevent some tax exemption status the members from the First and Second Estate enjoyed as they were always outvoted in their remonstrations[31]. The fact that the majority burdens of the French government fell upon the poorest in French society (the farmers and peasantry) fuelled the resentment toward the upper class.

In the face of unrest amidst severe economic difficulties and bankruptcy; Finance Minister Jacques Necker convened an Estates-General. The abrupt assembly of the meeting sparked the French Revolution, the peasant's decade-long struggle that eventually wrestled power from King Louis XVI. The assembly wished to conduct the Estates-General in the same mould as the preceding assembly, with each Estate deliberating separately yet having an equal vote. Fearing being outvoted once more, the Third estate refused to participate in the assembly under such conditions. The Third estate protested that they could only take in deliberations in a united sitting; the impasse propagated a six-week stalemate. This stalemate broke when some members of the nobility and clergy, notably Abbé Emmanuel Joseph Sieyès, began to break ranks with their estates in solidarity with the Third estate. On June 17th, this newly formed assembly renamed itself the National Assembly, bringing an end to political representation based on social classes. The National Assembly's

---

[31] Doyle, William - The French Revolution page 25

introduction of universal taxation symbolized its declaration of independence and sovereignty from the French Monarchy.

In its early years, the National Assembly was structured in the following way; the assembly consisted of the conservative group who were regarded as foes of the revolution, they were also known as "The Right" because they generally sat to the left of the presiding officer's chair. The Nationalists were pro-revolution and generally sat to the right of the presiding officer's chair (this is why they are called "The Left")[32]. The third group was the monarchists, those willing to follow the British model with a House of Commons and a House of Lords.

Maximillian Robespierre

Following a modus-operandi that would become prevalent with the 20th-century Marxists, as Maximillian Robespierre and the Jacobin club gradually gained power within the assembly, the need to purge thought criminals bubbled up to the surface. Amongst other things (like introducing a new calendar - The New Republican calendar); the new leadership passed laws that opened up a legal pathway to kill those opposed to their ideology while still maintaining some semblance of morality. As Rousseau advocated, the community was redefining morality.

The revolutionary armies that were initially set up to "guard the revolution" morphed into a group of out-of-control reprobates that soon became a thorn to the rulers. As the National Assembly (later renamed National Convention) decreed the Law of the General Maximum, a law which imposed price controls on all basic commodities nationwide to

---

[32] Ibid page 97
Scruton, Roger – Fools, Frauds and Firebrands page 2 (What is Left)

ensure the continued supply of food to the French capital. The unpopularity of this necessitated the deployment of the revolutionary army to enforce this decree. However, the army's ventures in the countryside devolved into murderous skirmishes against peasants and rebellious groups that weren't too welcoming to the idea of paying taxes to this newly established *quasi-aristocracy*. The opprobrium generated by the army's chaotic escapades forced Robespierre to abolish the revolutionary army. This also led Robespierre to conclude that French society was plagued by '*conspirators and treacherous people who profess(ed) themselves as friends*'[33] and felt that an urgent remedy was necessary to smoke out the rats. He went on to set up a more biddable centrally controlled law enforcement agency that would give him more control over the regions.

Amongst the many new laws passed, the Convention had one law, in particular, that was formulated to address and prosecute any conspirator working to reverse the revolution. History has shown us that all collectivist revolutions soon come across a need to preserve the revolution as public support begins to wane rapidly.

One decree in particular is The Law of Suspects, passed in 1793 by the National Assembly; the law gave the leadership powers to arrest all individuals suspected of working against (and thinking ill of) the revolution[34]. The trouble with this law lay in its ambiguity and malleable nature which afforded the leadership ample opportunity to weaponize it against personal foes of Maximillian Robespierre. This law sparked what is commonly known today as "The Great Terror" (or Reign of

---

[33] Haydon, Collin; Doyle, William – Robespierre page 160
[34] Thompson, JM – Robespierre page 533

Terror). The Law of 22 Prairial was passed the following year, a law that removed the final barrier that often gnaws at all aspiring despots, the individual's right to a fair trial[35]. The only way a suspect could beat these charges was for the individual to prove his innocence as the onus laid on the accused; I must remind the reader that Robespierre was a lawyer.

During this Reign of Terror, which took place from 1793 - 1794, anybody suspected of ideological impurity was accused of conspiracy and as a result, guillotined (head cut off) for being an enemy of the people. Fellow Jacobins were not spared from charges of plotting against the revolution; this was evident in the trial and eventual executions of the first president of the Committee of Public Safety, Georges Jacques Danton, and the leading revolutionary journalist, Jacques Hébert.

As Orwellian as it may be, Robespierre believed that the only way a government could bring peace to society was through terror; He concluded that since a good government enforces laws through instilling terror (man obeys laws out of fear of government), then that terror is virtuous because it is a product of a good government; the man was deadly serious;

> *"If the basis of popular government in peacetime is virtue, its basis in the time of revolution is both virtue and terror – virtue, without which terror is disastrous, and terror, without which virtue has no power... Terror is merely justice, prompt, severe, and inflexible. It is therefore an emanation of virtue, and results from the application of democracy to the most pressing needs of the country[36]"*

---

[35] Priestland, David - The Red Flag page 13
   Doyle, William - The French Revolution page 97
[36] Priestland, David - The Red Flag page 13

He established the Commission for Public Instruction, a commission designed to take control of all propaganda and "centralize moral law". Like in the Soviet Union 130 years later, this commission would produce plays, songs and political festivals that would guide the values of the society. As Jean Jacques Rousseau famously said; *Those who control people's opinions, control their actions*[37]

All who were in violation of this ideological outlook were arrested and some guillotined. In the period from the 24th March – 27 July 1794, close to 2627 people were beheaded (1376 in a span of 47 days)[38].

The Reign of Terror (Or Great Terror according to some historians) had done a lot to discredit the communist movement, but its avid followers still believed in its ideals and felt that its failings were a result of the Jacobin club's distortion. These French revolutionaries still believed that this ideology was the only way to defeat the inequality between the aristocracy and the lower class of France.

As Robespierre was preparing another purge list consisting of fellow parliamentarians who would be charged with counter-revolutionary attitudes and crimes, those on the list beat him to the punch and moved swiftly to arrest him first before putting him on trial; Robespierre was found guilty and sentenced to death. Pacing up and down his holding cell mulling over his impending execution, Robespierre could not stand the thought of being at the mercy of his 'backstabbers' so he sought ways to evade his due comeuppance. When he heard the footsteps of the

---

[37] Johnson, Paul – Intellectuals page 25
[38] Ibid (Priestland)
  Thompson, JM – Robespierre page 542

guards approaching his cell, he placed the barrel of the pistol which he had smuggled in firmly on his chin and fired one round in an attempt to blow his brains out. However, as he was about to fire the weapon, the guards who had now entered his cell, frantically leaped toward him causing the bullet to miss his brain - travelling right through his face completely shattering his jaw.

Paralyzed of speech due to the bullet wound, the now mute Maximillian Robespierre was eventually guillotined the following day.

As the dust settled briefly following such a chaotic period, the apostles of collectivism realized that their revolution had completely disintegrated. Many of those jailed were released, including the likes of Francois Noel Babeuf, Henri de Saint-Simon and Charles Fourier. One of the reasons offered for the failures of previous collectivist attempts such as those of The Diggers was the intellectual unsophistication of those that led the movements. This revolution was the first of its kind in the sense that its leaders were products of the Enlightenment Era, well-read in the works of Voltaire and the philosophy of human reason. An explanation was desperately needed.

A tactic that we would become accustomed to soon came into effect; that is every time an ideological revolution gets tested and fails, the failure is not attributed to its ideological foundation but squarely on the revolutionary leader's feet. They all condemned Robespierre's actions and went on to document their alternative views as to which route should communists follow in pursuit of Utopia. The criticism toward Robespierre seemed to have minimal effect on future collectivists as history shows that his tactics went on to be emulated by many future Marxist leaders, with dire consequences for their populations.

The criticism came from all angles, with Babeuf criticizing Robespierre for not prioritizing the agrarian approach, Saint-Simon excoriating him for not modernising the country's production methods while Fourier bemoaned his fixation on work instead of human creativity[39]. All these views had one thing in common, they all stuck to the belief that the society still had to be built from the top down, rammed down the throats of the un-consenting population for the sake of the omnibenevolent Utopian society. Babeuf doubled down on his agrarian-centric collectivist approach in the pursuit of absolute equality; As David Priestland wrote;

> **In the new society, money would no longer exist; everybody would send the products of their labour to the 'common storehouse', and then they would receive an equal proportion of the national product in exchange for their labour. Work would not be a chore because men would want to work out of patriotism and love of the community[40].**

The trouble with the old world is that it was quite difficult to envisage the actual size of a country; this observation is evidenced by Babeuf's genuine belief in the feasibility of the production model that he advocated for.

Man would not work for money, but out of love for their community and country. Babeuf, a founding member of the Insurrection Community of Public Safety, authored the thesis "Manifesto of Equals". The manifesto was not mere advocacy towards any ideological view, but a call for an uprising of the

---

[39] Ibid Priestland page 41
[40] Ibid Priestland page 18

French people (even through violent means) against the current leaders, in pursuit of a society never seen before. The following excerpts give a good idea as to why the authorities were greatly alarmed by such a piece.

"We aspire to live and die equal, the way we were born: we want real equality or death; this is what we need."

"And we'll have this real equality, at whatever the cost. Woe on those who stand between it and us! Woe on those who resist a wish so firmly expressed."

"The French Revolution is nothin but the precursor of another revolution, one that will greater, more solemn, and which will be the last."

"No more individual property in land: the land belongs to no one. We demand, we want, the common enjoyment of the fruits of the land: the fruits belong to all."

"Long enough, and for too long, less than a million individuals have disposed of that which belongs to 20 million of their kind, their equals."

"Let there no longer be any difference between people than that of age and sex[41]."

This is the work he would subsequently be executed for.

Note on the Germanics

We often criticize France for its role in adopting extreme and sometimes degenerate behaviours and philosophies but don't give her the credit she deserves for her ability and speed at which she self-corrects. France introduced the collectivist revolution into the conscious of the whole of Europe; she was

---

[41] https://www.marxists.org/history/france/revolution/conspiracy-equals/1796/manifesto.htm

expeditious in the spread of communism but was equally as expeditious in rolling back this ideology within its borders. France was able to instantly roll back the workers' revolution that many European countries battle with to this day by quietly restoring the monarch institution (that she had destroyed 10 years prior) through Napoleon Bonaparte in 1799. France's inherent ability to self-correct is the main reason why I believe France will continue to exist for many centuries to come.

Germany on the other hand, is blessed with efficiency; this does wonders in technological innovation and engineering but may also act as a straightjacket when the society is going the wrong way. Germany's inherent efficiency means that it will inevitably find ways to efficiently and assiduously implement any bad ideology or philosophy she wishes to implement. Germany can practice capitalism efficiently just like it can practice Nazism efficiently. When communism entered German society, the doctrine was proselytized efficiently; it morphed from being the layman's creed into the intellectual's creed.

On The Prussian Front

When communism was exported abroad, it arrived in Germany to a receptive society that suffered from high levels of inequality. As the industrial revolution gained momentum, German society saw the upper class (i.e. doctors and entrepreneurs) become wealthier at a faster rate than the working class as inequality increased. The consternation caused by this widening gap drove them to communism, which promised to alleviate this set of circumstances. In 1844, Ernste Dronke, a German writer and journalist estimated that 25% of the population in Berlin were beggars[42]. Communism as means

---

[42] Marx-Engels (Jones), The Communist Manifesto, page 34 (Intro by Stedman Jones)

for freedom morphed into communism as means to address class struggle, a struggle that would be well documented by Karl Marx.

The term "communism" is popularly accepted to mean a composition of the 10 creeds listed earlier in the chapter.

All these goals ought to be achieved through the use of militant tactics to seize power from the ruling class. This term was spread by Fillipo Buonarroti, author of Buonarroti's history of Babeuf's conspiracy for equality (written 1828) after having taken part in the Conspiracy of the equals in 1796. These ideas spread all over the country and resonated with the likes of Wilhelm Weitling, who introduced the Christian element to German communism in the form of his *Christian community of goods*[43], a written proposal that precipitated Weitling's *Mankind As It Is and Ought To Be;* a piece of work that garnered him great respect amongst German socialists.

Karl Marx and Freidrich Engels aimed to combine all these strains of communism while rejecting Weitling's injection of religion. This was because they had always viewed religion as the oppressor's tool to keep the oppressed subservient. In the Introduction to *A Contribution to the Critique of Hegel's Philosophy of Right* he wrote;

> **Religious suffering is, at one and the same time, the expression of real suffering and a protest against real suffering. Religion is the sigh of the oppressed creature, the heart of a heartless world, and the soul of soulless conditions. It is the opium of the people**

---

[43] Priestland David, The Red Flag, page 41
Marx-Engels (Jones), The Communist Manifesto, page 45 (Intro by Stedman Jones)

The abolition of religion as the illusory happiness of the people is the demand for their real happiness. To call on them to give up their illusions about their condition is to call on them to give up a condition that requires illusions. The criticism of religion is, therefore, in embryo, the criticism of that vale of tears of which religion is the halo.

They argued that mankind was naturally altruistic, cooperative and that with the right education; these qualities would come to the light and assume their predominance. Karl Marx, son of a lawyer Heinrich, and grandson of a rabbi, was born on 5 May 1818 in the Rhineland (lower Rhine) town of Trier in Prussia. Trier was then under French occupation and as a result, liberally governed in accordance with Napoleonic laws. His father enjoyed liberalism under occupation because it allowed him to flourish in his profession as a lawyer. However, things took a turn for the worse when Trier was absorbed by the conservative state of Prussia, which had laws that denied Jews all employment positions in the state service (unless they were granted exemption status)[44]. In his youth, Marx became a member of the Hegelian group of thinkers that subscribed to Georg Friedrich Hegel's theory known as *"The History of Mankind"*, which describes a sequence of events that outline man's progression from bondage to freedom. This process moves through struggles between ideas and social systems with the aim of incorporating the best of all aspects.

In 1842, Marx was appointed as editor of *Reinische Zeitung*, a liberal newspaper based in Cologne. This outlet gave him the megaphone to espouse his ideas and in his view, it became the voice of the peasants and downtrodden. This new venture would

---

[44] Priestland, David – The Red Flag – page 23

not last very long as the Reinische Zeitung was eventually shut down by the authorities. After having witnessed the very timid outrage of the German middle class, the disillusioned Marx together with fellow radicals, migrated to France in search of a community they believed was more open to their ideas.

Freidrich Engels, son of a wealthy Calvinist manufacturer, was a fellow radical member of the Young Hegelians society and became very close to Marx. Engels, thanks to his wealth and membership in the old-school British gentlemanly tradition; did not possess the combative streak witnessed in Marx. Heading the Manchester branch of the family business earned him the wealth that enabled him to often finance his impecunious friend's lifestyle with relative ease. Engels also brought the corporate /capitalism perspective to Marx's work; unlike Marx, he had a higher understanding of the higher class of society that Marx jealously derided from the outside looking in. Engels was one of them, he enjoyed all the activities one would associate with the British gentry; a connoisseur of wine, fine dining and fencing[45].

Alienated forces

Together, Marx and Engels produced writings commonly referred to as the "Paris Manuscripts", which documented their goals in the elimination of poverty and attaining of freedom. This was not just the freedom from autocrats, chiefs and kings, but the complete emancipation from control by "alienated forces" outside one's self. Despite the actual freedom we enjoy in today's world, we still have individuals engaged in a battle

---

[45] Heilbroner, Robert L. – The Worldly Philosophers page 97
Mises, Ludwig von – Theory and History page 121
Mises, Ludwig von Marxism Unmasked page 7

to *emancipate* themselves from *outside forces*. This manifests itself in form of victimhood, where individuals often revert to actual injustices in the past to support their claim that they still suffer those very same injustices today.

The disparities witnessed in household incomes in different communities, wages for women compared to men, or the number of women in boardrooms, are often attributed to external "forces" that work to oppose their progress. The personifying of the struggles of life that every man faces has made it easy for Collectivists (from Marx, Robespierre, Lenin, to Stalin and Mao) to vilify certain groups of society. The Jews were accused of theft and sabotage during WWI, often labelled as unpatriotic just like the Kulaks in Russia who were viewed as class enemies of the poor; today, the modern white male and his white privilege is the main *cause* of disparities witnessed in everyday life. Churches are not spared; their appeal to a higher authority undercuts the collectivist's call for the restructuring of the prevailing social order. The church was also blamed for the population's low levels of indignation toward the ruling class; the general population's submission to the perceived exploitative capitalist society; the previously mentioned "opium of the people"

Marx's biggest contribution to collectivism was in his technical approach to the question and defence of the concept of **Communal ownership of property**. Like many apologists that came before him, he based the case for collectivism on moral grounds, but his unique contribution came from his attempt at a methodical breakdown as to how property, value, labour, capital and production are all creations of the working class. His contribution was developing the best defence against the well-formulated denunciations from renowned philosophers and economists such as John Stuart Mill and Adam Smith. Unfortunately, one making the best case against something does not necessarily mean that they are making a good case in general; it means that one is making a flawed argument in a sea of terrible ideas. Karl Marx's 3 Volume Das Kapital (Capital) is collectivism's best answer to the economic problem facing a collectivist society; however, it remains a flawed defence because it is a defence of a terrible nonsensical ideology.

Das Kapital

The Marx-Engels *Communist Manifesto* was the declaration of values and Marx's *Das Kapital* served as a technical explanation of those values. *The Communist Manifesto* calls for the abolition of private property[46] and *Das Kapital* explains, in detail how they arrived at this position. *Das Kapital* looks at the issue of value; what is value, how it is created and by whom is it created. For example - Marx argues that total value is the summation of Use-value (usefulness of an article) and exchange value (value in the general open market - in the eyes of the people and what they are willing to pay); he maintains that an article must contain both values in order for it to have overall value[47]

> **We have seen that when commodities are exchanged, their exchange-value manifests itself as something totally independent of their use-value. But if we abstract from their use-value, there remains their Value as defined above[48].**

---

[46] In this sense, the theory of the Communists may be summed up in a single sentence: Abolition of private property. We Communists have been reproached with the desire of abolishing the right of personally acquiring property as the fruit of a man's own labour, which property is alleged to be the groundwork of all personal freedom, activity and independence.
[47] If the thing is useless, so is the labour contained in it; the labour does not count as labour, and therefore creates no value. - Marx, Karl – Das Kapital Volume 1 page 5
[48] Marx, Karl – Das Kapital Volume 1 page 3

The Manifesto asserts that private wealth is illegitimate because it is a result of ill begotten gains; a product created by labour but expropriated by the capitalist through exploitation[49].

> **[Labour] It creates capital, i.e., that kind of property which exploits wage-labour, and which cannot increase except upon condition of begetting a new supply of wage-labour for fresh exploitation. Property, in its present form, is based on the antagonism of capital and wage-labour[50]**

Capital explains this position and how an article's inherent value is directly proportional to the hours spent making it.

> **A use-value, or useful article, therefore, has value only because human labour in the abstract has been embodied or materialised in it. How, then, is the magnitude of this value to be measured? Plainly, by the quantity of the value-creating substance, the labour, contained in the article. The quantity of labour, however, is measured by its duration, and labour-time in its turn finds its standard in weeks, days, and hours[51].**

Marx realized that there lies an inconsistency in simultaneously believing that the labourer bestows an article with a definite (intrinsic) additional value[52] and the mere fact that consumers appraise the same article differently. If the sculptor spends three hours turning a R10 (ten rands) piece of wood into a R10 000 wooden sculpture of Auguste Rodin's *Thinking Man,* then why is it that some consumers are not prepared to pay R10 000 for it?

---

[49] Capital, therefore, it not only, as Adam Smith says, the command over labor. It is essentially the command over unpaid labor. All surplus-value, whatever particular form (profit, interest, or rent), it may subsequently crystallize into, is in substance the materialization of unpaid labor. The secret of the self-expansion of capital resolves itself into having the disposal of a definite quantity of other people's unpaid labor

[50] Marx, Karl & Engels, Freidrich – The Communist Manifesto (PROLETARIANS AND COMMUNISTS)

[51] Ibid, Kapital page 4

[52] Commodities, therefore, in which equal quantities of labour are embodied, or which can be produced in the same time, have the same value – Ibid page 4

So he resorted to this mental bifurcation of the meaning of value in order to hold these two contradictory beliefs and not go insane. In the case of the sculpture, the use value remains rigid and directly proportional to the labour hours spent, while the exchange value varies from one person to the next.

To this day, many collectivists still hold the belief that all value (and as a result, wealth) is a creation of labour; this is despite the presence of insurance industries, financial market industries, Facebook and various other products of the information age.

Marx argued that since wealth is a product of the working class, its produce (including property) should be controlled by the working class. But since Marx was more astute than we often give him credit for, he also knew that wealth is a product of profit. Then how did he square this circle? Well, by arguing that the labourer creates *surplus-value* by converting a raw article into a useful article (additional worth) which leads to profit once it's sold. He explains;

> **The capitalist buys labour-power in order to use it; and labour-power in use is labour itself. The purchaser of labour-power consumes it by setting the seller of it to work. By working, the latter becomes actually...a labourer. In order that his labour may re-appear in a commodity, he must, before all things, expend it on something useful, on something capable of satisfying a want of some sort. Hence, what the capitalist sets the labourer to produce, is a particular use-value, a specified article[53]**

---

[53] Ibid page 109

The product appropriated by the capitalist is a use-value, as yarn, for example, or boots. But, although boots -- the basis of all social progress, -- yet he does not manufacture boots for their own sake. -- Use-values are only produced by capitalists, because, and in so far as, they are the material substratum, the depositories of exchange-value. Our capitalist has two objects in view: in the first

The entrepreneur (the capitalist) was given very little credit for his or her mental equity and innovative skills, their role was reduced to a mere foreman looking over the true creators of wealth yet had some power that enabled them to expropriate the fruits away from their true benefactors. Marx's best explanation regarding this conundrum was that the capitalist is able to get away with this because of machinery and the division of labour.

Let us assume that some invention enables the spinner to spin as much cotton in 6 hours as he was able to spin before in 36 hours. His labour is now six times as effective as it was, for the purposes of useful production. The product of 6 hours' work has increased six-fold, from 6 lbs. to 36 lbs. But now the 36 lbs. of cotton absorb only the same amount of labour as formerly did the 6 lbs. One-sixth as much new labour is absorbed by each pound of cotton, and consequently, the value added by the labour to each pound is only one-sixth of what it formerly was. On the other hand, in the product, in the 36 lbs. of yarn, the value transferred from the cotton is six times as great as before[54].

In essence, he argues that when a capitalist hires a worker to make articles, and the worker is able to produce x number of articles per day, for the employer, that is the definite amount of labour they have employed; if the employer finds means to improve the worker's productivity (i.e. buying machinery) thus causing the worker to produce more articles a day, then the employer is cheating the worker because he is getting more out of the worker's labour than before. At this point, one must remember that Marx went to law school, because the sophistry in his spindle example ignores one basic fact of the employer-employee relationship. In the real world, when one purchases

---

place, he wants to produce a use-value that has a value in exchange, that is to say, an article destined to be sold, a commodity; and secondly, he desires to produce a commodity whose value shall be greater than the sum of the values of the commodities used in its production, that is, of the means of production and the labour-power, that he purchased with his good money in the open market. His aim is to produce not only a use-value, but a commodity also; not only use-value, but value; not only value, but at the same time surplus-value – Ibid page 114
[54] Ibid – page 126 Chapter 8

labour by employing an individual; one purchases the labourer's skills and time. One cannot purchase productivity because one cannot determine the labourer's productivity until a labourer commences to work. One may purchase a service relating to a specific job (i.e. hiring a contractor to paint your house) or purchase a service relating to time (i.e. weekdays 8 -5). However, Marx's cotton example shows that he seems to be of the belief that when an employer hires an employee; the employer purchases services both in the job sense and time sense. One sees how this distortion enabled him to logically reach the conclusion that machinery and innovation cheat the worker out of his or her labour.

The second culprit was of course the division of labour. He believed that the division of labour alienates the worker from the product because it spreads the creation of one article over many individuals. The article becomes a product of many men thus robbing the individual off a sense of accomplishment. The division of labour cheapens the value of a single labourer

> **The work is therefore re-distributed. Instead of each man being allowed to perform all the various operations in succession, these operations are changed into disconnected, isolated ones, carried on side by side; each is assigned to a different artificer, and the whole of them together are performed simultaneously by co-operating workmen. This accidental repartition gets repeated, develops advantages of its own, and gradually ossifies into a systematic division of labour. The commodity, from being the individual product of an independent artificer, becomes the social product of a union of artificers, each of whom performs one, and only one, of the constituent partial operations**[55]

---

[55] Ibid page 218 S1 TWO-FOLD ORIGIN OF MANUFACTURE

Marx accepted that division of labour improved production but still called for its abolition due to its perceived detrimental nature with regard to employment.

'To subdivide a man is to execute him, if he deserves the sentence, to assassinate him if he does not... The subdivision of labour is the assassination of a people'

Fundamentally, I believe Marx knew that the division of labour disproved his notion that labour is the true creator of value (wealth). Labour forms an intrinsic part of production, but is not the main creator of production. Yes, an article cannot be produced without labour, but this mere fact does not make the product a creation or a result of its feature. Just because A is a facet of B does not mean B is made from A, no matter how important of a feature A may be. The combustion engine is a fundamental component of the vehicle but that does not mean that the combustion engine creates the vehicle; Elon Musk's Tesla serves to support this point. The underlying foundation of Marxism is that a society must operate to the benefit of the workers, not consumers; so if the division of labour harms the workers, it should be abolished even if it benefits consumers by lowering the cost of living. Marxism aims to convince us that the rightful creators and as a result owners of wealth (property) are the working class, and so it is only just that the working class unite to wrestle this ownership from the current holders of property as the workers *had nothing to lose but their chains*.

Marx imputed all the struggles of life to capitalism, describing it as a system imposed by the state under the tutelage of the bourgeoisie class (upper class). A chapter in The Communist Manifesto reads as follows;

> "*the bourgeoisie has at last, since the establishment of Modern Industry and of the world market, conquered for itself, in the modern representative State, exclusive political sway. The*

> *executive of the modern state is but a committee for managing the common affairs of the whole bourgeoisie[56]".*

He felt that man had become slaves to capitalist societies; this includes money, the market and material things. Marx believed that this lack of freedom hindered man from connecting with his inner creativity and as a result was unable to form true human relationships as human exchanges all *became about money.* Lamenting how the bourgeoisie class;

> *...resolved personal worth into exchange value, and in place of the numberless indefeasible chartered freedoms, has set up that single, unconscionable freedom – Free Trade. In one word, for exploitation, veiled by religious and political illusions, it has substituted naked, shameless, direct, brutal exploitation.*

> *The bourgeoisie has stripped of its halo every occupation hitherto honoured and looked up to with reverent awe. It has converted the physician, the lawyer, the priest, the poet, the man of science, into its paid wage labourers.*

> *The bourgeoisie has torn away from the family its sentimental veil, and has reduced the family relation to a mere money relation[57].*

Grappling with Need

Work is the price one pays to eat; one needs to work to eat. Individuals that do not or cannot work need someone else to share what they eat with them; parent(s) work to eat and children eat what the parent(s) eat. This basic rule of life is a rule many individuals struggle to accept. The need for an individual to eat, produce and take care of family is a need that brings pressures that tend to overwhelm certain pockets of

---

[56] Marx, Engels - The Communist Manifesto I. Bourgeois and Proletarians page 221 Penguin classics
[57] Marx, Engels - The Communist Manifesto (page 222 Penguin classics)

society, making them resort to means and theories that promise to alleviate these pressures while guaranteeing more happiness and a life free of obligations.

Many, like Marx, see these pressures as creations of a capitalist society. The Need to Work and (have) money is viewed as undue expenses invoiced by an immoral capitalist system. It is worth mentioning that Karl Marx lived his whole life in debt; that he was never at a point of self-reliance and often relied on creditors and Freidrich Engels to finance his lifestyle. One can only imagine what this does to one's psyche.

Marx's disapproval and sheer resentment of the wealthy is highly likely to have stemmed from his relationship with his creditors, usury and the control creditors would exert over him due to unpaid bills. Marx would so often contact his parents and relatives for money that his mother is said to have said, in complete exasperation; I wish 'Karl would accumulate Capital instead of just writing about it[58]'. Marx-Engels' communism was a combination of the Liberation-communism and Rousseau-communism model; the former yearning for freedom and the latter yearning for equality and the abolition of private property.

Leap of Faith

To the rational man - a layman, this raises the obvious question of consensus, how would this society deal with conflict of interests; because one group having its way inadvertently puts the other group with contrasting interests under the subjugation of the winning group. Marx believed that since communism would eliminate class division, no conflict of interest would arise so consensus would not be an issue. But the fact that many followers of Marx resorted to despotic means in their

---

[58] Johnson Paul, Intellectuals, page 74

implementation of communism proves that this assertion was flawed. One must point out that Marx always stated that communism was to be achieved through the prevalent democratic channels. The Manifesto reads

> **We have seen …above, that the first step in the revolution by the working class is to raise the proletariat to the position of ruling as to win the battle of democracy. The proletariat will use its political supremacy to wrest, by degrees, all capital from the bourgeoisie, to centralise all instruments of production in the hands of the State, i.e., of the proletariat organised as the ruling class; and to increase the total of productive forces as rapidly as possible[59]**

But this still calls for a complete consensus; he believed that since there would be a complete consensus, there would be no need for the pursuit or observance of individual rights.

He believed that the prevalent conflict of interest was solely due to class division and nothing else. The unproductiveness of Karl Marx had a debilitating narrowing effect in terms of his outlook on life and views regarding the average working man.

Central Planning
Das Kapital (Capital) contained a few concessions with regard to his earlier writing, one of these was the notion that some jobs would not be carried out if work is only viewed as a form of self-expression and creativity, that for levels of production to be sustained, a directing authority would still be necessary;

> **As a general rule, labourers cannot cooperate without being brought together: their assemblage in one place is a necessary condition of their co-operation. Hence wage-**

---

[59] Marx, Engels - The Communist Manifesto II. Proletarians And Communists page 243 in Penguin classics

labourers cannot cooperate, unless they are employed simultaneously by the same capital, the same capitalist, and unless therefore their labour-powers are bought simultaneously by him[60]

This simple concession allows for the merging of communism (egalitarianism) and *statism (etatism)[61]*, it made it possible for future Marxists to maintain the façade of egalitarianism while building an obvious new ruling class. This explained why the Robespierres and Stalins were allowed to enjoy certain amenities not available to the working class; it explained why the pigs in George Orwell's Animal Farm still called themselves egalitarians despite their move toward governance for the benefit of the ruling few. This is how many workers today still believe in the idea of a worker's control over the factories despite many anecdotes showing that such moves (from capitalism to collectivism) are simply a move of exchanging one boss for another.

Collectivists believe that the state is only a force for evil when in the wrong hands and can be a force for good in good hands; good hands being the working class. So if state control is to be wrestled off the bad guys (the bourgeoisie class) and brought under the control of the proletariat, all the prevailing evils brought on by capitalism (the bourgeoisie class) will be extinguished. As Lenin wrote;

the state is an organ of class domination, an organ for the oppression of one class by another; its aim is the creation of an 'order' which legalizes and perpetuates this oppression[62]'.

So the state as an organ of domination, can thus serve as a morally good vehicle for dominating evil classes and ideas.

---

[60] Ibid Capital page 211 Chapter 13 (co-operation)
[61] (etatism) A political system in which the state has substantial centralized control over social and economic affairs
[62] Popper, Karl R – The Open Society and Its Enemies page 129 Chapter 17
    Lenin, Vladimir - State and Revolution page 725

I have not come across any writing, where Marx delineates this position as to how the elimination of class struggle would lead to a complete consensus; it is a complete leap of faith. Under communism – a Utopia, people would not work for money, but use work as avenues to express their creativity thus having a contribution in the building of their communities. He believed that the economy would not suffer because people would be working out of love for what they do. This would subsequently increase work rate and productivity, yielding economic growth. This would bring an end to the division of labour. In this communist society absent of the division of labour, man would do one type of job today, and a completely different line of work tomorrow, or as he wrote, (perhaps in jest);

> **He is a hunter, a fisherman, a herdsman, or a critical critic, and must remain so if he does not want to lose his means of livelihood; while in communist society, where nobody has one exclusive sphere of activity but each can become accomplished in any branch he wishes, society regulates the general production and thus makes it possible for me to do one thing today and another tomorrow, to hunt in the morning, fish in the afternoon, rear cattle in the evening, criticise after dinner, just as I have a mind, without ever becoming hunter, fisherman, herdsman or critic[63].**

It is in this leap of faith that Karl Marx is able to construct this disjointed argument and still make it sound plausible; it is a result of this disjointed ideology that we came to witness over 100 million people killed in the last 100 years.

---

[63] Engels, Freidrich & Marx, Karl - A Critique of The German Ideology (Private Property and Communism)

Marx was not calling for the destruction of capitalism and its strides, but to have communism built upon the benefits brought on by capitalism. Crediting capitalism for having destroyed the backward primitive feudalist way of life, and the innovation brought on by the industrial revolution. He praised the bourgeoisie class for being that revolutionary class that '*accomplished wonders for surpassing Egyptian pyramids, Roman aqueducts and Gothic cathedrals*[64]'.

He conceded that his model of society could not be established in a backward society ruled by autocracy. In-Line with Babeuf, he believed a "bourgeoisie revolution", like the French revolution would need to precede the proletariat revolution. Marx believed that a communist society would not be able to modernize industries but he was so exasperated by the prevailing levels of inequality that the abolition of income disparities took precedence over technological achievement and everyday quality of life. We see this today in discussions concerning climate change where we are expected to make sacrifices and relinquish liberties to central planners who promise to lead us from our current path that they insist leads to an existential crisis. He subscribed to social development in the following sequence; Feudalism - Capitalism - Socialism - Communism.

---

[64] The bourgeoisie has disclosed how it came to pass that the brutal display of vigour in the Middle Ages, which Reactionists so much admire, found its fitting complement in the most slothful indolence. It has been the first to show what man's activity can bring about. It has accomplished wonders far surpassing Egyptian pyramids, Roman aqueducts, and Gothic cathedrals; it has conducted expeditions that put in the shade all former Exoduses of nations and crusades. Communist Manifesto

Jobs and Economic crises

Marx gave credit to the bourgeoisie for having defeated feudalism and autocracy, but believed that they were ill-equipped to lead society into the Utopia world that he had envisioned. He believed that the bourgeoisie had established a society that would ultimately lead to their destruction[65]. Like a sorcerer who had unleashed powers they could no longer control, the industrial age was the power that was destroying small businesses, artisans and creativity in favour of the industrial factory owners. He argued that the industrial revolution would lead to greater exploitation of man and as competition between the employers increased; some employers would resort to machinery which would, in turn, replace workers. Marx warned of the periodic economic crises that result from the over-supply of produce by the factories to the market, putting small capitalists out of business while concentrating ownership to fewer hands.

At first glance, this insight seems accurate, but is quite misplaced because the extents of economic crises witnessed in the past 100 years were a result of government involvement (regulations) in the free market. As I will elaborate later in the book, the Overproduction phenomenon persists when the producer is isolated from the reaction of the market. The Soviet Union's central planners would overproduce a certain product that they incorrectly believed was in demand.

Marx's criticism of the labour market was quite accurate in the sense that we did see machinery replace some jobs[66], but he

---

[65] The development of Modern Industry, therefore, cuts from under its feet the very foundation on which the bourgeoisie produces and appropriates products. What the bourgeoisie, therefore, produces, above all, is its own grave-diggers. – Ibid

[66] i.e. watches were largely assembled by hand until the assembly became automated, or manual switchboard operators that used to connect calls by manually removing and plugging cables were replaced by electronic telephonic exchange systems

failed to take into account the new jobs that would be "invented" as a result of innovation and entrepreneurship; something other political economists[67] had accurately predicted many years before him

The invention of the internet paved the way for millions of jobs; from digital marketers, *and Youtubers* to various online businesses we take for granted today. The smartphone is another technological innovation that carved the way for new industries such as that of App developers and those operating in the social media industry. He failed to see, that innovation leads to more jobs, and more industries and that even though automation may eliminate some jobs, the unused labour is absorbed by the industries that are introduced by the innovation pioneered by the newly freed labour; he failed to foresee that employment as a whole increases. I remember watching this program one night called *Life Below Zero*, a program that follows the lives of people who live in this snowy Alaskan community where the temperature rarely goes above -5°C. In this one episode[68] in particular, I was astounded by how much of a struggle the inhabitants had to go through just to get drinking water. One individual, Sue Aikens was out in the wilderness for the whole day in search of drinking water. It was a struggle that would even shock African communities without running water. For these inhabitants, the challenge was in finding frozen water holes. Since the whole area was covered in snow, this whole exercise involved walking around with an iron rod occasionally impaling the ground to see if any water would come gushing out from the ground underneath. I contrasted their lives with mine and realized how fortunate I was to have been a benefactor of the technological innovation that gives me running water; I also realized how this innovation freed up my time and enables me to spend it on other activities that were of greater value for myself as well as my community.

---

[67] David Ricardo, Adam Smith, John Stuart Mill
[68] Life Below Zero season 5 episode 4

Marx also accurately predicted monopolies but did not see how the free market system periodically goes through a correction, which in turn presents many smaller players with opportunities and ways of "equalising" the playing field. History has given us numerous examples of big corporations that went out of business as a result of economic crises and failure to innovate, subsequently making the way for new businesses to emerge. How the smartphone disrupted the camera film industry or how Microsoft and Apple disrupted the monopoly held by IBM computer and Nokia/Blackberry.

Marx believed that these 'downsides' of capitalism prepared the ground for communism, that the workers would be so disenfranchised that, they would rise up to seize control of the production process now ideally suited for central planning[69]

The state would improve the economy in accordance with a "common plan" and all workers would be mobilized in "industrial armies". Military discipline (code word for coercion) was a necessity to ensure that this central plan was carried out efficiently.

In 1847, revolutionary events took place in Switzerland, Italy, Paris, Vienna Budapest, Krakow and Berlin the following year; where members of these societies appeared to have developed a sudden appetite for freedom of speech. The unrest eventually led these monarchies to capitulate by granting some liberal freedoms. The calls for social reform eventually forced Russia's Tsar Alexander II to commission an act that led to the abolition of serfdom in 1861. Engels and Karl Marx sought to ride this wave and moved back to Germany where they revived the

---

[69] above, that the first step in the revolution by the working class, is to raise the proletariat to the position of ruling as to win the battle of democracy. The proletariat will use its political supremacy to wrest, by degrees, all capital from the bourgeoisie, to centralise all instruments of production in the hands of the State, i.e., of the proletariat organised as the ruling class; and to increase the total of productive forces as rapidly as possible

newspaper Marx had previously been appointed as editor, calling it the *Neue Rheinische Zeitung.*

Marx had hoped for a proletariat revolution following King Louis-Philippe's removal in 1848 by the disenchanted French middle and working class. The new government declared a republic, passing many laws favourable to the working class (i.e. subcontracting -a method used by employers to pay more wages - was banned) and the working day was reduced to 10 hours[70]. But he was to be bitterly disappointed when another insurrection of 15000 workers was crushed by the new government with thousands killed and some imprisoned in Algeria[71].

Karl Marx and Freidrich Engels tried to foment a revolution of their own in Germany (Elbefeld and the Rhineland proletariat) in 1849, only to be crushed by authorities once more. This spirit of revolution was to be imitated by neighbouring countries like Italy and France only to face similar fates as those of their German counterparts. Revolutionary fervour was of great concern to the monarchs and autocracies governing at the time, so any sense of a revolution was ruthlessly crushed. The Crackdown knocked the wind out of Marx's sail and he retreated from the limelight spending much of his time writing Capital, a book Engels had commissioned him to write in 1845.

The Red Flag

There was to be a glimmer of hope in 1871, when France elected a government consisting of self-declared socialists for the first time. After Paris had been surrounded by Prussians in one of the longest sieges, the Parisian government signed an armistice that left The Parisians outraged. This was the reason why the following elections resulted in the election of 81 new members, two-thirds of those being socialist. For the first time,

---

[70] Priestland, David – The Red Flag page 35
[71] Ibid, (Red Flag) page 35

the red flag (which symbolises a militant United proletariat) flew above a seat of government. These socialist officials received workers' wages and were subject to dismissal by the people.

Enemy of the people and their leaders
Many dictatorships in modern economies still subscribe to the four stages of the progressive sequence and believe it is a natural process. They continue to believe that any deviation from this sequence should be ruthlessly crushed and that any reforms that seek to expedite this process must be greatly encouraged. Anybody that poses a threat to the pursuit of this sequence is rendered evil, selfish and admonished as nothing but an enemy of the people, those against collectivism are viewed as cold heartless, selfish and immoral people. One of the biggest Marxist parties to form was the Social Democratic Party of Germany (SDP). The late 19th-century industrial revolution greatly increased the size of the industrial working class and the ideas of this party resonated with millions of employees. One of these was the notion of workers taking over the ownership of the means of production.

But the 1878 assassination attempt on the Kaiser's life resulted in a crackdown on workers' organisations. Anti-socialist laws were implemented and the SDP was banned. Although the laws were repealed in 1890, the party and workers continued to face immense discrimination.

By the early 1900's Europe had seen s rise of a few Social Democratic parties that embodied the German party. The Austrians, Czechs, Dutch, Swedish Finnish and Norwegians all had Marxist parties gaining ground in their country's electorate. Marxism's rise in popularity can be accredited to Freidrich Engels, who upon Karl Marx's death took it upon himself to establish Marxism as a political force. Engels would often engage in lengthy correspondence with European socialist politicians, writing hundreds of letters of criticism and advice from his base in London.

On the Revolution

Engels later found a companion in Karl Kautsky, born in Prague to a theatrical family; Engels found his easy-going nature and eloquence in a wide range of subjects quite refreshing. As David Priestland noted; *If Engels founded the Marxist 'church', then the first 'pope' of socialism, as he was called at the time, was Karl Kautsky*[72].

Kautsky injected Darwinism into Marxism by highlighting their similarities; the natural progression of human history, and believed, just like Marx, that there would be no need for violence to topple the Capitalist bourgeoisie system because capitalism would ultimately be destroyed by its own weight. Kautsky argued that Marxists should push for reforms through non-violent ways for a revolution to take place when the economic conditions were right.

The question as to how the worker's revolution would arise remained a much-debated topic amongst Marxist circles because some believed, like Kautsky, that participating in politics only serves to legitimize *bourgeoisie establishments.'*

This debate moved from the realm of theory into reality when the workers had to actually choose between nationalism and imperialism in the advent of World War One. In certain regions, this war pitted the proletariat against the socialists as various socialist parties in parliaments across Europe had to vocalise their support for the war efforts against other fellow socialist countries. In essence, the French and British Socialists were asked to side with their Imperialist state and go to war against German Socialists. And when they voted in the support of the war efforts, nationalism and imperialism had won over the unity and brotherhood of the proletariat.

---

[72] Priestland, David – The Red Flag page 53

It seemed like Marxism had been defeated in World War 1, however, the hardship and drudgery that was brought on by the extensively prolonged trench war was perceived as a creation of imperialism; this consternation re-energised Marxist movements across Europe. Collectivism, as an ideology was in the ascendance, it was widely taught and accepted in certain circles of European and North American society. We saw the rise of Benito Mussolini and the black shirts giving rise to collectivism in Italy and the neighbouring society, the Bolsheviks and an exiled leader Lenin returning to topple a 300-year-old dynasty; the rise of a mediocre painter and his brown shirts getting into the driving seat of a European power, not to lead the collective to the promised land as intended, but to suffering, death and complete devastation. The United States was also well in its leftward trajectory under the presidency of Woodrow Wilson.

Even though Marxists differ in some respects, we can get a fundamental understanding of what Marxism is just by looking at what collectivists believe in irrespective of the contradictions one might pick up in Marx's work. Towards the end of the First World War, Tsar Nicholas II abdicated his throne, the worst decision ever taken by man with the sole exception of Adam and Eve; ultimately paving the way for the Bolsheviks, under the leadership of Vladimir Lenin to walk into power. The USSR (Union of Soviet Socialist Republics) was formed and would rule Russia and most of Eastern Europe and Southern Asia for the next 70 years.

Chapter 3: Colonialism and the Collectivists

The USSR soon became the biggest exporter of the Marxist-communist ideology worldwide; from South America, Europe-Caribbean islands to Africa. During this time, Africa was battling a cancer of its own. The whole continent apart from a few countries like Ethiopia and Liberia were under the control of foreign nations. The Scramble for Africa resulted in more than 90% of Africa colonized.

The Philanthropic beginnings

Having outlined the History of Collectivism, we may now explore how and when it was exported to African shores. To understand Africa today is to know and understand her past; her borders and the origination of the ubiquitous doctrines and policies implemented in the past that still affect her today. Although African history goes back far beyond contact with the Wazungu (white people), one only needs to go back to the point of initial contact to study the roots of what shapes modern Africa today; that point is African colonization.

One often wonders why it took so long for the outside world to develop an appetite for Africa, private diary inputs and letters by various prominent explorers start flooding the market in the 16th century. Yes, we read about The Kingdom of Kongo, Ndongo, Egypt, Ethiopia and other coastal countries from ancient texts (including the Christian Holy Bible); however, these exploits were localized to the coastal areas of Africa. One makes the same observation when reading about earlier South African history, Cape Town in particular. For example, when the Afrikaners (mostly Dutch farmers that had settled in Cape Town) embarked on their "Great Trek" to escape the newly establish British rule, their migration inland was perceived as a migration into the wilderness; a perilous journey into the abyss.

Various factors could have been the reason for the delay in exploring the continent. One factor in particular is the unique African climate that laid a fertile ground for bacteria combined with the treacherous terrain which effectively warded off many aspiring explorers toward other continents such as South and North America. Expeditions into the interior of Africa aggravated the effects of ailments such as malaria, dysentery, typhoid and smallpox; these treatable infections often became death sentences in the perilous African terrain.

When the British government funded the 1841 missionary expedition set out to '*open up*' Niger in West Africa; 130 of the 145 Europeans aboard the three ships (the Albert, the Wilberforce and the Soudan) contracted malaria, the disease killed 40 of the 130[73].

In *Wealth, Poverty and Politics*, author Thomas Sowell also alluded to the unique navigation challenges exploration ships faced when operating in African rivers. How the shallowness of the waters (coastal and sometimes inland) proved to be dead-ends for most commercial ships. He wrote;

> *Moreover, the coastal waters around sub-Saharan Africa are often too shallow for oceangoing ships to dock. In such places, large ocean-going ships must anchor offshore, and have their cargoes unloaded onto smaller vessels that can operate in shallow waters. But this time-consuming process, and the greater amount of labour and equipment required, has been more costly— often prohibitively costly[74].*

Ships that managed to navigate past the coastal waters still faced dangers as they could at any point find themselves abruptly confronted with cascades and escarpments that could bring the whole expedition to a screeching halt.

---

[73] Johnson, Paul - History Of Christianity page 363
[74] Sowell, Thomas - Wealth, Poverty and Politics page 17 (Waterways Ch. 2)

But as the religious missionaries sought to spread their faiths across the globe, it was only a matter of time before they turned their focus to inner Africa. It was amidst such fervour that the Anglican Church Missionary Society launched an African campaign in 1840, amongst the various dignitaries (such as Prince Albert and Prime minister Sir Robert Peel) was a young David Livingstone[75], whose evangelicalism and anti-slavery crusades would go on to have a forever-lasting impact worldwide. As he once asked, *"Can the love of Christ not carry the missionary where the slave-trade carries the trader?"*

From what started as religious missionaries on a quest to spread their religion and combat slavery, the philanthropic European presence in pre-colonial Africa morphed into a pestilence that threatened the sovereignty of African rulers across board. As the Scottish physician and Christian missionary David Livingstone sailed around Africa in his infamous quest to discover the sources of the Nile River, these travels exposed him to the daily tribal life of Africa and the continuous barbaric village raids that were carried out to fuel the slave trade.

In an effort to rescue Africa from the slave trade, Livingstone led the crusade for the need to "open up" Africa, an aim to bring what he termed the 3C's - Commerce, Christianity and Civilization - to the continent to liberate her from her troubles[76]. In his 1857 address to the University of Cambridge, he said;

> *"I beg to direct your attention to Africa. I know that in a few years I shall be cut off in that country, which is now open. Do not let it be shut again! I go back to Africa to try to make an open path for commerce and Christianity[77]"*

It was also in the guise of philanthropy that more nefarious actors like King Leopold founded the Congo Free State; a self-aggrandizement pet project that greatly multiplied his personal

---

[75] Ibid, Johnson page 363
[76] Packenham, Thomas - The Scramble for Africa page xvii
[77] Ibid Johnson 363

wealth (due to the sudden explosion of the rubber trade necessitated by the rise of the automobile) at the expense of the natives. In his desperation for profit, King Leopold's ABIR feudal lords often severed the limbs of plantation workers suspected of slackness, indolence and subterfuge.

In his last days and still searching for the answer to a mystery that eluded many great men before him, that is the source of the Nile River; David Livingstone was struck down with another bout of pneumonia. Though common in Africa; and to David Livingstone who survived it before; this was one battle he would not win. It was a somewhat tragic end to such an illustrious life; the tragedy did not lie in his failure to find the source of the Nile, for he had many achievements[78]. The tragedy lay in his solitude; it is tragic for someone with a cult hero status, largely celebrated worldwide, to die in the wilderness, suffering in seclusion unbeknown to their loved ones; wandering in search of a goal they would never achieve.

David Livingstone died May 1873 having lived a glorious life full of achievements; amongst the long list of achievements as an explorer were the "discoveries" of Lake Ngami in modern-day Botswana north of the Kalahari Desert. He also "discovered" the Victoria Falls in 1855, the river Lualaba in Congo, the central Zambezi valley leading across the continent and Lake Nyasa which spans across the borders of modern-day Malawi, Tanzania and Mozambique. Although venerated as an explorer, David Livingstone's greatest achievement was in his efforts to curb the African slave trade. His vivid depictions of the barbarity ubiquitous in Africa brought the world's attention to the slave trade, calling it the 'open sore of the world. The Missionary enjoyed a different experience of African life compared to the European tourist or slave raider. His experiences differed in the sense that he had skin in the game.

---

[78] Packenham, Thomas - Prologue The Scramble for Africa Prologue

Colonialism and the Collectivists

The Missionary's experience differed from other Europeans because his mission was to win souls and the Explorer's aim was to win territory. For him to accomplish his mission work, the missionary had to live amongst Africans, he had to speak the language of the African, and in speaking his language; he felt the African man's anguish.

The search for David Livingstone - erroneously presumed dead - sparked a sensation that increased the world's interest in the African continent, including one Henry Morton Stanley, a Welsh-American journalist from the New York Herald. As Livingstone's letters back home seemed to dry up, ramblings of his demise appeared more credible, igniting calls for the repatriation of his remains. Henry Stanley set sail for Africa in search of his idol, an expedition which culminated in his infamous November 1871 meeting with David Livingstone in the small town of Ujiji, near Lake Tanganyika south of Kigoma in present-day Tanzania. That's how Henry Stanley landed on African shores, the quest to rescue his idol birthed the journey of Henry Stanley the explorer; he would later make it his mission to complete Livingstone's quest in finding the source of the Nile River.

Exploration expeditions became conquest expeditions, incentivizing governments into funding these projects; many European nations might have missed the boat in the conquest of the Americas but were adamant that they would not miss out on this particular opportunity. More Europeans joined this race as they saw the conquest of Africa as means to outcompete each other in the quest for European dominance. Africa had untapped natural resources that offered opportunities to grow their economies, cheap labour (slavery), expand their army and ultimately, expand territory.

The sudden interest in the "Dark Continent" (a sobriquet coined by journalist-turned-explorer Henry Stanley) that birthed the Congo State, inadvertently precipitated what was to be later known as the "Scramble for Africa". Explorers like Henry Stanley, acting on behalf of King Leopold II of Belgium, and Pierre Savorgnan de Brazza acting on behalf of the French, raced to "capture" as many territories as possible for the sole benefit of their funders. They raced to sign multiple peace treaties with local chiefs to hold a claim on these territories on behalf of their governments.

Pierre Savorgnan de Brazza was another explorer who rose to prominence as a result of his exploits. With the aid of the French government and French private enterprises, the Italian native explored the Central African region which culminated in the signing of a treaty with King Illoh Makoko of the Batekes (Teke) in 1880[79].

The king's signature represented a victory for the French over the Belgians, who had funded Henry Stanley's campaign to capture this very same territory on their behalf. For his success, Brazza was rewarded with French citizenship and the capital of the Republic of the Congo, the Ncuna settlement; was later renamed Brazzaville in his honour. This territory paved the way for the French Conquest of Central Africa.

The Berlin Conference
As the Scramble for Africa continued well into the 19th century, it became evident that the current state of disorderliness increased the risk of conflict as African leaders would often sign treaties with multiple government agents. The rush for the Congo led by Henry Stanley and Pierre de Brazza merely accentuated the dangers of this state of affairs - not having a clear outline as to what constitutes a treaty or the prerequisites

---

[79] Ibid - Packenham page. 107 Prologue

of a valid treaty; basically, a documented code of conduct that would assist in settling any disputes in the race for territories. In an attempt to obviate this impending car crash, the German Chancellor Otto von Bismarck rapidly convened a diplomatic summit of European powers, formally calling it the General Act of the Berlin Conference (today commonly referred to as the Berlin Conference)

This conference involved discussions that gave birth to "the Berlin Act"- a treaty that outlined the code of conduct during the conquest and competition for pieces of Africa; this code of conduct outlined what constitutes an annexation and the steps that must be followed for an annexation to be recognized. It stipulated the responsibilities and laws each imperial nation should adhere to for their new treaties to be recognized. I don't think the reader should be surprised by the fact that not one African leader was present at this conference; the reader should also not be surprised by the fact that African leaders did not recognize this act. The Berlin Act includes the following points[80];

1. *The notification of annexation of territory which would be sent to other powers*
2. *Effective occupation to validate this annexation*
3. *Freedom to trade with all nations including the Congo basin*
4. *Freedom to navigate than Niger and Congo Rivers*
5. *Suppression of slave trade by land and sea*

The continent would go on to "welcome" many explorers, subsequently haemorrhaging 90% of its territory within a 10-year period. Carl Peters is one German teacher-turned-explorer who precipitated the German effort toward expanding the German Empire on African shores. He would go on to sign treaties with various local kings and chiefs that established the German Colony of East Africa (in modern-day Tanzania)[81]. The

[80] https://courses.lumenlearning.com/boundless-worldhistory/chapter/the-berlin-conference/
[81] Ibid - Packenham pg. 277

German Dr Gustav Nachtigal colonized Kamerun (Cameroon), Togo (Little Popo /Togoland) and Angra Pequena (South-West Africa)[82]. On the other hand, General Louis Archinard of France wrestled the Tukulor Empire and the French Soudan (today Mali)[83] away from Sultan Ahmadu.

Right to Conquer!

As Britain and France rapidly amassed territories subsequently growing the size of their empires, latecomers like Italy and Germany scrambled for the gerrymandered (have a look at the Caprivi Strip of Namibia) leftovers that did not offer the same opportunities found in the Congo basin, West, North or South of Africa. Their appetite for imperialism reached its peak when Italians tried to conquer famine-prone Ethiopia multiple times despite ample evidence that the colonization of Abyssinia would be of little economic value; especially when one considers the geographical landscape and costs of ruling the territory.

Like the Third Reich in Germany that sought to avenge the WWI defeat; Mussolini made the most of the Italian people's chagrin following the humiliating 1896 defeat at the hands of Menelik II of Shoa (Shewa) in the battle of Adwa. In this battle, the world once again witnessed an African indigenous people successfully repel the hostile advances of a European-Western power. Mussolini's annexation of Abyssinia was another message to Africans that no treaty or World League[84] would come to their aid once a European power had its eye set on their territory.

The October 1935 Italian invasion of Ethiopia was born more out of revenge than mere conquest, or at least that's how the world (including The League of Nations) viewed it. One could see this in their widespread insouciance to this aggression as it

---

[82] Ibid - page 143
[83] Ibid - page243
[84] World league expressed its utmost condemnation and nothing else.

was in no doubt a violation of the Treaty of Versailles[85] as well as the world peace championed by The League of Nations. The apparent opprobrium towards the Italians was undermined by their unwillingness to enforce any sanctions that would have *disincentivised* any further aggression toward Abyssinia. After all, when has (world) opinion ever helped anyone under attack?

Despite the multiple statements of condemnation, it appeared as if deep down, they empathized with Italy's need to avenge the humiliation it had suffered in the 1896 defeat at the hand of Menelik II. It's as if they were in agreement with the Italian sentiment that asserts that successfully repelling an invasion by a European superpower is an act which cannot go unpunished.

It was quite evident that the Western world was of the opinion that Indigenous persons repelling an invasion by a European power was a greater insult (and violation) to the world order than Italy's unwarranted aggression towards the Empire of Ethiopia. In essence, Britain and France understood that Italy was avenging the same humiliation they themselves had suffered a few decades earlier at the hands of *primitive* armies. The British remembered that the annexation of the Zululand in South Africa was preceded by the humiliating defeat the far-technologically superior British army suffered at the hands of the spear-wielding Zulu *impis* under the leadership of King Cetshwayo ka-Mpande in the infamous battle of Isindlwana. The French also remembered their initial encounter with Samori Toure and the Wassoulou-Mandingo Empire, an empire that was in present-day north and south-eastern Guinea and parts of north-eastern Sierra Leone, Mali, northern Côte d'Ivoire and southern Burkina Faso.

---

[85] The Treaty of Versailles was one of several peace agreements that officially brought The First World war to an end.

Transfer of Colonies

The scramble for Africa led to the establishment of settler colonies and reached its apogee in 1904 when Africa had its largest percentage of territory at the hands of Colonial Powers. From Cape-to-Cairo and Niger-to-the-Nile, the whole territory of Africa was under the rule of Europe. The fall of one empire did not bring liberation to the subjects, but only presented an opportunity for another powerhouse to occupy the position vacated by the previous coloniser. The fall of the Ottoman and German empires may have liberated the Turks and Saudi's but it only brought the Africans and Middle Easterners different rulers in the form of the British, French and white minorities in Africa (i.e. Zimbabwe and South Africa).

The mandate system that was established following the World War I peace treaty transferred German and Ottoman colonial empires to British and French custodianship. Modern-day Togo, Libyan, Ghanaian, Nigerian, Rwandan, Burundi and Cameroon territories were transferred into the hands of the French and British, while South-West Africa (Namibia) was given to the minority-ruled South Africa. The only Africans deemed qualified to gain independence or custodianship were the white Africans.

It is for these reasons that South Africans lay some blame at the feet of Great Britain with regard to the suffering that followed. As Britain prepared to hand over the Cape and Natal colonies to the white republics (to form a unified South Africa), the Herbert Henry Asquith government acquiesced to the newly formulated constitution that denied black natives and Indians the right to vote. Under the new constitution, the few people in the Indian and black population who were deemed *'fit'* to vote in the Natal and Cape colonies had this right curtailed[86].

---

[86] Ibid – page 665

The lack of representation in the House of the Union Parliament and access to the voting booth left the black majority powerless to neither prevent nor defeat the apartheid system. The timid reaction to Ian Smith's Unilateral Declaration of Independence on the 11th of November 1965 was in effect Britain handing over Southern Rhodesia (today Zimbabwe) to the white minority in the same fashion Britain handed over South Africa to the South African white minority. The Europeans handed over colonies to a white minority that gave little thought to the interests and well-being of the native (black) population.

Compartmentalizing Morality

It is often stated how rapid the events of 1914 escalated into an all-out war (WW1), and although such sentiments have a lot of truth to them, I think this observation overshadows a fundamental principle that modern governments still violate today; that is of trying to compartmentalise morality. To put actions into compartments believing that since these actions are restricted or localized to certain compartments, the consequences that result from such actions will also be localized into those compartments. We see this in the local drug dealer that devotedly takes care of his daughter while simultaneously selling drugs to other kids her age, or the rabidly racist preacher that disowns his son for marrying out of his race while simultaneously preaching the messages of Jesus Christ every Sunday. In this instant, WWI broke out because something that had been deemed moral was suddenly implemented on the wrong people - the Serbians - forcing the whole European Continent to confront the concept of colonization with some skin-in-the-game.

Compartmentalizing morality makes one believe that they can still uphold overall moral values despite acting immorally in another field, so long as that one immoral act is localized to a singular domain. They believe that certain actions are ethical provided that there is consensus and that any revocation of such consensus brings an end to such actions. "It is okay to do it because everybody does it and it will stop being okay if everybody stops doing it". Basically, there was a consensus amongst world powers that the colonization of foreign territory was not an unethical act by virtue of the fact that all world Superpowers were doing it. The General Act of the Berlin Conference rubber-stamped its legality. Compartmentalization led Imperial nations into believing that they could still champion and hold onto the moral high ground despite their barbarous actions in the colonization of Africa. Versailles treaty found that Germany's military 'aggression' and "expansionary" policies were the ultimate causes of the First World War[87]. This *military aggression and expansionary* policy which was standard and moral in the Africa compartment became immoral in the Europe compartment.

The belief that a power that does not respect the autonomy of African/Asian borders would somehow respect European borders was very naïve, short cited and portrayed a deep sense of a lack of self-awareness. In retrospect, the hostility witnessed in the early 20th century should not have been a surprise to anyone, morality is a value habituated by practice, and it cannot be compartmentalized into specific domains*[88].

Back to Africa
Once these countries were colonized, the colonial governments passed laws on African territories that benefited the colonizers. They would apply tariffs on other countries (colonized by fellow Europeans) as means to raise money. The "increase" in population provided ways to improve military presence to aid their military ventures elsewhere. Britain exponentially

---

[87] Johnson, Paul - A History of the Modern World page 106 (Waiting for Hitler)
[88] [For those that invoke the notion of "taking a life" to counter this point - I would reply in the affirmative, it is immoral to take a life for personal gain (or gratuitous) and the life of the innocent - but it is moral to take the life of a criminal, soldier or one that threatens your life. In the biblical realm, we speak of killing and murder. A combat soldier kills an enemy, but murders his noisy neighbour.]

increased its military manpower through the absorption of India, West and Southern Africa; this British expansion also fuelled Jan Smut's aspirations of establishing a Southern African British empire.

Treaties and Conquests

Since many African leaders were illiterate in European languages, their reliance on translators left them open to the chicanery prevalent in most explorers who were all-so desperate for their fruitful territory. Many African leaders accused of having signed away their sovereignty actually signed documents believing that they were entering into different agreements entirely. King Lobengula's (the Matabeleland king of modern-day Zimbabwe) "concession" of exclusive mining rights to Cecil John Rhodes's British South Africa Company is one case in point where the verbal promises made to the Matebele King were different to the promises made on paper. The king was under the impression that the company was solely after mining rights at the outback of his kingdom for the meagre price of £100 a month, 1000 Martini-Henry rifles, 100 000 rounds of ammunition and a gunboat on the Zambezi nearby[89]. This 'misunderstanding' promulgated the eventual invasion and conquest of the Mashonaland and Matebeleland, founding Rhodesia (modern-day Zimbabwe).

In some instances, it was later discovered that these leaders signed these documents believing that they were entering into protectorate agreements, an agreement that brings a kingdom or state under the protection of another sovereign state in return for resources, access to pathways and various other assets. Since Pre-colonial African society was plagued with slave raids from infamous slave traders like the infamous Tippu Tip, the warlord Mwenda Msiri of Katanga and other Arab slave traders from the

---

[89] Ibid, Packenham page 384
https://zimfieldguide.com/bulawayo/were-lobengula-and-amandebele-tricked-rudd-concession
https://www.sahistory.org.za/archive/rudd-concession-king-lobengula-matabeleland-1888

Zanzibar region; protection from an imperial power was a very attractive option for weak tribes living in constant fear of night raids. Tribes would also sign treaty-of-protections to fend off virulent rival tribes that were constant thorns to their way of life. Samuel Maherero, chief of the Herero tribe gave little thought into putting the cross on the treaty that offered protection against their constant nemesis, the neighbouring Nama tribe[90].

Imperialists that failed to present documents that would justify any takeover simply resorted to coercion and invaded the territory, forcing the natives into giving up their sovereignty. This invasion was sometimes met with fierce resistance in certain parts of the continent. We read of the great battles of *Isindlwana*, where the Zulus in South Africa defeated the great British Royal army. We read about the battles between the Tukolor Empire (under the leadership of Sultan Ahmadu) and the French imperial force, battles that preceded the colonization of modern-day Mali; or the above-mentioned Mandingo Empire under the stewardship of Samori Toure.

Complete annihilation

We read about rebellions that attempted to extricate peoples from colonial rule such as the Maji-maji in modern-day Tanzania. A rebellion instigated by Kinjikitile Ngwale, a medium who managed to convince the native population that he was possessed by a snake spirit called *Hongo*, which gave him the insight to develop a secret potion that would give the men an advantage in their bid to drive the German settlers out their land. He managed to convince quite a large number of natives and clan leaders that his potion *maji* (water in Swahili mixed with some castor oil and local seeds) had the power to turn bullets into water. Through his secret campaigns disguised as traditional consultations, the witch doctor managed to garner so much support that the natives (including the Matumbi and

---

[90] Ibid, Packenham page 605

Ngindo people) were emboldened enough to spark the infamous Maji-maji rebellion in modern-day Tanzania[91].

Another rebellion that attempted to drive the Germans out was the Herero Uprising in modern-day Namibia. The daily torment the Herero people had suffered at the hands of German rulers slowly eroded their compliance; the raping of Herero women that went unpunished, the habitual floggings and murders were such common occurrences that Chief (or *Kaptein*) Samuel Maherero was left with no other alternative but to plot a daring uprising in an effort to drive out the barbarous German colonials. The revolt experienced initial success; however, the German reinforcement proved to be too strong for the rebellion. This ill-fated rebellion paved the way for General Lothar von Trotha, the most brutal leader to have ever walked the African continent[92]. In his open letter to the Maherero people, von Trotha wrote the following:

> I, the Great General of the German soldiers, address this letter to the Herero people. The Herero are no longer considered German subjects. They have murdered, stolen, cut off ears and other parts from wounded soldiers, and now refuse to fight on, out of cowardice. I have this to say to them … the Herero people will have to leave the country. Otherwise, I shall force them to do so utilizing guns. Within the German boundaries, every Herero, whether found armed or unarmed, with or without cattle, will be shot. I shall not accept any more women or children. I shall drive them back to their people – otherwise, I shall order shots to be fired at them.[93]

General von Trotha's subsequent *Vernichtungsbefehl* (extermination order) was testament to his resolve in sticking to every word of this letter; it sparked the heavy-handed brutal reprisals that culminated in the setup of concentration camps

---

[91] Ibid – Packenham 407
https://www.blackpast.org/global-african-history/maji-maji-uprising-1905-1907/
[92] Ibid - Packenham page 608
[93] Ibid - Packenham page 611

and the now-infamous genocide of the Namibian tribes as most were hunted to near extinction, or driven to the perilous Kalahari Desert to meet their demise[94].

Despite any resistance that African rulers put up, it could never match the might of the great Imperial nations that could always rely on their superior weaponry and extensive sources of reserve troops from other colonies.

French Army general Louis Archinard's invasions of North African empires led to the colonial conquest of the West African territory. Not even the might of Samori Ture (Toure), founder and leader of the Wassoulou Empire could prevent the annexation and eventual destruction of the once mighty African empire. The destruction of great armies would reverberate across whole regions, sending a clear message to neighbouring kingdoms thus thwarting any morale necessary for assembling an army strong enough to fend off invasions. The final defeat of the once great Zulu nation at the Battle of Ulundi sent shockwaves across the whole Southern Africa region; following this defeat, many chiefs were more inclined into settling for peace rather than risking complete annihilation.

Ethnic Tensions

Contrary to Europe and the western world, the lack of nationhood in Africa was the biggest reason why its resistance efforts failed. Simply put - an attack on the Igbo or Zulu tribe was not an attack on Nigeria or South Africa overall. The Hausa people did not feel like an attack on the Igbo hundreds of kilometres away was an attack on the Hausa tribe; the Ba-Sotho people did not feel like a British-led attack on the Zulu tribe 100 kilometres away was an attack on their 'people'. If African tribes were united under one nation, its fall to invading

---

[94] Hull. Isabel V.; Absolute Destruction; page 56

powers would have definitely been delayed if not repelled completely.

The pre-existing ethnic tensions did half the job and the art of *Divide, Conquer and Rule* - a skill Europeans honed over 400 years of imperialism and exploitation in Asia, the Americas and the Pacific regions - did the rest. The divisions between African ethnic tribes were so pronounced that it left them vulnerable to exploitation. The Europeans would go on to conquer Africa in just over a 15-year period.

The hatred between some Ethnic tribes was so pronounced that tribes would partner with invading Europeans in an effort to defeat rival African tribes. We already discussed how the Herero would align with the Germans to get protection from the Nama tribe and how the Bambara were influential in the eventual defeat of the great Tukolor Empire when the Bambara merged forces with the French. The native's participation in colonial wars was a common phenomenon, we read about the French army's use of 'tiralleures' or 'laptot; indigenous infantries or troops recruited in French colonial territories. We read of the general term "askari" which is reserved for indigenous soldiers serving in the armies of European colonial powers.

Menelik's rapid consolidation of Ethiopian chiefdoms transformed the Ethiopians from a bunch of defragmented tribes into one solid united monarchy; a monarch that was strong enough to defeat General Oreste Baratieri's Italian forces at the 1896 Battle of Adwa.

Civilize the savage
At the dawn of the 20th century, most parts had been colonized by these 7 European powers; Germany, Britain, Italy, Spain, Belgium, France and Portugal. These European countries had established colonial states which were bureaucratic, racist and authoritarian in their very nature; often driven by the fact that

their governing was not in service of the governed but to the citizens of the colonial power. Each power appointed governors that served the interest of the colonial power's leader, these appointees could be local, foreign, or a local but overseen by a foreigner sent by the office situated in the Colonial power's capital city (i.e. London/ Paris)

As these Europeans took over these territories, they enforced their ideology with the aim of civilizing the savages, a mission of bringing in David Livingstone's 3 C's; Commerce, Christianity and Civilization.

In a similar mould, France implemented its own version of civilizing the savages by embarking on its mission to evolve the natives into becoming civilized French Africans[95]. The anti-slavery campaign offered the moral justification for colonization amidst criticism from other nations that would occasionally highlight the injustice of this practice. There was a perception that when left alone, Africans would simply go back to their 'savagery ways' of killing each other. King Mwanga's (of Buganda) burning of Christian male pages who resisted his sexual advances was one occurrence that propagated this belief and was an event that strengthened the case for the colonization of the Buganda region[96].

By the time Hitler invaded Poland, much of African territory was still under European control. Even though countries like Egypt and South Africa had been granted autonomy, no other country was under self-governance. France still controlled most of Western and Northern Africa; the Belgians in Congo, Burundi, and Rwanda; the Spanish in Morocco, and Equatorial Guinea; Italians in Somalia and Eritrea; the Portuguese in the West African Islands Mozambique Guinea Bissau and Angola

---

[95] Ibid - Packenham page 115
[96] Ibid - Packenham page 415
  https://www.bugandawatch.com/2015/05/21/my-two-cents-worth-katikkiro-mukasa-was-behind-many-mwanga-executions/

with Britain scattered all over Africa (from Somalia to Libya to Nigeria to Ghana to the Southern part of the continent).

Brother in arms

Despite many attempts at insurrections and violent resistance movements, such efforts remained futile. Even the severed hands of the farmworkers in Leopold's Congo Free State could not generate enough opprobrium to strengthen the call to de-colonize African territory; once again, the removal of one European power only led to the appointment of another European power. The Colonial power proved to be too strong and quashed any uprising with relative ease. The two World Wars did little to compound liberalism's call to bring any real change; colonised countries needed a friend, a brother in arms.

As these guerrilla uprisings continued, another battle was brewing in the post-World War II world in the form of the Cold War. This non-combative *war* involved the 2 superpower nations (USA and USSR) competing for influence and dominance in the globe. Their nuclear capabilities only added to the anxieties felt all over the globe, the clash between these two countries was not just a battle for superiority and dominance but a battle of ideologies; collectivism vs capitalism; USSR led by its Marxist party and the United States, a society that championed free market liberalism (to some extent). In an attempt to subvert the other's ideology, they proceeded to destabilize each other's position on the world stage. This came to a head in the Korean War, the Vietnamese war, the Cuban revolution and the overall decolonising of Africa. The partitioning of post-WWII Germany and Korea brought one half under the leadership of a US-backed government and the other half under a Soviet-backed government; thus aggravating this battle of ideologies

Non-Alignment Movement

Other world leaders grew cautious of this precarious situation as time went on, so much so that Indonesia's President Sukarno convened the first Afro–Asian Conference (aka Bandung Conference) which took place on 18–24 April 1955 in Bandung, Indonesia. The delegates of the 29 countries from the African and Asian continents aimed to develop and promote economic relations outside the sphere and influence of the two "warring" superpowers[97]. The conference laid the ground for the eventual creation of the Non-Aligned Movement, a forum of 120 developing world states not formally aligned with or against any major power bloc[98] (USA vs USSR)

Anything But Red

African leaders tried to remain neutral in the Cold War but their need for assistance and resources to supplement an armed struggle incentivized them to align with a power bloc most willing to offer such assistance. In most cases, the Soviet Bloc was often more prepared to offer the military training and finance required to wage a successful guerrilla-liberation war. Leaders in need of resources believed that they could exploit the Cold War to their favour, often pitting Western and Eastern bidders against each other. Liberation freedom fighters realised that western countries were prepared to offer whatever resource at their disposal (including supporting dictators such as Ngo Dinh Diem in South Vietnam) so long as this assistance would undermine if not defeat any communist influence lurking nearby. Western nations would grant aid to certain nations while simultaneously instigating *coupes de tat* against democratically elected governments elsewhere. Whoever proved to have adopted the superpower's ideology was deemed worthy of support.

---

[97] McTurnan, Kahin - The Afro-Asia Conference
    Johnson, Paul - History of the Modern World
[98] Ibid - History of the Modern World

Colonialism and the Collectivists

This was evident in the case of Mobutu Sese Seko (Joseph Mobutu), who would go on to exploit this conflict to its fullest, utilising the American CIA to aid his meteoric rise to leadership. Since most liberation movements were aligned with Marxist governments, any attempt to counterpoise this communist influence drove the US government into the arms of the incumbent colonial powers; the arch-nemesis of liberation revolutionaries. They would enter into such a partnership with the "other side" regardless of the side's depravity. This sad state of affairs (many were to follow) was once again witnessed during the Congo Crisis, when local politicians with the backing of western powers, angled for the Succession and fragmentation of the Democratic Republic of Congo.

With the backing of Belgian troops, regional premier Moïse Tshombe felt emboldened enough to declare independence on behalf of The State of Katanga[99]. Even though the United Nations condemned Mr Tshombe's actions, their denunciations proved to be useless and the subsequent trips to the US failed to produce any results. Patrice Lumumba's courting of Premier Nikita Khrushchev for Soviet assistance to restore law and order was just the ammunition needed to convince Belgium and US intelligence agencies to initiate steps that would guarantee his removal from office[100].

Following a Belgian Commission that was set up to investigate Belgium's responsibility in Lumumba's assassination, the final report concluded that *'Some members of the government, and some Belgian actors at the time, bear an irrefutable part of the responsibility for the events that led to Patrice Lumumba's death[101]'*, Foreign Minister Louis Michel noted in his address to Parliament.

---

[99] Arnold, Guy - Africa; A Modern History page 94
[100] Ibid page 97
[101] Ibid page 100
   https://www.nytimes.com/2002/02/06/world/world-briefing-europe-belgium-apology-for-lumumba-killing.html

Though the CIA denies any form of responsibility in the murder, the report concludes that *"the assassination could not have been carried out without the complicity of Belgian officers backed by the C.I.A"*. Madeleine G. Kalb's **The Congo Cables** also went to great lengths to document the case for C.I.A's involvement in the assassination. Kalb alleges that Richard Bissell, then special operations chief of the CIA asked his special assistant to *'prepare biological materials for possible use in the assassination of an unspecified African leader[102]'*.

Mobutu Sese Seko used the *'Anything But Red'* policy to his advantage, realising that for as long as he was anti-communist, his instigating of the 1965 coup d'état, the suspension of political parties and numerous human rights violations followed by a 32-year rule would draw little opposition from Western powers[103]. The same was witnessed in Ghana and the civil wars of Angola and Mozambique, as the battle of ideologies prolonged wars that would have quickly reached their resolutions if the combatants were left to fight on their own.

The Clash of ideologies witnessed in the cold war was once again visible in Angola's Civil War following Angola's independence from Portugal. A struggle for power ensued amongst three groups; the MPLA (The People's Movement for the Liberation of Angola) - led by leader president Agostinho Neto with the backing of USSR and Cuban communists; the second group was UNITA (National Union for total independence of Angola) led by Jonas Savimbi who was backed by the US and the apartheid South African government; while the third group, the FNLA (The National Front for the Liberation of Angola) received financial support from the Mobutu Sese Seko government[104]

---

[102] Ibid Arnold page 98
[103] Ibid Arnold page 99
[104] Ibid Arnold page 490

The hand of the eye of Moscow
In *Toward the African Revolution*, Frantz Fanon stated;
> *"the competitive strategy of Western Nations, moreover, enters into the framework of the policy of 2 blocks, which for 10 years has held a definite Menace of atomic disintegration suspended over the world. And it is surely not purely by chance that the hand of the eye of Moscow is discovered, in an almost stereotypical way, behind each demand for national independence, put forth by the colonial[105]"*

In the Western world, the Marxist ideology surged in popularity, its influence grew from a position of weakness to one bringing dread to the Margaret Thatchers and Ronald Reagans of the world. It soon became a movement popular amongst your freedom fighters, youth and oppressed peoples before it would be adopted by the ruling government. It gained a foothold in Western society through academia as the influx of Marxist professors that obtained employment in western universities produced graduates that were sympathetic to the Marxist cause. Some of these graduates found their way into political office and were able to champion redistributive policies similar to those championed by Karl Marx and Freidrich Engels. Portuguese, French and Italian communist parties gradually came under criticism for their apathy towards the state of the colonised proletariat in the *third world*. These parties were seen as extensions of the class of the old imperialist/neo-colonial forces who served the interest of the ruling class. So just like the First World War, kin and kith took precedence over working-class comradery. The proletariat's allegiance to their nation took precedence over the universal worker's revolution.

Annus Mirabili
Sekou Touré's opting for full independence over the quasi-independence under the French carapace led to what we now

[105] Fanon, Frantz - Toward the African Revolution page 124

commonly refer to as Africa's *Annus mirabilis* (wonderful year), the year 1960 when a string of francophone countries were granted independence from the French[106]. Cameroon, Chad, Central African Republic, Benin, Burkina Faso, Congo Brazzaville, Côte d'Ivoire, Gabon, Mali, Madagascar, Mauritania, Niger, Senegal and Togo all embarked on a path of self-governance, self-restoration and finally; the opportunity to build societies that would give all its inhabitants equal rights and freedoms.

The January 1966 Afro-Asian (Tricontinental) Latin American people's Solidarity conference that was held in Cuba Havana became one of the first major conferences that were convened with the aim of extricating colonized nations from the grips of imperialism. An event attended by over 500 delegates from 82 countries; the conference delegates averred their positions concerning violence during revolutions, the armed struggle and the dangers of neo-colonialism posed by the incumbent colonial powers and the United States[107]. Simply put, oppressed nations and peoples had the right and were at liberty to exhaust all avenues at their disposal in the waging of popular armed struggles to defeat the aggression and suppression by imperialism and its lackeys.

Common Foe

Since countries that championed the free market system (Capitalism) were the same nations practising imperialism (France, Britain and US neo-colonialism), it should not have been a surprise to see Africans conflate the practice of Free Market economics with the ills of colonialism. As many imperial nations (i.e. Great Britain, France, Belgium and the US) championed Capitalism, Most Africans became convinced

[106] Ibid – Arnold page 17
[107] https://www.marxists.org/subject/china/peking-review/1966/PR1966-04h.htm
https://africanactivist.msu.edu/organization.php?name=Organization+in+Solidarity+with+the+People+of+Africa%2C+Asia%2C+and+Latin+America

that the free market system (capitalism) is a fundamental characteristic of imperialism; capitalism was inadvertently linked to the African man's hardships and servitude. In essence, one of the reasons many Africans developed a fondness for Marxism lies in their common hatred for colonialism; in the colonial powers, the African and the Marxist had a common foe. The USSR managed to convince many that it abhorred colonialism despite being a colonial power itself. In 1956, the USSR invaded Hungary after the country experienced an anti-communist revolution as certain factions of the population expressed desires to break free from the USSR[108].

The Capitalists in African Civil wars

President dos Santos's MPLA were the eventual victors of the Angolan Civil War. Because the MPLA was a democratically elected government, the whole cause and destruction of the civil war was put at the feet of UNITA and its backers the US and South African governments. It is alleged that a total of $250 million[109] was spent on covert operations in Angola[110]. This happened at a time when the USA and South Africa were seen as bastions of capitalism in the western world and Africa respectively. The fact that these two countries were capitalist while bearing much guilt in the destabilizing of newly formed independent nations did not help the free market system advocates in Africa at all.

The United States' alignment with the Apartheid South African regime undermined its moral standing and capitalism's claim of (moral) superiority over Collectivism. The ideological battle between Marxism and Capitalism was also on display in the Korean and Vietnamese wars. In both wars, the communist's goal was to unite the countries initially divided post-WWII (West-East Germany, North-South Korea, Vietnam etc.), while

---

[108] Priestland, David - The Red Flag page 257
[109] Quite a large amount in the '80s
[110] Ibid – Arnold page 586

the capitalist faction wished to keep the countries split to prevent the formation of another communist bloc. In Africa, the "free market" appeared to be against the African man's freedom; In Asia, capitalism appeared to be against unity. The South African apartheid government labelled anti-apartheid activists as communists, lumping liberal men such as Nelson Mandela in the same group as men like Vladimir Lenin, Stalin and Pol Pot. It becomes obvious why one would see a friend in Marxists and why many Africans saw Marxism, a collectivist ideology, as more humane compared to the so-called free market system.

Another proxy War was witnessed in Mozambique in the clash between FRELIMO (The Mozambique Liberation Front, from the Portuguese Frente de Libertação de Moçambique) and Renamo (Resistencia Nacional Mocambicana); a battle where Renamo was backed by the apartheid South African government and Portuguese exiles.

> *Capitalism is a development by refinement from feudalism, just as feudalism is development by refinement from slavery. Capitalism is but the gentlemen's method of slavery. - Kwame Nkrumah*

The colonized believed that their colonization and ultimate exploitation was for capital gain, just like the Marxist that believed that their exploitation in the factories was carried out for capital gains. The colonized people believed that it was capitalism and the rapacious pursuit of wealth that corrupted the colonizer's moral compass. In *Ujamaa: The Basis of African Socialism,* Julius Nyerere wrote;

> *A millionaire can equally well be a socialist; he may value his wealth only because it can be used in the service of his fellow men. But the man who uses wealth for the purpose of dominating any of his fellows is a capitalist[111].*

---

[111] https://ethics.utoronto.ca/wp-content/uploads/2017/11/Nyerere-UjamaaThe-Basis-of-African-Socialism-1962.pdf

Colonialism and the Collectivists

Regardless of whether the colonizers had imperial or liberal societies back home, one could not dispute the fact that they were societies built on capitalism; simply put, the fact that Colonial powers were Capitalist made it difficult for the colonized African to hold capitalism in high esteem. Patrice Lumumba's US-Belgian-led deposition from power didn't help to ameliorate this reputation. Pre-independent colonies had political systems and laws that benefited the ruling class and had little regard for the needs of the colonised people, so upon gaining independence, these nations felt a need to recalibrate this imbalance, this left its leaders looking for a model that would fill this void. People had been exploited and disenfranchised for years and the newly elected leaders were looking to remedy this injustice.

The newly independent nations sought a political system that would redress the prevailing levels of inequality, and redistribute the wealth currently concentrated in the hands of the few - the infamous 1%; while ensuring that they can build a society that offers equal opportunities to every citizen within the land. When one reads Julius Nyerere's *Ujamaa:* The Basis of African Socialism; one notices that he was of this atavistic mindset when he wrote

> *"sociologists may find it interesting to try and find out why our societies in Africa did not, in fact, produce any millionaires – for we certainly had enough wealth to create a few. I think they would discover that it was because the organization of traditional African society – its distribution of the wealth it produced – was such that there was hardly any room for parasitism[112]"*

The newly independent nations believed that David Livingstone's vision of the 3C's led to the undermining and sometimes complete decimation of their cultures and traditional

[112] https://ethics.utoronto.ca/wp-content/uploads/2017/11/Nyerere-UjamaaThe-Basis-of-African-Socialism-1962.pdf pg. 2

practices. The newly elected leaders wanted a system that would aim to restore lost practices and incorporate the people's culture and traditional values, so collectivism was most attractive because it offered a political system that promised civil progression while restoring the lost society. This in effect merged modern government with tribalism.

The Arusha Declaration

Uhuru Monument, Arusha, Tanzania, August 7, 2011 (From www.blackpast.org)

This was well documented in modern-day Tanzania, when the newly elected (in 1961) Prime Minister Julius Nyerere published a political ideology seeking to achieve this very same goal. He titled it The Arusha Declaration, a policy in pursuit of socialism and self-reliance. This publication discussed the concept of Ujamaa (extended family or Brotherhood in Swahili) and socialism.

It declared that African socialism was a model for African development. Kwame Nkrumah was another leader who was open to socialism or rather, African Socialism. The Arusha Declaration's one of many objectives was

..to see the government exercises effective control over the principal means of production and pursue policies which Affiliate the way to collective ownership of the resources of the country[113].

In essence, *Mwalimu* Julius Nyerere sought to move his nation back to its pre-colonial collectivist state; an agrarian society that aimed to fight poverty strictly through agriculture. It's obvious that the author's inclination toward the collective ownership of production was heavily influenced by the works of Karl Marx and Freidrich Engels. In Part 1 of their book titled *The German Ideology*, the duo asserts that:

"The ideas of the ruling class are in every epoch the ruling ideas, i.e. the class which is the ruling material force of society, is at the same time its ruling intellectual force. The class which has the means of material production at its disposal has control at the same time over the means of mental production, so that thereby, generally speaking, the ideas of those who lack the means of mental production are subject to it. The ruling ideas are nothing more than the ideal expression of the dominant material relationships, the dominant material relationships grasped as ideas."[114]

As discussed in Chapter 2, the subversion of human capital (entrepreneurial skill, knowledge, intellect and experience) enables collectivists (especially Marxists) to put labour as the paramount force in production. It enables them to purport that the value of a product is derived from the input of labour. How else could they buttress the claim that the factory workers are the real owners of the factory and overall production?

When a leader inherited an independent state, they soon realized that most natives had been relegated to a proletariat labourer status as the economic resources were in the hands of the ruling

---

[113] https://www.marxists.org/subject/africa/nyerere/1967/arusha-declaration.htm
[114] Ibid, The German Ideology – *Ruling Class and Ruling Ideas* chapter
http://www.marxists.org/archive/marx/works/1845-gi/part_b.htm (6 of 8) [23/08/2000 16:33:59]

class while the workers lived in abject poverty. Leaders that sought to assuage this imbalance found refuge in the ideology that proclaims labour's *paramountcy* over the human capital; the collectivist ideology offered a perfect solution to achieve this goal. It is no surprise that once Julius Nyerere embarked on a path to restore Tanganyika, he found a home in the Marxist doctrine. As Part 2b of the declaration reads;

> *..the major means of production and exchange are under the control of peasants and workers…….……. to build and maintain a socialism, it is essential that all the major means of production and exchange in the nation are controlled and owned by the peasants through the machinery of the government and cooperatives[115]*

Julius Nyerere introduced a villagization scheme that forcefully relocated large sects of the population to the collective farmlands (co-operatives) designated by central planning authorities. This villagization policy aimed to regiment a society into pursuing the collectivised goal of lifting the masses from poverty and redistribute the wealth held by the "top 1%" of the post-colonial era. Mozambique and Ethiopia followed suit.

Ghana's Kwame Nkrumah, Modibo Keita of Mali, Leopold Senghor of Senegal and Sekou Toure of Guinea were other leaders that advocated for African socialism. In his 1981 speech, Samora Machel of Mozambique took a socialist stance when he proclaimed;

> *" the victory of socialism is a victory of science, it is prepared an organised scientifically, the plan is scientific organisation of this victory... Everything Must Be organised, everything must be planned Everything Must Be programmed[116]"*

---

[115] https://www.marxists.org/subject/africa/nyerere/1967/arusha-declaration.htm
[116] Ibid – Priestland page 353
Machel, 18 November 1976 - quoted in Hall and Young, Confronting Leviathan, p76,

Colonialism and the Collectivists

As the Soviets and Cubans continued to support liberation movements across all of Africa, the Marxist ideology gained the sympathy and support from the rest of the continent.

The Second Chimurenga
By 1980, the following countries had embraced collectivism and adopted socialist policies.; Angola, Tunisia, Mali, Benin, Ethiopia, Ghana, Congo-Brazzaville, Algeria, Madagascar, Mozambique, Somalia, Mauritania, Somalia, Guinea, Tanzania, Zambia, Seychelles, Cameroon, Cape Verde Islands, Guinea-Bissau, Libya and Sao Tome and Principe Island.

For most African nations, decolonization came at a high price as a result of the prevalent inequities in military resources. It was always understood that the belligerents fighting for liberation had higher casualties compared to those from the government. The liberation forces' plight was compounded by the logistical nightmare of having to smuggle in armaments, having to deal with food shortages and economic losses that resulted from the constant interceptions of ammunition in transit.

The liberation armies in the Portuguese colonies had to bomb the country to the ground before their right to self-determination was eventually recognized. The liberation struggle left most of these countries bankrupt and saddled with land-mine-infested fields. South Africa and Zimbabwe[117] were left under the curatorship of the minority group that implemented barbaric, racist segregationist policies that produced circumstances that continue to affect many black people to this day. This forced the majority to enter into another long-term struggle for their 2nd

---

[117] When Zimbabwe Declared independence from the British, the British did little to stop this, thus granting Zimbabwe independence

independence, or Second Chimurenga as our Zimbabwean brothers and sisters called it.

Once the colonial forces were defeated, the Marxist revolutionaries set their sights on "enemies" within, the African aristocrats and monarchies. One thinks of Mengistu Mariam's DERG military junta removing Emperor Haile Selassie I from power or Colonel Muammar Gaddafi's toppling of King Idris I of Libya.

The Non-Marxist Liberation Movements

Although the Marxist movement perforated all African societies, claiming that all liberation movements were Marxists would be ignoring a large part of our liberation history. Collectivism in all its formats was crucial in the emancipation of Africa; even in times of war, the nation collectivises to defeat an invading enemy. Liberalism and capitalism failed to come to Africa's aid in its time of need as it brought nothing but exploitation. Collectivism (the Marxist variation in particular) offered arms and training to those in bondage, and through this, was able to fully embed itself in the decolonised Africa's DNA. It is quite important to understand this bond so we can comprehend the challenges we face in uprooting collectivism from Africa.

Chapter 4: Collectivism and the African Worldview

On Worldview

Collectivism is so depressingly ingrained in the African DNA that it would be futile to proselytize the capitalist doctrine without having a firm understanding of the African worldview (or "Weltanschauung").

A worldview (or mindset) can be altered but is somewhat sticky. It's sticky in the sense that there is a level of inertia when it is confronted with new and sometimes conflicting information. The levels of inertia vary from one individual to another; this inertia is fairly dependent on the individual's age, culture and dispositions. A child's present worldview is less sticky compared to that of a 60-year-old because of the logical fact that a child's worldview is not derived from as much information as with a 60-year-old; the mere sight of an aircraft changes a 1-year-old child's world view while the 60-year-old remains ambivalent to such sightings. The amount and similarities of anecdotes is directly proportional to the stickiness of the worldview; well that is the case until a black swan event[118] comes along. In fact, as black swan events prove, the lack of anecdotes over a prolonged length of time also shapes our worldview.

So, a worldview is sticky but amenable, its stickiness is not only dependent on the individual's overall disposition but the novelty of the new information they come across. In this chapter, the

---

[118] Popularized by Nassim Nicholas Taleb, a Black swan event is an event (often unpredicted by the majority) that disproves prevailing axioms; an event that makes you realise that you don't know what you thought you knew.

aim is not to argue the notion of one worldview holding a form of superiority over another, but to study how a current mindset predisposes one into accepting foreign ideas and ideologies. The current litany of worldviews results from cultural cultivation over millennia.

In making this point, the aviation industry comes to mind. As an avid follower of air crash investigations (and being a pilot myself), a few aircraft accidents that took place as a result of pilot error come to mind; these are normally classified under the *Controlled Flight into Terrain (CFIT)* category of accidents because they 'occurred as a result of a fully functional aircraft under the complete control of an aircrew member (pilot) *inadvertently flown into terrain, water, or an obstacle[119]*. In some of these accidents, when the investigators combed through the flight data recording devices trying to unravel the events that preceded the disaster, they discovered that the co-pilot, who's the captain's subordinate, would take notice of the captain's errors but could not find the courage to voice their concerns despite being fully cognisant of the perilous nature of the situation they were currently facing. The investigators had to call on behavioural psychologists for an explanation of this perplexing behaviour. They discovered that the crew's cultural background discouraged the questioning of figures in higher authority.

In *Outliers*, Malcolm Gladwell discussed a similar phenomenon when he looked at the Colombian Airliner Avianca flight 052 that crashed in January of 1990. Within a few hours into the investigation, authorities quickly discovered that the aircraft simply ran out of fuel. The investigators knew that fuel

---

[119] Skybrary (https://skybrary.aero)

exhaustion is not something that happens abruptly, they aimed to find out why an aircraft equipped with high-end fuel gauges and warning systems carried on flying past a myriad of airports to a point where it simply dropped out of the sky as a result of running out of fuel (fuel depletion).

As they went through the data recordings, they discovered that as the aircraft approached John F Kennedy International Airport (JFK) in New York City, the traffic congestion meant that it had to be placed on a few holding patterns[120]. Unfortunately, these holds resulted in a 77-minute long delay (apparently not unusual in New York) to the time of arrival; the aircraft spent much more time in the air than it had initially anticipated. The delay was followed by a missed approach[121] that further increased the time the aircraft spent in the air. The extra time the aircraft spent in the air eventually led to the total depletion of the aircraft's fuel[122].

What puzzled investigators even more, was the fact that they knew that the aircrew was cognizant of the low levels of fuel, the state and nature of the emergency, but somehow failed to relay this urgency to air traffic control. Whenever pilots communicated with the Air Traffic controller, they never outlined their predicament explicitly, i.e. saying something like *"Pan-pan, pan-pan, pan-pan, Avianca 052 would like to declare an emergency, running low on fuel, endurance 30 minutes, Avianca 052".*

---

[120] In aviation terminology, a hold is when an aircraft is requested to fly in a particular pattern (normally a circle) over specified airspace. In times of high air traffic, this serves as a bottleneck for the airport, giving air traffic controllers more time to accommodate aircraft wishing to land on the runways.

[121] An aborted landing – a pilot cancels landing intentions when he or she believes that they cannot land the aircraft safely; this may be the result of a runway incursion, a sudden change in wind direction or misjudging the approach flight path or angle

[122] Gladwell, Malcolm - Outliers Chapter 7 page 217

They would instead use what linguists call *"mitigated speech"* whenever they attempted to relay their predicament to the Air Traffic Controller. As Gladwell wrote;

> **The term used by linguists to describe what Klotz [Mauricio Klotz first officer tasked with communication with ATC] was engaging in in that moment is "mitigated speech," which refers to any attempt to downplay or sugar-coat the meaning of what is being said. We mitigate when we're being polite, or when we're ashamed or embarrassed, or when we're being deferential to authority[123].**

Because mitigated speech has a tendency of downplaying the true meaning of what is being said, its use in emergencies is highly inappropriate as the person on the receiving end of the message might not grasp the true nature of the situation. In this case, the pilots were being 'deferential to authority'. Had the pilots declared a formal emergency when asked to circle over Norfolk, Virginia, ATC would have given them priority over other aircraft waiting to be cleared for landing; putting them 1st in line thus greatly shortening their time in the air.

To unlock the riddle as to why the flight crew was unable to relay their state of emergency to the air traffic controller, psychologist Robert Helmreich argued that to understand the first officer's behaviour, one has to take into account the individual's background and worldview, Helmreich wrote:

> *"The high-power distance of Colombians could have created frustration on the part of the first officer because the captain failed to show the kind of clear (if not autocratic) decision-making expected in high-power distance cultures. The first and second officers may have been waiting for the captain to make*

---

[123] Ibid Chapter 7 page 226 (Outliers)

decisions, but still may have been unwilling to pose alternatives[124]"

What this and other similar incidents (such as the KoreanAir flight 801 accident) highlight is that despite Aviation's practice of high standards and outstanding safety record, the industry encountered difficulties in certain cultures and communities as a result of pre-existing traditions and worldviews.

Foreign Concepts

One of the main reasons cited for capitalism's failure to take hold in Africa is that capitalism failed as a result of Capitalism's very nature; its pursuit of the betterment of one's own life at the 'expense' of the collective, the traditional values that require self-sacrifice for the sake of the collective. They claim that Capitalism failed due to the values it teaches, values deemed wholly antithetical to the African way of life. Collectivism just seemed more natural, more humane and ultimately, best suited for African society.

> *"Africans have no more need of being 'converted' to socialism than we have of being 'taught' democracy. Both are rooted in our past—in the traditional society which produced us[125]"*
> *-Julius Nyerere*

In essence, it has been alleged that the failure of capitalism in Africa is due to the basic fact that capitalism was too foreign a concept for African people. This appears true at a glance, but when compared to other areas of African life, one realises that the continent has had *too-foreign* concepts penetrate the

---

[124] Ibid Chapter 7 page 242 (Outliers)
The International Journal of Aviation Psychology Vol 4, Issue 3 (1994); Anatomy of a System accident: The Crash of Avianca Flight 052 - Robert L. Helmreich
[125] Julius Nyerere's - "Ujamaa—the Basis of African Socialism

continent experiencing little resistance (or stickiness) in gaining ground. A typical example is that of the Christian religion, which propagated the worship of a strange man from ancient Israel over the worship of (local) ancestors or animistic deities such as weather systems (i.e. rain) animals and sculptures; a practice that had been in practice for thousands of years.

So having taken all of this into account, it still begs the question; why was it so easy for the Marxist message in particular (a European ideology) to imbed itself in African life? In the previous chapter, I detailed the relationship between Africa's colonisation, the liberation movement and its link to Marxist regimes like those of Communist China, the USSR and Cuba. But this does not fully explain our society's failure or refusal to embrace Capitalism. Africa has rejected capitalism to the same extent as how the Chinese and South Americans have rejected it. South America has witnessed Chile under the dictatorship of Augusto Pinochet, move from being a poor socialist country into becoming one of the leading economies in the continent; but we continue to see South American countries churning out socialist policies (despite the free market system's history of eradicating poverty); remaining loyal to collectivism by continuously embracing political parties that promise more redistribution and bigger governments.

To help answer this question, I would like to further examine the concept of foreign ideas, their introduction to new civilizations and why some of these foreign concepts experience mixed receptions in new societies.

It is not a matter of intelligence or as some would say - IQ; a discussion best left for another day. But we have to accept that some cultural practices and beliefs weld themselves so deeply into a people's Weltanschauung that some foreign concepts have no hope of breakthrough. Think about atheism in Africa, it's quite extraordinary that atheism has struggled to gain a foothold in Africa despite advocating against an unproven concept – the existence of a supernatural power.

Christian Values and pre-existing worldviews

The spread of Christianity is one example in particular. Originating from the Middle East, evangelicals ventured outside their borders intending to spread the teachings of Jesus Christ all over the world. With time, their message gained more traction in some areas compared to other areas. The biggest hurdles the religion had to overcome were the basic fact that it was a religion proselytized by a vanquished people, a religion that venerated mercy, love and forgiveness; or to paraphrase G.K Chesterton - a religion that teaches lions to live harmoniously with sheep[126]. One can comprehend how belligerent tribes such as the Germanic, Zulu and Buganda regions grappled with the commandment that teaches "Thou shalt not murder". We understand that belligerent tribes saw killing as a necessary part of nature; that killings and conquests were simply results of the stronger gene overcoming the weaker. It's interesting to note that the image of Jesus Christ had to be remodelled from the *meekish* lamb-like spiritual teacher into a sword-swinging warrior in order to elevate His prestige so that the population can find it easier to accept Him as Lord. One sees this when looking at famous works such as that of Stuttgart Psalter and the

---

[126] Chesterton, Gilbert K. - "the lion lay down with the lamb" page 84 of Orthodoxy

classic poem called *Heliand* which aimed to depict Jesus as a militant warrior.

The two world wars in the 20th century perhaps prove that maybe this was a teaching they never fully came to grips with. But one also has to weigh in the fact that in times of crisis as the Christian faith faced possible defeat by the newly risen Ottoman Empire, it was these very same people that defended the faith. The Holy Roman Empire protected Catholicism and continued to be a major source of resources in the Christian crusades that aimed to repel the Ottoman expansion. It is also thanks to their perseverance, today's world benefits from the existence of the layman's Holy Bible, a product initiated by the German priest Martin Luther when he translated the bible from Latin to vernacular languages[127]. Today's printing press, an invention from the same era as the vernacular Holy Bible, went into its initial use when the Johannes Gutenberg printer precipitated the printing revolution; which played a key role in ushering the Renaissance, Reformation and the so-called Age of Enlightenment.

One can refer to Christianity's struggles in India as a second example of a foreign concept's struggles in gaining ground amongst a new people. Christianity's advocacy for kinship across bloodlines came into direct conflict with the teachings and ethics espoused by the caste system (Varna), a belief system practiced for thousands of years. The caste system is a socially constructed hierarchal social status (to which one is bound from birth till death) that propagates the notion that the social status one holds today is directly correlated to - and determined by - one's previous life. It is a belief that if one is suffering, enslaved

---

[127] Johnson, Paul - History Of Christianity page 223

or poor today, then that suffering is a morally just result of the egregious sinful life the person lived in their past life. It also teaches that the wealthy one enjoys this prosperous life as a result of having lived righteously in their previous life. This is the caste system John Bowker describes as *the overlapping but separate classification of people by birth, known as jati (birth), with brahmans (aka ritual experts) twice-born at the top and Untouchables (dalits) at the bottom*[128]. It was quite difficult for a 'higher caste' member of Indian society to accept that another member deemed to be of a lower caste was in fact their equal, their brother. Perhaps the privileges and a sense of superiority they enjoyed dis-incentivized accepting such a message, as Thomas Sowell once said;

> **"It is usually futile to try to talk facts and analysis to people who are enjoying a sense of moral superiority in their ignorance[129]."**

On the other hand, the members deemed to be the lower caste found the Christian message liberating as it extricated them from the determinism inherent in the caste system, it liberated them from a life of rejection, perdition and total damnation. Although Christianity brought a message of liberation to those in the low caste, its message undermines the elite status of those in the upper caste. For the upper class, those placed at the top of the hierarchy; the acceptance of Christianity was an abnegation of the benefits that come with having a high social status.

The belief in reincarnation is shared amongst the followers of both Buddhism and Hinduism. Once again, Christianity in India shows how a prevailing culture can diminish a foreign concept's

---

[128] Bowker, John – Beliefs That Changed The world page 129 Caste system-
[129] Could not verify source

chances of success in a new society. This is not meant to be an admonishment of Indian culture, Hinduism or India's "failure" to adopt Christianity; this discussion aims to highlight that despite being exposed to Christianity more than a thousand years before missionaries landed on African shores, today India has a smaller percentage of Christians compared to Sub-Saharan Africa.

Living For The Collective

One discovers similar challenges when studying the evangelization of the Capitalist (Free Market) system in new societies previously devoid of anything similar. Chinese society has never abnegated collectivism regardless of the prosperity it has enjoyed from the little capitalism it implemented in the 20th century. Even after having witnessed Hong Kong rise from being a primitive impoverished fishing (village) island to becoming one of the bastions of the capitalist world (with many inland Chinese citizens risking death by swimming from the mainland to Hong Kong), The Communist Party of China is today stronger than it has ever been. The millions of deaths under Mao's regime did little to bolster capitalism in Chinese minds.

From Taoism to Confucianism, the Ancient Chinese society has always believed in running a society in the same way a patriarch runs a household. Confucianism holds filial piety as one of its main creeds - the Five Constants; the virtue of respect for one's parents, elders and ancestors. This relationship is clearly delineated in Stephan Feuchtwang's Handbook on Religion in China;

> *Basing his theoretical formulations on fieldwork conducted in*
> *both Yunnan and Jiangsu provinces in the 1930s, the*

113

anthropologist Fei Xiaotong observed that peasants understood morality as best attained through superordinate control of subordinates and moral modelling (Fei 1992: 30). The superordinate control of subordinates meant that those who were higher in the hierarchy corrected the mistakes of their subordinates. Furthermore, ethical rules were embedded in particular hierarchical relationships such as those between parents and children and rulers and subjects.

Moral modelling meant that those higher in the hierarchy were supposed to create morality through exemplary living, which would radiate outwards to influence others. As such, morality was situation-specific and depended on the particular identities and relationships of the actors rather than on abstract and universal standards (Fei 1992: 74). Parents, for instance, had particular obligations to care for and teach their children. In return, these children were indebted to their parents forever[130]

In family life;

For instance, the idea of xiao or filiality exemplifies this. Children are indebted to their parents for the gift of birth and for raising them. Therefore, they must repay them not only through support in old age, but through support in the afterlife through proper death ritual and ancestral worship. Moral modeling is related to filiality as well, since both parental investment and subsequent filial piety are actions that others should follow[131].

Quite similar to Africa, it propagates self-sacrifice for the benefit of the collective; the adulation towards the ancestors and the self-sacrifice for the benefit of a supreme leader. The Ancient Chinese and Japanese peoples had always believed in a

---

[130] Feuchtwang, Stephan (Editor) - Handbook on Religion in China page 126 & 355
[131] Ibid page 129

top-down planned society that governs the individual's actions right down to their ambition and moral codes. Again, for these societies, capitalism's message of the pursuit of individual freedom, interests and wealth was too blasphemous a message worth considering.

Imperial Japan

History has also shown that the same societies that shunned certain foreign ideologies in particular domains also went on to accept other foreign ideologies in other areas, thus proving that their rejection of those certain foreign ideologies was due to substance and not mere intransigence or incorrigibility. It is also worth studying how other societies found the teachings of capitalism (even in its fragmented form) more palatable than those discussed above (India, China, and Sub-Saharan Africa).

At the dawn of the 19th century, Japan re-immerged from its 220-year seclusion and sought to rebuild itself into an expansionist superpower once again. The merging of the Shintoism doctrine (religion) with the Bushido samurai warrior code morphed Japan into the belligerent military empire that went on to invade and occupy neighbouring countries; culminating in the infamous Rape of Nanking where Imperial Japanese troops raped and massacred over 300 000 Chinese citizens[132]. When Japan was faced with 2 foreign concepts (Christianity and capitalism), it adopted one foreign concept (capitalism) but rejected the other. Their belligerence was open to adopting concepts from the free market system despite having vastly rejected Christianity.

---

[132] Johnson, Paul - A History of the Modern World page 224

The Spirit of the Migrant

After going through examples of communities where foreign concepts failed to gain traction, my analysis would be incomplete if I did not explore the societies that readily accepted foreign concepts or ideologies with little reluctance. The USA is a good example; one wonders how a slavery practicing colony rose to become one of the main bastions of Capitalism. Perhaps the United States' disillusionment with the British monarchy served as the main catalyst for a revolution that fertilized the ground for individualism, the individualism that welcomed the spirit and values of the free market system. The societal fragmentation or long-term instability meant that individualism had little competition once it was introduced; an individualist spirit that produced the following creed; *"Life, Liberty and the pursuit of Happiness"*, a well-known phrase in the United States Declaration of Independence. A people that were uprooted from their base were more open to a social system that produced prosperity than ancient civilizations that were imbedded in ritualistic doctrines, autocracy and royal relational entanglements that plagued Europe to the point of self-destruction during the First World War.

Perhaps it should not have been a surprise to witness the former white colonies such as the USA, Australia and Canada more open to the capitalist spirit of liberty and individualism. If one looks at these societies, one realizes that they are in essence, nations formed by migrants. And if we look at the migrant, we see an individual that has acted in a manner that abnegates the collectivist society that he or she is migrating from. The action of the migrant is that of an individual pursuing liberty, happiness and individual success (this remains true even for those escaping imprisonment - thus pursuing liberty). This is the individual that has walked away from the security offered by the collective in pursuit of liberty fully cognizant of the risks involved. The migrant is the individual who escapes the trappings of the pre-existing worldview in pursuit of a better life. It should not have been a surprise to witness former white colonies built by migrants, outside the aegis of an imperial power, more open to the free market doctrine pontificated in Europe. The prevailing migrant society in fact welcomed the doctrine of the Free Market because it was already inherent in their very nature.

Pre-Colonial African life

In essence, foreign ideas get varying receptions when entering new societies, and it's with this in mind that we move on to the African continent. How was life in Africa prior to the colonial era?

From Egypt to modern-day South Africa, man lived under a leadership figure in the form of a chief or king (sometimes called Sultans or Pashas in the northern region). In these societies, the king was a supreme ruler that provided security, land and in some instances food to his or her subjects. The individual was ultimately the king's responsibility; in times of drought or famines, any disillusionment was directed towards the ruler. The African lived under a centrally planned, top-down, collective society that guided moral codes and beliefs. Julius Nyerere was accurate in his assessment, that socialism was "rooted in our past—in the traditional society which produced us". Like the Ancient European aristocratic society, the leaders were surrounded by a group of advisors (lords-bureaucrats) and tribal elders that were tasked with giving (moral) guidance to the king.

Like many tribes worldwide, they venerated their ancestors and practised beliefs and rituals aimed at alleviating famines and periodic suffering that the natural world would sometimes dish out (i.e. epidemics). As an agrarian civilization of little technological development, it experienced little inequality because most members were equally poor; except for advisors and landlords who were given bigger lands. The community members were allotted land that they could pass down their lineage for as long as they had the favour of the ruler; however, it was not a society that gave many opportunities to climb up the social ladder - such is the perils of lineage.

On the issue of liberty, with the exception of Ethiopia; serfdom was not as commonly practised as it was in Europe, but Africa had its fair share of slavery. As discussed in chapter 3, Slavery was one of the major motivations that drove David Livingstone's philanthropy as he egged Britain to colonize territories in Africa.

When one had the misfortune of being a member of one of the weaker tribes, one constantly lived in fear of slave raids and the perdition that came with slavery. The tribes in the equatorial belt were in constant fear of slave raiders who would pillage their villages, and kidnap their brothers and sisters with the aim of selling them to white and Arab transatlantic slave traders. One of the causes of this *pestilence* was Msiri of Katanga (1830 – December 20, 1891), a Nyamwezi[133] warlord renowned for his copper, ivory and slave trading. He was able to exploit the slave trade to fund his expeditions against agents of King Leopold and France in the Congo basin during the race to conquer the Congo[134]. Through his trading, Msiri, together with his militia, was able to get his hands on European rifles and gunpowder; this afforded him a great advantage in his conquest of neighbouring tribes. Such conquests led to the formation of the

---

[133] One of the Bantu groups of East Africa. They are the second-largest ethnic group in Tanzania.
[134] Ibid Packenham page 400

Yeke Kingdom (also known as the Kingdom of Katanga or Garanganze) in modern-day DRC. However, actions during these times coupled with the alleged cruelty of mutilating the limbs and ears of his subjects served as justification for his eventual murder[135]. Mirambo of Nyamwezi and Tippu Tip (from Zanzibar) were other warlords that raided villages for slaves to trade for ammunition.

Slave raids were one of the major reasons why some chiefs would often beg to sign protectorate treaties - basically signing away their sovereignty. Weary of constant skirmishes with the neighbouring tribes and imminent annexation by the Germans, Chief Akwa and Chief Ndumbe Lobe Bell of the Duala people each approached Britain intending to enter into protectorate treaties. They hoped that a treaty would fend off the Germans from their respective chiefdoms and get them more backing in their wars[136].

In pre-colonial Africa, you were safe in the collective and you were much safer in a strong collective. This is a truth that ingrained itself in the African psyche for so long that one slowly begins to understand why individualism appeared so abhorrent. The concept of individual freedom is so foreign that I have yet to come across a vernacular word describing the phenomenon. The African has never lived in an autarkic society, their lives and existence always served as mere organs or cogs of the ruling authority. This reminds me of a practice that used to take place in South Africa; following the death of his mother Nandi, Shaka Zulu ordered that a few more women be buried along with the Queen mother to keep her company and act as servants in the afterlife[137]. This practice paid little credence to human life and emphasizes the point that there was simply no respect for

---

[135] Ibid Packenham page 403
    http://www.nrzam.org.uk/NRJ/V3N5/V3N5.htm F S Arnot and Msidi 430 (a rebuttal)
[136] Ibid Packenham
[137] http://historyza.blogspot.com/2015/08/nandi-mother-of-shaka-zulu.html
    https://www.encyclopedia.com/women/encyclopedias-almanacs-transcripts-and-maps/nandi-c-1760s-1827 https://www.zululandroute66.co.za/directory/grave-of-shakas-mother-nandi/

individualism. One can understand why Capitalism's claim that the notion of self-interest works to the benefit of the whole society was a hurdle this ideology could never clear in the African worldview. To this day, with our history, Africa still rejects the Free Market System.

We've established that collectivism had its benefits as it was quite essential to the survival of African tribes. As I lamented in my previous chapter, it was precisely the lack of nationhood-unity that left Africa vulnerable to the cancerous conquest of imperialist Europe. It was much easier to conquer the Zulu Impis compared to invading Ethiopia. A united nation, a country, operating in unison was tougher to conquer than an un-collectivised society.

The Tsonga people in South Africa were a weaker opposition to foreign tribes than the Zulu due to a lack of a centralized authority. They only became a formidable force once Soshangane conquered a **faction** and transformed it into mighty people that were a fierce thorn to the Portuguese and British invaders in the subsequent years.

The Zulu people lament the factionalization of the Zulu tribe as the last ailment that cleared the path for the total colonization of Kwa-Zulu Natal and South Africa. So to the African mind, the message of individual liberty was a rallying cry for Africa to adopt what it perceived to be the cause of their defeat, the root of the complete capture of the continent by foreign invading forces.

Atavism and progress
We've also witnessed bastions of capitalism; champions of individual freedom, equal rights and liberty, with the same breath, subjugate a completely innocent people. We've

witnessed the champions of liberty stripping Africans off their land, alienable rights, (self) worth and human dignity.

The collectivist message was appealing to the African not because it promised sovereignty and personal freedom; the collectivist message was appealing to the African because it promises to give back a life that was taken away by colonialism. It was not that Marxism was a new foreign concept looking to gain ground in Africa, but a new ideology that preached a message that was in tandem with a worldview that had already existed in Africa for thousands of years. It is a worldview that's never left. Marxism is a collectivist ideology that offered Africa a way of returning to the pre-colonial collectivism era while embracing modernization. It is another reason why many African liberation movements utilized Marxism as a vehicle toward their independence; the collectivist mindset is the reason why newly independent nations utilized Marxism and various other forms of collectivism as vehicles toward the restoration of a society they believe they've lost.

After having laid out the compatibility of the African mindset to Collectivism, the next chapter will aim to explore collectivism in its various forms.

Chapter 5: Other forms of collectivism

Fascism and its African Disciples

The failures (and horrors) of collectivism have resulted in many believing that when one talks of collectivism, they are simply making reference to socialism and socialism alone. Despite its collectivist roots, modern activists and journalists believe that a fascist is simply a leader that displays authoritarian characteristics, a leader that governs through decree unbounded by any pre-existing laws. They believe that a leader is deemed a fascist despite lacking the main feature necessary for Fascist rule, the element of Collectivism. The underlying reason why this collectivist element has been removed is to make the fascist libel stickier to whomever it's applied to.

Benjamin Netanyahu, Donald Trump and Jair Bolsonaro are leaders (Netanyahu & Trump now former) that typify this phenomenon; both are constantly berated as neo-fascists despite moving their governments closer to free market capitalism[138]. We've witnessed leaders labelled as Fascists despite having shown no characteristics nor implemented any policies aligned to Fascism. Robert Paxton, the Columbia professor and author of *The Anatomy of Fascism* is one of the many writers that bestowed Trump with the fascist label; he offered the following definition of Fascism in his book:

> *Fascism may be defined as a form of political behaviour marked by obsessive preoccupation with community decline, humiliation, or victimhood and by compensatory cults of unity,*

---

[138] https://www.theguardian.com/commentisfree/2021/jan/16/if-trump-looks-like-a-fascist-and-acts-like-a-fascist-then-maybe-he-is-one
https://www.peoplesworld.org/article/democracy-dies-under-brazils-neo-fascist-bolsonaro/
https://www.iol.co.za/news/opinion/brazils-bolsonaro-laying-the-groundwork-for-fascist-state-49294677

energy, and purity, in which a mass-based party of committed nationalist militants, working in uneasy but effective collaboration with traditional elites, abandons democratic liberties and pursues with redemptive violence and without ethical or legal restraints goals of internal cleansing and external expansion. (p. 218)[139]

One is free to disagree or better-yet vote against these *right-of-centre* presidents, but one should also agree that calling Benjamin Netanyahu, Donald Trump and Jair Bolsonaro fascists is quite an egregious libel. A look at one of the leaders that introduced the 1st Fascist movement into governance will help illustrate how paramount collectivism is in building any Fascist state.

Benito Mussolini, the Italian journalist turned dictator led the National Fascist Party into power from 31 October 1922 – 25 July 1943. He founded and later implemented the Fasci movement (meaning bundle); a collectivist ideology philosophized by intellectuals such as Giovanni Gentilè. An ideology that would go on to be replicated all over post-liberation African societies; an ideology that popularized the following infamous quote;

"Everything for the state; nothing against the state; nothing outside the state.[140]"

One might wonder, if everything is for the state, how does fascism differ from socialism? Well, like his German counterpart, fascists realized that it is much easier to have control of what is produced rather than taking over the means of production. In the fascist state, Churches were free to worship,

---

[139] https://www.vox.com/22225472/fascism-definition-trump-fascist-examples
[140] Sabine, GH – A History Of Political Theory page 1495

private citizens could own private property, and agricultural and private industries were left to their own accord so long as they were not in contravention of the leader's national (economic development) plans. But this fact raises another question, if Fascism makes an allowance for ownership of private property and a privatized means of production, why call it a collectivist movement? Fascists might be sympathetic to the moral teachings of Marxism and its condemnation of inequality, but Fascists are not quite as illiterate in economics when compared to their Marxist comrades; they are fully cognizant of the fact that great wealth can only be produced in a free market system.

A fascist is a hyena that lingers on the outskirts waiting for the lion to make the kill; springing into action once dinner is served seeking a share of the spoils. In comparison with communism, where the complete element of production is hijacked by "the workers"; these unscrupulous actions are not as detrimental to the market; so long as the hyena doesn't take a huge chunk of the spoils, thus dis-incentivizing further hunting (investments). By 'allowing' the producers to keep their produce, the government still maintains fair levels of incentive schemes necessary for cultivating a productive market economy. With all this in mind, Fascism still falls short of Capitalism.

The Fascist government maintains veto power over the produce yet still allows the producer to consume their produce so long as their consumption does not go against the agenda of the state. In essence, the entrepreneur is still free to employ their skills in production despite the fact that they are not the sole owners of the enterprise they establish, they are just mere custodians of the enterprise which ultimately belongs to and serves the state.

Fascists are collectivists because they believe that the life and work of the individual are the property of the state, that the wealth of a country belongs to the collective. As Giovanni Gentilè summed it; Fascism is a **'total conception of life'**[141]. In democracies, the state is the servant of the individual, while in a Fascist state; the individual is the servant of the state. The individual is a mere cog that serves to form the great "Bundle" called a Fasci; a great state

The Roman bundle of sticks ("fasci") was adopted as a symbol by Italian fascists.(Getty Images: Bettmann)[142]

Its humiliating collapse towards the end of World War Two led many admirers to eschew the title and name of Fascism while still holding on to the same views advocated by Mussolini – that is *"nothing outside the state, nothing against the state";* the notion that the individual is a servant of the state.

I accept that the modern leaders that hold the same view might not call themselves Fascists in name, nor believe that they are

---

[141] Scruton, Roger - Fools, Frauds and Firebrands p118
  G. Gentilè, Che cosa e il fascismo? Discorse e polemichi, Florence p. 39.
[142] Image from https://www.abc.net.au/news/2017-03-07/italian-fascist-symbol/8330802

fascists, but one cannot deny that their philosophy and way of governance is in sync with the school proselytized by Benito Mussolini and the fascist movement. Some African leaders might have not called their movements Fascism per se; however, their subordination of individual liberty to the state's plan was in accordance with the principles of Fascism.

When Kwame Nkrumah instructed a retrial of the infamous Kulungugu Bomb attack, nothing in natural law or the constitution gave the leader moral justification to order this retrial. But because a conviction served the interest of the state (and leader), the principles of natural law were subverted in pursuit of the state's political aim. When a government decrees a specific way of life to its citizens, those actions are fascistic regardless of the leader's intentions or whether the leader subscribes to fascism or not. One instantly grasps this concept when one thinks of the racist individual; we accept that an individual may be racist even if he or she has never applied that label to themselves. We acknowledge that one is racist if their actions and beliefs echo those preached by the most overt racist groups in our midst. From Kenneth Kaunda's Zambian Humanism to Nyerere's Ujamaa, both doctrines regiment the populace into that shape and vision prescribed by the leadership without the populace's consent.

National Socialism
As mentioned in the Fascism discussion, other schools of collectivism realized that it is much easier to have control over produce rather than taking over the means of production. Where Marxists - an internationalist movement, fought for the whole proletariat class across national borderlines; the National

Socialists led the crusade for the proletariat within their national borders. The Marxist participates in class-warfare while the National Socialist participates in race-warfare; one believes in class superiority whilst the national socialist believes in a nation and/or racial superiority.

The German fascist variant is the obvious example; it adopted the moral philosophies of the Italian fascist state with the sole exception of whom it considered as the rightful members and beneficiaries of the collective product. The Nazis took their localized collectivism a step further by demarcating their population into racial groups where the state worked to uplift one racial group.

The Nazi state was for the working man and that particular working man could only be one of the "Aryan race", the Herrenvolk[143] that the Nazi Party leader, Adolf Hitler believed to be the 'pure German race'; the master race. That is the ideal Aryan individual with pale skin, blond hair and blue eyes. He believed that members of this race carried a racial superiority over non-Aryans and thus had a duty of conquering and annexing territories that belonged to other nations.

The 25 Point Programme of 1920 drawn up by Hitler and Anton Drexler gives one a clearer picture of the party's vision for the German state and the kind of policies the party stood for and would implement in order to achieve their ambitions, the programme amalgamated the doctrines of Nationalism, Socialism and Anti-semitism. The 25-point plan reads as follows:

---

[143] the German nation as considered by the Nazis to be innately superior to others. - Oxford

Other Forms of Collectivism

1. The unification of all German-speaking peoples into one greater Germany.

2. The abrogation and destruction of the Treaty of Versailles and St. Germain

3. Colonies and land to feed Germany's population

4. Only members of the race (only those of German blood) can be citizens. No Jew can be a German.

5. People in Germany who are not citizens must obey special laws for foreigners.

6. Only German citizens can vote, be employed or hold public office.

7. Citizens are entitled to a job and a decent standard of living.

8. No immigration of non-German must be allowed. Anyone who has come to since 2 August, 1914 must be removed

9. All citizens have equal rights and obligations.

10. The duty of a citizen is to find employment

11. All unemployment benefits should end.

12. All profits made during the war must be confiscated

13. Nationalisation of public industries

14. Large companies must share their profits with the workers

15. Pensions must be improved

16. Help for small shops and businesses; large department stores must be expropriated to support this

17. Property reform to give small farmers land, provision of a law for the free expropriation of land for the purposes of public utility, abolition of taxes on land and prevention of all speculation in land.

18. Criminals, usurers and profiteers must be punished by death

19. The substitution of German common law in place of the Roman Law

20. Improve education so that all Germans can find employment.

21. Improve people's health by outlawing child-labor and forcing people to do sports.

22. Abolition of the mercenary troops and formation of a national army.

23. German newspapers must be free of foreign influence

24. Freedom of religion for all religious denominations within the state so long as they do not endanger its existence or oppose the moral senses of the Germanic race.

25. Strong government with unrestricted authority over Germany[144].

---

[144] Druck, J. B - Weiß'sche Buchdruckerei - Das Programm der NSDAP p 17
https://encyclopedia.ushmm.org/content/en/article/nazi-party-platform
https://alphahistory.com/nazigermany/nazi-party-25-points-1920/

For those looking at this ideological movements through the left-right ideological spectrum, any attempt to classify Nazism as a right-wing or left-wing movement generates great debates in social and political circles. The Nazi movement's incorporation of racism, a phenomenon historically associated with right-wing (conservative) movements; and its incorporation of socialism, a phenomenon historically associated with movements of the left, does not help in settling the debate.

Those on the left, desperate to designate the Nazi movement under the Right -wing carapace normally point to Nazism's racial element, its anti-immigration policies and Hitler's intense hatred of Marxism and Bolshevism as proof of Nazism's true ideological affiliation; while those on the right point to the socialist policies (nevermind the name) as proof that National Socialism is a left-wing movement. Those who fail to realize that collectivism can be in the form of a left or right-wing movement will never get their heads around the Nazi party's ideology or where it fits in the left-right ideological spectrum. Whichever way one looks at the party, it is evident that the Nazi party remained a collectivist movement because it subjects all its citizens to the will of the state. Like their Italian counterpart, the individual is a mere cog that serves to form a great "Bundle" called a Fasci - a great state.

Africa was fortunate that no leader implemented the National Socialist doctrine, even though it had its admirers in DF Malan's South African Nationalist party. Leaders within the National party lamented the fact that South Africa sided with the British instead of the Axis powers in both World Wars[145]. However, its ignominious defeat in 1945 and the murder of 6 million Jews

---

[145] vd Westhuizen, Christi – White Power pg. 21 & p 26

gave secret admirers enough reason to shun the movement as a whole.

Other localized Socialism movements

The other forms of localized collective movements limited their ideology to a criterion different from that of the Nazis which used race as a qualification for membership into the working class. The birth of the Baʻathism movement in the 1940s paved the way for the growth of Arab Socialism, a variant of a collectivist movement that localized their socialism down to the Arab world, subsequently leading to the formation of the pan-Arabism movement.

Leaders such as General Gamal Abdel Nasser of Egypt championed the Pan-Arabism movement and socialism in the Arab world. To the great chagrin of Israel, France and the United Kingdom; Gen. Nasser nationalised the foreign-owned Suez Canal, thus sparking what was to be known as the Suez Crisis (aka Tripartite Aggression/ Sinai war). In response to Nasser's actions, the 3 countries invaded Egypt to seize back control of the Suez Canal and depose the leader. The widespread condemnation from the international community (The United Nations, the United States and the USSR etc.) forced the western powers to withdraw from the country; a retreat and publicity that Nasser would not let go to waste. This garnered the Egyptian great prestige in Africa, thus adding to his image as a leader in the Arab world[146].

Various leaders such as Ahmed Ben Bella and Houari Boumédiene, both former presidents of Algeria adopted this form of Socialism. Political leaders such as Salah ben Youssef also played a key role in the formation of the Tunisian National

---

[146] Ibid –Arnold p 37

Movement, another Pan-Arabism movement largely responsible for instigating Tunisia's war of independence from France.

Tribalism

One form of collectivism Africans are all too familiar with is the collectivism demarcated in tribal lines - Tribalism. Tribalism is one form of collectivism that has plagued the African continent for millennia. As discussed in chapter 3, despite its merits as means of survival, a tribal society subjects the population to the will of the ruler (State). Everything within the tribe, nothing outside the tribe, nothing against the tribe; a tribal society is inherently a fascist society. The will of the ruler is imposed on every individual within the society.

Africa has witnessed leaders from one tribe rule to the sole benefit of their own tribe at the expense of members from other tribes. The inter-tribal civil wars that plagued Africa were a result of individuals from one tribe rising to power with the intention of utilizing the power granted by the office they held, to instigate pogroms against rival tribes. The Shona-Matebele tribal friction in Zimbabwe led to the Gukurahundi[147], also commonly referred to as the Matebele massacre; a pogrom that was carried out by the Zimbabwe National Army from early 1983 to late 1987 under Robert Mugabe's Zimbabwe African National Union (ZANU) government[148]. This was a pogrom largely supported by the Shona-speaking people. Although there are different estimates, the consensus of the International Association of Genocide Scholars (IAGS) is that more than 20,000 people were murdered.

---

[147] Meaning "the early rain which washes away the chaff"
[148] https://www.bbc.com/news/world-africa-27519044

This was not the 1st time ethnic tensions led to genocide and would sadly not be the last; the political office meant directorship of the army, presenting the best opportunity to 'settle' ethnic rivalries. Since gaining independence in 1972, the Hutu and Tutsis of Burundi used the presidency to perpetrate genocides against one another as a result of ethnic tensions. In 1972, the Tutsi - dominated army and government instigated a pogrom against Hutus, killing an estimated total of 100 000 people (some estimate 150 000). When the 1st democratically newly elected Hutu president Melchior Ndadaye was assassinated on 21 October 1993; his supporters, predominantly Hutu, responded violently by going on a killing spree against the Tutsi. The events descended into a civil war as the army (still predominantly Tutsi) retaliated by launching attacks on Hutus civilians and rebels. The whole 90's episode resulted in the deaths of 25 000 Tutsis[149].

As witnessed in the Balkan regions in the 19th and 20th century, ethnic rivalries in one region would lead to wars across borders as tribal affiliations superseded nationality. The Civil wars in Congo and Rwanda were largely influenced by tribes in neighbouring countries.

The thousands of Hutus that escaped the 1972 *Ikiza* carried their scars with them, as they made their way to neighbouring countries. The Tutsi genocide of the Hutus in Burundi precipitated the Rwandan genocide 22 years later, when the Hutus perpetrated a genocide against the Tutsi, murdering

---

[149] Ibid – Arnold 9 367
https://www.sciencespo.fr/mass-violence-war-massacre-resistance/en/document/burundi-killings-1972
http://atrocitieswatch.org/the-1972-and-1993-burundi-genocides/

around 70% of the country's Tutsi population with rifles and machetes.

One should also point out that despite ethnic tensions; a majority of countries made up of various tribes did not deteriorate into the barbarism discussed above. This is largely because a large percentage of African countries are heterogeneous societies (except for countries like Lesotho, Swaziland, Botswana, Egypt and Morocco), the political office always presented an opportunity to exact one tribe's **Will** even though that **Will** would be to the detriment of the other countrymen from different tribes. The ascension to power is also commonly used as a yardstick to measure one tribe's superiority over another.

The collectivism of a tribal kind often drives individuals into rejecting presidential candidates on the sole basis of tribal affiliation. In South Africa, the ANC knew that nominating Jacob Zuma (a Zulu man) as a candidate would guarantee the party a victory in the Kwa-Zulu Natal province due to the fact that a lot of members from the Zulu tribe would be more open to voting for him than if it were a candidate from a different tribe.

During the Thabo Mbeki years, one would hear individuals lament the fact that the first 2 South African presidents; Thabo Mbeki and Nelson Mandela, were from the Xhosa tribe. People would assert that it was imperative that the president that succeeded president Mbeki be from a different tribe because it was high time *"Xhosas gave others a chance"*. This thinking is perpetuated by the belief that when a member of a tribe ascends to the presidency, he or she will govern for the sole benefit of that tribe. This would be quite bewildering if one was not familiar with South Africa's history. The country was under the grip of one tribal pro-Afrikaner movement that heralded tribal affiliation paramount to anything else and implemented the apartheid system that would work to benefit one tribe, the Afrikaners and their interest, over the other tribes.

I would not like to see Africans disassociate themselves from their tribal identities; I subscribe to the spirit of the rainbow nation which teaches that we embrace our tribal identity, our tribal history and yet work towards building one country. For instance, I am a Tsonga man that enjoys reading my Tsonga history and listening and dancing to the fast-paced Xitsonga music, but this should not allow me to employ my tribal affiliation in matters of politics and leadership selection. One should be able to identify a weak, dangerous or corrupt leader even if the leader is from one's tribe, one should be able to reject a candidate despite holding the same tribal affiliation and opt for another candidate belonging to a different tribe. Tribalism is a collectivist ideology that fails to distinguish the individual's identity or characteristics; it employs a macroscopic view of society and all its members.

Democratic Socialism and its African Disciples
And lastly, we look at Democratic socialism, another Marxist Trojan horse that utilizes subterfuge to trick many voters into collectivism. Adherents of the socialist doctrine hell-bent on eschewing the Marxist and Fascists movements still believed they could attain a socialist society without the coercive, despotic and brutal elements found in the USSR and Fascist Europe. Their naivety leads them into believing that the path to a Utopian society can be paved through the democratic process.

Governments that actually put the socialism doctrine into practice and experienced the socio-economic regression that naturally followed are disassociated from the socialist movement overall; their failures are attributed to corruption, despotism and the all-too-common excuse of foreign interference. In their perorations they declare; *"They were not true socialists"* or *"they did not implement it correctly"*; as they attempt to resell the utterly discredited doctrine to the credulous masses.

In *The Soviet Union Versus Socialism*, Noam Chomsky, one of the many thought leaders that worked tirelessly to disassociate the failures of the USSR from the Socialism doctrine wrote the following;

> *…. the essential element of the socialist ideal remains: to convert the means of production into the property of freely associated producers and thus the social property of people who have liberated themselves from exploitation by their master, as a fundamental step towards a broader realm of human freedom.*

> *The Leninist intelligentsia have a different agenda. They fit Marx's description of the 'conspirators' who "pre-empt the developing revolutionary process" and distort it to their ends of domination; "Hence their deepest disdain for the more theoretical enlightenment of the workers about their class interests," which include the overthrow of the Red Bureaucracy and the creation of mechanisms of democratic control over production and social life. ………..*

> *…Failure to understand the intense hostility to socialism on the part of the Leninist intelligentsia (with roots in Marx, no doubt), and corresponding misunderstanding of the Leninist model, has had a devastating impact on the struggle for a more decent society and a liveable world in the West, and not only there. It is necessary to find a way to save the socialist ideal from its enemies in both of the world's major centres of power, from those who will always seek to be the State priests and*

social managers, destroying freedom in the name of liberation[150]

Unlike the socialism that enslaved and repressed their countrymen, they claim that their democratic socialist society will be governed with the consensus of the voters, strictly adhering to the "general" will of the population. The oxymoronic feature of democratic socialism is accentuated by the promise that people will be governed with the consensus of the voters so long as these voters don't stray from the creeds of socialism. But an obvious question soon arises, what happens when the "general will" of the people advocates for lowering taxation?

In Africa, the socialists that were wary of the communist movement in Africa opted for the democratic socialism doctrine. The African socialism of Chad's François Tombalbaye, that of Léopold Senghor from Senegal or the African Socialism advocated by Thomas Sankara of Burkina Faso; had one thing in common, they subject the population to the will of the leadership, subsequently making them inherently authoritarian.

For as long as the will of all members of the population is aligned with the will of the leadership, the society experiences great levels of social cohesion. There is little friction caused by the variety of ideals within members of the population because there is little conflict of ideals. Basically, if we all want the same things to the same extent, then a collectivised effort towards the attainment of that particular thing is quite sensible, that's why collectivism works in wartime periods - we all want to repel the force invading our country.

When the country is under an invasion by a foreign army or is in the grips of a war for its liberation, a large majority of the population will view victory as the ultimate priority (the thing

---

[150] https://chomsky.info/1986____/

they want the most), since this priority is in line with the leader of the population, any sacrifices the leadership demands of its population will be met with less resistance because the population will already be in a state where it is more inclined to make sacrifices that would bring closer to the attaining of the thing it wants most - victory. The population is less sensitive to the authoritarianism of the leadership because the diktat of the leadership is not that dissimilar from the sentiments of the general populace. It is only once these wills and ideals start to diverge that the population grows more sensitive to the imposition of the leadership's will. This also explains why Theocracies and homogenous collectivist societies are able to govern harmoniously in particular instances.

The variety between each individual's hierarchy of ends greatly increases, reducing the commonalities required to establish the "general will" of the people. The makeup of a majority decreases to a mere 51%, thus bringing a growing minority under the rule of a thin majority. It is for this reason that collectivism always leads to authoritarianism, those looking to pursue ends different from those of the leadership suffer reproach, government coercion and ultimately - government repression. President Julius Nyerere - a good man - had no choice but to resort to coercive means to achieve his ends and pursue the villagization program he had planned for his country, he found himself employing the authoritarian tendencies he had deeply lamented in the pre-independence years in Tanganyika.

There are certain creeds that a society needs to hold true and indefeasible (un-debatable) in order to defend its civilization from any elements of authoritarianism. It is only through the defeat of these creeds can the path be cleared for any form of authoritarianism to gain a foothold in society to ultimately take over the government and all its structures. Respect for private property, freedom to choose, the right to eke out a living (a right we somehow lost during the peak COVID lockdown days) and equal immutable and inalienable human rights are some of the creeds that ensure tyrannical movements never rise to power.

Chapter 6: Shortcomings of Collectivism

So now that we understand Africa's marriage to collectivism and explored collectivism's importance in liberating the African continent, this chapter will explain the shortcomings that come with this union. Africa's adoption of Collectivism could only be considered good if it was effective in achieving its goals; which is to upend the ruling class, a ruling class which dealt with the native population unscrupulously. However, after a careful study of the last 100 years, it's safe to conclude that Collectivism's track record *in power*, as a form of governance, is barren of any positive results.

One may ask, what are positive results, or to put it more clearly, how do you define positive results? Well, it's fair to say that one is said to have succeeded in their endeavours when they have concluded what they wished to conclude (I guess even a burglar is said to be successful if they rob a house without getting caught). In essence, you are successful when you have achieved your intended goals - when you arrive at your intended destination. And it is based on this understanding that I can safely conclude that collectivists cannot be deemed to have been successful because they didn't achieve their intended goals. And in this chapter, I will prove why it never will.

The Promises

Collectivists aim is to build an egalitarian society. If one looks at the world in its present state; with the prevailing presence of need, suffering, cancer, pain, disappointment, betrayal and of-cause, veganism; one can fully empathize with their.... say "uneasiness". A part of me wishes that this idealist society was tenable, and a part of me doesn't. A part of me wishes that this altruistic joyous society which is free of poverty; simultaneously egalitarian in opportunity and outcome existed.

As I stated in chapter 2, they attribute current levels (and existence) of poverty to capitalism, arguing that the capitalist society enables landlords and owners to get rich off stealing from the poor working class. The opprobrium resulting from the current levels of inequality is also directed toward the very same capitalist system that has lifted many from poverty; a state that all humanity shared from the earliest of times. The very fact that capitalism doesn't uplift all peoples from poverty at-once, is characterised as its inherent flaw. We are told that a collectivized society, with a collectivist socio-economic doctrine, is the sole doctrine that can fix this flaw; and that its veneration of egalitarianism will be the main reason it will leave no room for such inequalities to arise again.

The advocates of collectivism promise to create a society that will maintain the structures built under capitalism with the sole exception of property ownership. It is only the labour-centric mindset that can take (and make) this claim and promise with earnest conviction; the promise that everything will remain unchanged with the exception of property ownership, that everything will be owned communally. From policing, health care facilities, and education right down to the levels of production; the current bearers of private ownership of property will be replaced by the workers (working class).

They promise that their society will be one of little suffering and toil for the working class as the products of their labour will be equally shared amongst the society, thus freeing the society from the greedy entrepreneurs that would have unjustly kept it for themselves.

One only needs to crack open a history book to see the outcome of their previous attempts, the history of the USSR, Cuban, Zambian Angolan, Tanganyika and Mozambican collectivist societies in the past leaves us no choice but to accept that the pursuit of the above-mentioned ideals has produced very little positive results. Documenting the shortcomings of collectivism in depth would likely transform this chapter into a whole separate book, but since this is not an economics book, I'll explore these factors at a macroscopic level.

Those advocating for any form of governance should aim to make a good moral case for the implementation of that form of governance, its ideology and the policies it wishes to pass. The candidates must make a rational case by proving to the people that its ideals and goals are tangible; that they are attainable economically and logically. An ideology that fails in **either** category should leave the populace with no other choice but to reject the ideology in its entirety. The first step is to make the moral case against collectivism (including Marxism and all its variants) and why the approach of a centrally planned society (and economy) cannot possibly produce the results collectivists aim to produce.

1. Incompatibility with the human being

I briefly discussed Collectivism's incompatibility with human nature and would name this as one of the greatest shortcomings when studying the socialist governments of the past. The greatest shortcoming of the collectivist intelligentsia is their misunderstanding of the common man, we can call him James. It is the collectivist intelligentsia's misunderstanding of basic nature of the human being.

"If socialism is against human nature, then human nature must be changed" - Unknown

Let's take a look at the main creed of collectivism, the aim of Equality; the creed that preaches the equality of man, both in opportunity but more importantly; equality in outcome as well. The question is; is this consistent with human nature and can we get the average man – James, to willingly adopt this creed?

Well, when one looks at man's everyday activity, one quickly realizes that it is just not natural to expect equal outcomes in any endeavour in which human beings partake since human beings are born with various levels of inherent gifts, qualities and characteristics; there are many factors that may lead to one person out-performing their peers. Parents raising more than one child can attest to the fact that children are born with certain inherent characteristics - those raising an unhappy child can attest to this even more; a kind of firmware setup that no amount of teaching or nurturing can override.

The one difficulty we come across in any attempt to guarantee equal outcome lies in the fact that outcome is directly correlated to input and opportunity; this may sound simplistic until we realize that the average man also has a direct input on opportunity. For example, Jimmy and Sarah may be given the equal opportunity of attending the same prestigious high school; however, Sarah's dedication to her school work will assist her in achieving better grades, thus having better opportunities than our dear friend Jimmy. Sarah had a direct input in her opportunity.

In an aim to circumvent this inherent problem, the wiser collectivists have rebranded the advocacy for *Equality* into advocacy for *Equity*.

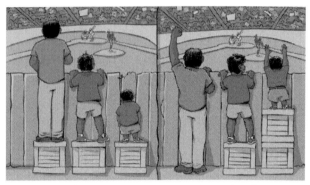

ANGUS MAGUIRE // INTERACTION INSTITUTE FOR SOCIAL CHANGE - https://www.mentalfloss.com/

The advantage of the advocacy for **Equity** is that this allows one to give no regard to input, thus completely muddying any lenses that may wish to look into the morality of this aim. For instance, how can one judge its fairness or morality if one does not consider starting points; how one individual got to their current socio-economic standing in the first place (input)? Its sole creed is equality of ends, or as US vice president Kamala Harris said;

"Equitable treatment means we all end up at the same place"[151]

The advocacy for Equity is inherently more evil than the advocacy for Equality because it deliberately disregards the individual's work (input). The advocate for equity states that *"I accept that Vusi may have worked harder than James to attain this management position and that both men may have been granted the same (equal) opportunities, however equity suggests that James must reap an equal amount of rewards as Vusi"*

The egalitarians have realized that an individual's knack for directly enhancing or destroying given opportunities will always make it difficult for society to achieve equal opportunity and

---

[151] https://web.facebook.com/KamalaHarris/videos/equity/1731574083660306/?_rdc=1&_rdr

equal outcome. To understand inputs, when must delve into human characteristics that dictate one's efforts.

Degree of Want

We accept that people have various tastes, interests and wants; but we should also accept that even in instances where 2 individuals can have the same wants, the 2 individuals' degree in desiring to attain that want will differ. The effort they put into attaining that need or want will differ. My local gym is full of people with the desire to lose weight, but not all of us will exert the same energy (and effort) towards attaining that want; we might be prepared to spend a few hours (or to our disgrace.. minutes) on high-intensity workouts, but we'll draw the line when it comes to high kicking aerobics classes and the consumption of kale smoothies. Just like in the case of Jimmy and Sarah, despite equal opportunities, the variance in effort will result in a disparity in outcomes.

For the collectivist society to attain an egalitarian society, the central planning authority will have to prejudice the higher achiever by either limiting his or her productivity; or by reducing the fruits of their achievements down to the level of the outperformed. For the average man to run the same time as Usain Bolt in a 100m sprint, we would have to suppress Usain Bolt in some form (even through violent means), to achieve an equal outcome. In essence, they would simply have to rob the higher yielder by expropriating some of his yield for redistribution amongst the lower yielders.

The above case scenarios involve those with the same desires, but what about those with different tastes entirely? The collectivist society presumes that the conditions in its society will be favourable to all mankind and that individuals with different desires will be accommodated. If I were to not dedicate much time and effort towards an activity as a result of my lower ambition, would it not be immoral to confine the fruits of my more dedicated peers to the same level as mine by forcing them to share their excess yield with me? This is a moral standard no egalitarian can ever pass. As Walter Williams wrote;

How does something immoral, when done privately, become moral when it is done collectively? – Walter Williams

Something immoral at a small scale cannot become moral at a bigger scale. This simple notion needs no elaboration, if it is immoral to do it to my neighbour, it should not be done holistically. If the general populace understood these alienable rights, as Africans we would be in a better position to identify a bad leader in the making, no matter how charismatic they may be.

2. Inhibits Freedom

Collectivists fail to accept the fact that individuals in any society are driven by different factors that lead them to make different choices in different domains. This fact becomes problematic in a collectivised society, as Ludwig von Mises put it;

The essential mark of socialism is that one will alone acts[152].

The Mises quote alone was worth the long hours I spent slaving through the man's colossal treatise, *Human action*. It explains that a collectivized society can only act in one direction at a time; even when it attempts to diversify, it ultimately moves toward one direction. For instance, it cannot diversify a war effort as it does not allow for some to not partake in that war effort; governments that embark on "green energy" don't diversify their investments by growing their coal sectors - there are numerous examples. All collectivist governments are

---

[152] Mises, Ludwig von - Human Action p728

inherently authoritarian because they subject the whole population to the will of the central planning authority.

The Covid 19 pandemic should put all of this into perspective, regardless of one's views regarding the necessity of the lockdowns; I believe it's fair to say that in the implementation of the lockdown, ONE WILL ACTED. Those against the lockdowns had no choice but to live under the lockdown regulations whether they willed it or not.

Acting Man

In the opening chapters of Mises' Human Action, we learn that from the day man is born, man faces uneasiness; you may call this uneasiness a want or a need[153]. Whichever way one classifies it, any set of circumstances one experiences that one wishes to change may be called uneasiness. We classify the wish to alleviate a particular uneasiness as the "**WILL**" - it is important to note that when he **Wills** to alleviate this uneasiness, he has a particular goal in mind, this goal is what we call an '**END**'. And lastly, the steps man takes towards the alleviation of this uneasiness is called "**ACTION**". Prior to acting, man evaluates his current circumstances, his capabilities and the opportunities available to him so he can determine the kind of action he should take to come as close as possible to meeting this end.

When Amaju wakes up one morning, he soon faces uneasiness; the man realizes that he is hungry. He wishes to rid himself of this gnawing sensation in his stomach that is slowly weakening his body, this is his **WILL**. He determines that eating food is the

---

[153] It's practically the same thing

best way of getting rid of this sensation, thereby getting something to eat is his **ENDS**. So Amaju weighs up all resources at his disposal to determine which of these resources offer the highest possibility of success; he then settles on catching one of the rabbits that keep running up and down his majestic habitat. He builds a rabbit trap, the building of this trap is his **ACTION**. Now if a central planning authority in a collectivist society only governed Amaju, it would surely be of great assistance to Amaju and would efficiently plan the attainment of food on his behalf. However, if there were a million Amajus, the planning authority would find out that it would have to assess each circumstance as some areas would be devoid of rabbits; the authority's efficiency in planning would wane as the number of Amaju's multiplied. It is for this reason that the individual man is better suited in assessing his or her position and is most capable in forging the best path into alleviating any uneasiness they may suffer.

Hierarchy of Needs

An average society consists of many *Amajus* who experience different types **and** levels of uneasiness (needs). As discussed in my last point, each individual faces different levels of uneasiness. Another point worth mentioning is that one individual has many needs, with each need given the highest priority at particular times; and each need having varying effects in hampering the individual's levels of satisfaction.

For instance, the uneasiness caused by the need for water (thirst) will hamper my satisfaction to a greater extent compared to the uneasiness caused by the need for a faster internet connection. However, once I get my glass of water, I will be at liberty to pursue my mobile network provider to discuss my slow internet situation; at this particular time, this need gains priority over other needs. Economists generally call this the Law of Diminishing Marginal Utility, which states that as consumption increases, the marginal utility (usefulness and subjective value) derived from the consumption of each additional unit declines. So the next time your wife swears that she needs those new pair of shoes, just know that she truly means it. At each instant, the individual's needs are hierarchal and are satisfied in order of importance. Once a need is satisfied, man acts to satisfy the next level of need. The psychologist, Abraham Maslow, accentuated this hierarchy when he published what has become known as Maslow's Hierarchy of Needs in 1954[154].

Maslow's Hierarchy of Needs

Maslow was correct in giving this hierarchy a pyramid shape, putting emphasis on the fact that what lies on the base of the pyramid holds a greater significance compared to what lies at

[154] FAA-H-8083-9A, Aviation Instructor's Handbook p17
Erusmas, B ; Strydom, Johan, Kloppers, Sharon - Introduction to Business Management page 13
pic - https://www.simplypsychology.org/maslow

the top. The pyramid shape symbolizes the various degrees of importance. There are some aspects in Maslow's Hierarchy of Needs that I personally don't agree with, however, I do believe that it was quite profound in the sense that he outlined that the individual does have a hierarchy of needs. My disagreement stems from the fact that I believe each individual ranks each of his needs differently from those stated by Maslow. I think suicide bombers, mercenaries and prisoners on hunger strikes proved that Food and security is not always Basic a need for everybody.

There are instances where our physiological (Basic) needs may be identical, but each individual's Hierarchy of Needs start to diverge from the next person as we move up the pyramid. For some individuals, their hierarchy is identical to that stated by Dr Abraham Maslow, however, we've witnessed individuals with a hierarchy set that is different from Maslow's as one goes up the pyramid. Once the basic needs of safety and security are met (everybody wants to survive first), the next level of needs start to look different from the needs of our fellow man. While a majority might follow the next level of "Belongingness and love needs", some individuals (i.e. bullies, dictators and sadists) might repudiate Belongingness and Love Needs', opting for prestige and being feared (Esteem Needs) instead.

Specialisation
We have no qualms with the fact that the Will of safety, policing and the judiciary system is a *Will* pursued through collectivised means because it is a basic primary need and Will we all inherently share. That's why even in Free Market societies, the police, courts, and penal systems (basically all law and order)

remain the sole responsibility of the central authority. It is only once these systems are in place (with law and order maintained), can the people pursue their personal various other needs (in their varying order of importance(s)). In our current society, we have individuals like environmentalists that are predominantly (and religiously) preoccupied with the well-being of the planet. This is their Will - these individuals make personal decisions and sacrifices to ensure that they upkeep the well-being of the planet through various ways, i.e. going green and reducing carbon emissions; this is their Action. These individuals will even pursue career choices that aim to advance their environmentalism.

In that very same society, you will have individuals, let's call them Africans, preoccupied with technological progress and the first world status is their Ends. These 'Africans' will argue that since fossil fuels are largely responsible for the First world's socio-economic status of many western countries, the same technology should be developed in developing countries to eradicate abject poverty in the same way the western countries eradicated their abject poverty. The *Africans* will prioritise technological progress over environmentalism and will wish to satisfy the need to eradicate poverty before they satisfy the uneasiness that results from the effects of climate change. This is precisely why the concern regarding climate change is a 1st world problem, their need of eradicating abject poverty has been satisfied and the need to reduce carbon emissions takes precedence over the need to eradicate poverty. These individuals believe that since capitalism is the only proven way one can be lifted from abject poverty, they should continue to advocate for the capitalist model in 3rd world countries.

In essence, society has individuals pursuing totally different (and in some instances, opposite) Ends. A society consists of individuals that develop various visions for society; we have those that pursue veganism or vegetarianism advocating for the ban on the consumption of animal products, genuinely believing that this act is unnecessary, immoral, out-dated and barbaric. Vegans and vegetarians will advocate for carbohydrates as a main staple food that can replace animal products completely.

On the other hand, we've got individuals believing that the consumption of meat (ketogenic diet) is most beneficial to the human body as compared to carbohydrates. They will point to studies that support their claim that the high consumption of carbohydrates has led to the growing obesity pandemic and increasing levels of diabetes and cardiovascular diseases. These "ketogenics" will be as feverous in their advocacy for the ketogenic diet as vegans and vegetarians are in their advocacy for the overall green movement.

One may also look at those who are of the view that mechanisation-automation is the scourge of modernity; their belief that automation should be abnegated by all means to preserve, or better yet, increase job opportunities for the sake of employment. Their views run contrary to those that believe that mechanisation or automation benefits society by decreasing the cost of production and consequently, the cost of living. Whichever view they may hold, the decisions and sacrifices these individuals make will ultimately be affected by their above-mentioned views.

If you think the above conflicts of interest are problematic, wait until we come to religion – which includes atheists. Think about the devout Christian, who believes that her religious teachings take precedence over secular teachings. This Christian shares the same society with the atheist that equivalently holds secular values as sacred as the Christian holds hers.

These examples expose the complexities involved in the individual's decision-making process; the individual's lifestyle and career choices. These examples highlight that even though individuals share a common environment and pursuit of happiness; their ends and in some respect means, are quite different. The ends of veganism is a society that does not consume animal products, this is of course a vision that is in conflict with the meat (and dairy) eating population. If each one of these interest groups were to impose their wills on the other groups through a centralized power, it is quite evident that the other groups would be living under the tyranny of the ruling group. At this moment, the African can barely keep his lights on while the environmentalist continually chastises him for his carbon emissions and reliance on fossil fuels.

Even in instances where the whole society *Wills* for one End to the same extent, individuals will prescribe different means by which the ends will be attained. For example, the wish to eradicate crime might be unanimous; however, individuals will prescribe different actions which they believe if taken, will bring the society closest to achieving that goal.

Difference in Priorities

Human beings also have varying priorities; one woman might wish to pursue a career in banking, while another woman may wish to stay at home to look after her children. Some individuals will want to pursue a career that will maximize their earning capacity (e.g. highest return in terms of remuneration), while other persons might pursue a career that they believe will be most fulfilling but not financially rewarding (e.g. Nuns, rabbis and sociologists). Ultimately, humans often prioritise certainty over uncertainty in terms of employment over entrepreneurship. A central planner has no right to dictate what priority tops the list of each individual.

Collectivists place the state above all, while the human being lists their family or work as the highest priority. Regardless of one's view of nationalised mandated Medicaid, one cannot dispute the fact that for the individual; this mandate prioritised health insurance over rent and food. This was contrary to most individuals' priorities, individuals who would normally prioritise shelter and food over health insurance. Subsequently, one finds individuals with insufficient money for their shelter and food after paying for the nationalised healthcare programs. A collectivist government fits every man into a strait jacket, when we in fact come in many diverse forms

Two individuals may be as equally disillusioned by the current levels of poverty but may have different ways as to how poverty may be alleviated. The collectivist aims to address inequality because they believe that all human beings are as equally disillusioned with the current levels of inequality as they are. But the above-mentioned examples do not support this belief; they prove that some individuals pursue certain lifestyles or endeavours fully cognizant of the fact that such endeavours may not reward them in any financial sense. These examples prove that if a central authority were to pursue certain ends, they will inherently deny certain individuals the right to pursue ends contrary to those of the central planning authority. The fact that social scientists and scholars are yet to reach a consensus concerning poverty or general happiness highlights the complexities involved in personal decisions people make every day concerning their personal lives.

The subjugation of the whole society into the vision of the collectivist state is in no doubt a violation of the right and freedom to choose a path which they believe will bring them the most happiness; it denies them Liberty. This regimentation is no different to the regimentation involved in the slavery days, where the slave was denied the right and freedom to carve out a path to economic and personal freedom. This is the biggest reason why the moral case for a collectivist state collapses, a collectivised state inhibits freedom.

Kgomo Ya Moshate

As I write this chapter, the country is going through the current coronavirus pandemic and the South African government has taken steps to implement what they call *a lockdown*[155]. The government implemented a curfew and banned all sales and transportation of liquor and tobacco products. The government banned outdoor exercising while ordering all businesses (restaurants, saloons, call centres, small businesses etc.) they deemed "non-essential" to close down.

Covid 19 put authoritarianism into perspective, especially for those of us unfamiliar with an openly authoritarian state. I do not wish to enter the fiercely debated issue of lockdowns as I've noticed that this subject stokes up passions similar to those witnessed in certain religious circles, but my aim is to point out how governments struggled to draft lockdown regulations that did not harm any part of the population. Because the government made stopping the spread of the coronavirus their highest priority, the individual's need to eke out a living became secondary. Those prohibited from making an income were simply asked to be patient and wait it out, as a result, the

---

[155] A lockdown is a set of regulations the government implemented in reaction to the pandemic, one of the strictest lockdown regulations worldwide.

government imposed its priorities, its Hierarchy of Needs order on the whole population.

Those that were prepared to take the risk of contracting the virus to feed their families felt like they were heavily constrained by the regulations that prevented this aim. To President Cyril Ramaphosa's surprise, he came up against similar amounts of opprobrium after lifting some regulations (e.g. lifting curfew and restoring economic life) as he did when he imposed it. Those that opposed the easing of the lockdown regulations felt like the government was in this case pursuing materialistic endeavours at the expense of human life; they felt like the government was relegating safety down to a level below material wealth. This whole episode reminded me of the old Sepedi /Setswana allegory *Kgomo Ya Moshate, wa e gapa o molato, wa e lesa o molato;* which translates to *"The Royal Cow, you strike it, you're at fault, you leave it alone, you're at fault"*.

See in this catch-22 situation, if you, a commoner, came across a royal cow grazing in the communal maize fields; you were at fault if you chase it away from eating the crops because you dared to chase away the king's cow. But you were also at fault if you left it alone because you allowed it to eat the communal crops. You're basically at fault no matter what you did.

The lockdowns became President Cyril Ramaphosa's *Kgomo Ya Moshate*, whenever his government imposed its hierarchy of needs on society, it fell afoul to those with a different hierarchy of needs. During the Lockdown, One Will Acted;
1. The government's primary Will was to minimize deaths from the Coronavirus by minimizing its spread. The government prioritised minimizing the spread of the virus over individual liberty and the right to eke out a living was secondary
2. The government prescribed a specific way in which the pandemic would be combatted, consequently prescribing

the means (It's Will) by which its aim will be attained. This left no room for other individuals to combat the pandemic in alternative ways

3. The ultimate end the governments wished to attain was the eradication of the virus. This is evident in its aim of minimizing the spread of the virus. Those who believed that the aim should be to learn to live with the virus were restricted from exercising (and in some domains - i.e. social media-, expressing) their views.

After breaking down this collectivised effort, it was quite clear that for as long as the government continued to impose regulations during the pandemic, it always infringed on the basic human rights of its citizens, all in the name of pursuing an end that might not be worth the sacrifice.

3. Inherently Coercive

"Socialism in general has a record of failure so blatant that only an intellectual could ignore or evade it."
- Thomas Sowell

During the early stages of a collectivist government, the conflict of specialisations soon bubbles up to the surface. The impracticality is made bare as the central planners subsequently realize that their ideals will not be met. Man's specialisation may lead him to eschew the vision of the central planning authority. These planners are left with two options; 1. Abandon the current path of central planning that has led to social disintegration; 2. Make a few adjustments while remaining committed to their current path.

Unfortunately, history shows us that a majority of these central planners always opted for the second option, the misfortunes brought upon that society were not blamed on the shortcomings and irrationality of their policies; but were said to have resulted from the actions of the ideological enemies that wished to subvert their revolution. Robert Mugabe laid all the blame squarely on Britain and other western countries for the economic downturn Zimbabwe experienced in the later years of his presidency.

In essence, it is not the ends they tweak, but the means. As the Russian dissidents always quipped, *'In socialism, the past always changes; it is the future that is certain'*. The individual with the conflicting vision or ideal is not regarded as merely someone with a different opinion or specialisation, but as a selfish evil enemy of the people (thus the state) that needed to be defeated by any means necessary. Any persecution and censorship of these ideological enemies is regarded as a rightful attack against the enemies of the state; all forms of violence are justified.

The fact that all collectivist societies are inherently authoritarian is a fact most collectivists struggle with or simply refuse to accept. In the previous chapter, I discussed Democratic Socialism and how the socialist democrats believe that the path to communism and a Utopian society can be attained through the democratic process. They assert that their government will not go down the same perilous road taken by previous failed socialist dictators because Democratic Socialist societies will be governed according to the "general will of the people". The Democratic Socialists of America's official website explains the movement's vision as follows;

> *"At the root of our socialism is a profound commitment to democracy, as means and end. As we are unlikely to see an immediate end to capitalism tomorrow, DSA fights for reforms today that will weaken the power of corporations and increase the power of working people. For example, we support reforms that:*

- *decrease the influence of money in politics*

- *empower ordinary people in workplaces and the economy*
- *restructure gender and cultural relationships to be more equitable.*

We are activists committed to democracy as not simply one of our political values but our means of restructuring society. Our vision is of a society in which people have a real voice in the choices and relationships that affect the entirety of our lives. We call this vision democratic socialism — a vision of a more free, democratic and humane society.

We are socialists because we reject an international economic order sustained by private profit, alienated labor, race and gender discrimination, environmental destruction, and brutality and violence in defense of the status quo.

We are socialists because we share a vision of a humane international social order based both on democratic planning and market mechanisms to achieve equitable distribution of resources, meaningful work, a healthy environment, sustainable growth, gender and racial equality, and non-oppressive relationships.[156]"

The visions of all other Democratic Socialist parties are no different. They believe that for as long as they are committed to governing in accordance with the general will of the people; their socialism will not be coercive as it is willed by the people (democracy). However, the perusal of this claim makes one realize that this is simply not possible. I would like to point out an element of duality in the democratic socialist's creed, the pursuit of government by consensus and the commitment to governing along the creeds of socialism. This duality can be maintained for as long as the will of the people and the prescription of the socialist ideology do not come into conflict. Basically, when all the people in the society are socialists and one man is as committed to socialism as the next man.

---

[156] https://www.dsausa.org/about-us/

Conflict of Creeds

"It is impossible to prevent a possible conflict of civilizations, because it is impossible to prevent a possible conflict between ideals - *G.K Chesterton (Heretics)*

Unfortunately, this is not the case in normal society because there always comes a point where creeds come into conflict and friction arises. An example would be property ownership and privatised healthcare. What happens when "the will of the people" wills for something inherently opposed to the socialist creed; say they will for lowering taxes, private property and the freedom of opting out of socialized healthcare? At this point, the leadership would have to choose one creed over the other; they would have to choose to abnegate one commitment - say, commitment to governance by consensus in order to maintain a commitment to the other - say, commitment to Socialism. The central planning authority will abnegate the commitment to governing by consensus by choosing to impose the above mention policies on the population against their will.

These examples show that the two creeds can be in sync until there comes a point where the population grows disillusioned with the leadership or the policies inherent to socialism. And so, as the government loses the consensus of the people (the one creed), it is faced with two more options, maintain its commitment to governing by consensus of the people - thus maintaining the "democratic" element; or maintain its commitment to socialism without the consensus of the people.

A government that chooses the 1st option, which is to maintain its commitment to governing by consensus of the people will thus bring an end to the democratic socialism doctrine. It will stray from socialism in pursuit of what the people want. This was the case when the leadership of the Kibbutz community in Israel abandoned total communal ownership once the societal cohesion started to disintegrate. Once the members of the community started to live through the experiences of having their earnings confiscated for redistribution, they were confronted with the inherent unjust reality of egalitarianism; this injustice led to infighting, communal strife and the disintegration of a community that once shared strong bonds and high levels of social harmony.

The leadership that opts for the 2nd option - which is maintaining its commitment to socialism, will have no other alternative but to impose its policies on its citizens without a consensus. Without consensus, the policies will now have to be imposed on the citizens against their will; any form of resistance will be repressed, if needs be, violently. So, despite any promising rise, all Democratic Socialists eventually devolve into violent regimes that repress any form of opposition. They realize that maintaining the socialist doctrine means going down the same path travelled by the Marxist dictators they had initially disavowed.

Appeal to authority

To maintain any credibility, the central planning authority has to be held in high regard in the eyes of its people and its plans have to appear well thought through; the authority has to appear benevolent, omniscient and ultimately, honest. It is no surprise that as the state expanded in its power and authority, the leaders grew more irascible and resistant to criticism and negative feedback – leaving them more open to censorship. Like a cult, those within are encouraged to disassociate themselves from the heretics of society - the harbourers and proponents of contrarian views. In every instance where they were in power, heretics were chased from public spaces, the press and opposition parties were repressed, with show trials for those suspected of "wrong thinking" jailed or often killed. Steve Biko's advocacy for black pride and black consciousness was such a threat (so heretical) to the collectivist apartheid government that giving the man a fair trial was deemed too risky.

Bed of Procrustes

Since the collective planning authority is only able to pursue one set of hierarchy-of-ends, when it is in pursuit of this one end, it will have no other alternative but to coerce those with a different hierarchy of ends - who wish to pursue their own ends through their own means - to align themselves to the means set out by the planning authority. Means that can only lead to the hierarchy laid out by the collective authority.

In the collectivist tribe, once a tribal council is set out on a warpath against the neighbouring tribes to avenge a slight to the king's prestige, the local farmer within that tribe was given no choice but to cease all his activities and means of making a living and join the local army; at the risk of losing his life, head for the hills in pursuit of the ruler's ends. This alignment is conducted through conscription where any resistance is suppressed through violent means.

The society becomes one giant bed of Procrustes. The bed of Procrustes is an allegory that speaks of a Greek mythological figure named Procrustes, who owned an iron bed which he compelled his victims to lie on (according to some accounts, visitors that he drugged). On this bed, all his victims' height had to fit perfectly on the bed, if a victim was shorter than the length of the bed; Procrustes stretched the victims' limbs for the body to fit perfectly. Alternatively, if the victim was longer (taller) than the bed, he would cut off the legs to make the body fit the bed's length. In either event, the victim died. For Procrustes, his bed represented his vision of man, his reality, and if the victim did not fit the bed perfectly, the victim had to be altered into this "reality" as the vision was never at fault.

This allegory elaborates on the dangers of ideological determinism in general. From Marxism, Statism to all various forms of collectivism, the leaders are so committed to their goals that no amount of contrary data or information will cause the leadership to abort its course of action. The vision is so virtuous that no facts or reality can undermine its omnibenevolence.

4. Breeds A State of Terror

"We must smother the internal and external enemies of the Republic or perish with it; now in this situation, the first maxim of your policy ought to be to led the people by reason and the people's enemies by terror."
- Maximilien Robespierre

For us to build a society that values and protects everybody's alienable (God-given) rights, we need to have laws in place that can be enforced. Although I am in agreement with the libertarian creed that argues for privatized police enforcement, I acquiesce to the notion that this can also be achieved by a central authority. Why, because the need for security (law and order) is a primary need we all share to the same extent - I accept that the pursuit of such ends, just like in war times, can be collectivised. In essence, not many of us would have problems with the government if law and order were its sole mandate. In the words of Immanuel Kant; *"Man is free if he needs to obey no person but solely the laws".*

Morality Matters
In a normal society, we accept that all citizens are expected to follow pre-determined laws and regulations and that it is imperative that these laws be comprehensible for the layman to understand. We accept that laws should be clear enough so that

each member of society can anticipate what actions the law enforcement would take against a member if they were to be in violation of those laws, the citizen must also be put in a position where they can anticipate the sanction that will be passed once one is found guilty of having violated a certain law. In cases of ambiguity, we affirm that the state's elected judges are expected to follow a rational process of reason to reach a fair and just judgement before imposing a just and fair sanction. Ultimately, the government should be bound by the laws it passes.

Now, these facts raise an interesting question, if government is to be bound by law, then who makes the law? And, are the lawmakers bound by any law?

Well, the answer to the first question is - government; government makes laws. Although most countries employ a *Separation-of-Powers* approach to guard against tyranny, the legislating branch of government still forms part of government thus making my answer true. However, the second question remains unanswered.

In attempting to answer this second question, one immediately realizes that for lawmakers to be bound by any law, there has to be a law that operates outside the carapace of the lawmakers. We can call it an objective law, historical philosophers might refer to it as Natural law; a law that "exists" outside of man in the sense that it cannot be created nor destroyed by man - an Objective Law that is indefeasible and applicable to all human beings walking this planet. In short, it is a law that makes you understand that gratuitous murder is wrong irrespective of current public opinion or current state law regarding gratuitous murder.

...Furthermore, does legality establish morality? Slavery was legal; apartheid is legal; Stalinist, Nazi, and Maoist purges were legal. Clearly, the fact of legality does not justify these crimes. Legality, alone, cannot be the talisman of moral people"   - Walter Williams

We take its existence as a given even though the average human being cannot always articulate it (apart from the religious believers who attribute this law to instructions given by a Deity). We call this morality. You will notice that this law applies to you against your will as you never subscribe to it willingly, this law has the ability to induce debilitating (and in extreme cases - delirious) levels of guilt whenever one violates this objective law called morality. It's one of the main teachings Fyodor Dostoyevsky's *Crime and Punishment* wanted to portray. In this classic novel, Rodion Raskolnikov had seemingly gotten away with murder (literally) after having murdered his landlord; he had escaped all forms of suspicion from his neighbours and all members of his community, apart from himself. But despite this remarkable feat, the very fact that he could not escape suspicion (and guilt) from his inner self is what led to his undoing. This book showed that even if one can evade or renounce man's law; like Rodion Raskolnikov, one can never escape nor renounce natural law. Raskolnikov's conscious constantly gnawed at him to a point that it drove him to sheer madness, thus inducing punishment; and in the end (spoiler alert) his imprisonment was his rescue.

It would be nonsensical to seriously argue that governments are bound by laws that they "create". If government created laws, then it would have the power to make amendments at a whim whenever certain laws became inconvenient. Africa has numerous examples of leaders who amended laws that imposed term limits the moment their presidential term became subject to these laws. Democratic governments can make amendments to their laws but will ensure that they can prove how their amendments will actually bring these laws closer to this objective law called morality, it's the only way they can convince their electorate into voting for this law. Remember, one can subscribe to manmade law, but is not given an option in subscribing to the objective law described above. It's either we abide by the objective law or we lose our sanity, we cannot keep both. The politician's arguments may be valid or flawed, however, the one thing proponents from each end of the spectrum will have in common is an extent of conviction in their ideals, that their ideals are more in line with morality. If one looks at the current debates concerning *Capitalism*, the issue of Inequality always comes to the forefront. The adversaries of Capitalism will argue that the inequality Capitalism creates in-fact violates moral law regardless of its ability to raise people from poverty, thus making the whole system immoral. On the other hand, the apologists argue that inequality does not violate objective law, to the contrary, they would assert that (as Don Watkins and Yaron Brook wrote) *Equal(ity) Is Unfair©* as it takes away people's justly gained rewards.

It's our commitment to this objective law that prevents us from making arguments such as *"I believe this amendment must be passed into law for this and that reason despite its immorality"*. So to answer the question "are the lawmakers bound by any law?" the conclusive answer is – YES; lawmakers are bound by an objective law called morality.

This takes me to the next point; Who or What created this law? Who or what is the moral giver? it is the answer to THIS question that further explains why collectivist societies that govern in accordance with the will of the "people" have no guardrails prohibiting them from governing by terror. In my discussion regarding debates concerning Capitalism, my scenario showed how two people can hold firm beliefs on the existence of morality yet have polarized moral opinions regarding the very same subject. It seems like these two individuals have an internalized way of seeing the world, a worldview that helps them make sense of morality. This internalized way of seeing the world may differ from one person to another. This "internalized firmware" acts like a compass; and in this context, two sailors may firmly believe in the existence of the North Pole, but navigating to the North Pole is highly dependent on the setup and calibration of their compass. A flawed compass will mislead the sailor in the same way a flawed moral compass misleads the human being.

It is for this reason that past societies emphasized the importance of religion, it was because they understood that religion can affect one's moral compass. A moral compass is the same reason why libertarians emphasize the importance of individual liberty; they understand that a belief in individual liberty can affect one's moral compass too. A human being that respects individual liberty is inadvertently a decent human being because they will be averse to the expropriation of people's lives for the benefit of their personal ideals.

The collectivists' commitment to ruling according to the collective will cause them to reject individual liberty, thus corrupting their moral compass. A movement with a broken moral compass will end up committing acts that violate morality. Their commitment to governing in accordance with "the will of the people" (people being the state itself - the planning authority) gives the collective authority moral justification of changing laws in accordance with that will. Whatever the state dictates is claimed to be the will of the people, it is bound by a flawed moral compass that leads it to nowhere, just like the seaman with a defective compass in the above-mentioned scenario.

Because the people are able to will for anything, the State can pass any law regardless of its immorality, this is why tyrants were able to instigate pogroms against other civilians with little opposition. Apartheid in South Africa was implemented and continually defended through the 'democratic' process in-spite of its cruelty toward humanity. The malleable constitution is amended at a whim so that whatever the planning authority proclaims via diktat readily becomes law. As time goes on, the population grows less familiar with the laws; they do not know which of their future actions may lead to their persecution.

History confirms that Collectivism always leads to despotism. From Maximilien Robespierre, Vladimir Lenin, Joseph Stalin, Adolf Hitler, Benito Mussolini Robert Mugabe, Mengistu Mariam and quite sadly, Kwame Nkrumah; collectivist rulers always abused the judiciary to persecute ideological enemies as those not showing absolute support of their regimes had trumped up charges levelled against them. Laws were amended and were so vague that practically anybody could be prosecuted for having violated them. Laws that make way for the establishment of the *Counter-Revolutions and Sabotage commissions* formed by the Cheka under Lenin (and Trotsky) that led to 1000 executions in 1 year alone.

The ambiguity puts the average member of society in a constant state of fear as they witnessed many persecuted for practically nothing. One of the things that always surprised Westerners touring collectivist states was the lack of chatter amongst the general population as they carried on with their day-to-day activities. This general lack of casual interactions echoed the general air of suspicion ubiquitous within these authoritarian countries. Zimbabweans would often be overcome with terror whenever one criticized President Mugabe in their presence, as many believed that the president possessed magical powers (and spies) that enabled him to thwart any plans to challenge his rule. The former Minister of Home Affairs of Zimbabwe, Dumiso Dabengwa revealed *"People were told there were magic binoculars which could tell which way they voted and there were no-go areas for other parties[157]"*.

In Collectivism, the population can no longer anticipate the actions of the planning authority as they have come to the terrifying realization that the planning authority is not adhering to any higher law or code of ethics - the population lives in a constant state of terror.

5. Results in Shortages and Economic collapse

When one reads through history, it's only a matter of time before one comes across Marxism's horrendous track record concerning deaths resulting from Marxist policies. The collectivists (Marxism in particular) are estimated to have killed over 100 million people in the last 100 years; no other forms of government come close to having "accomplished" this feat. A portion of these deaths was a result of repression, however, the other greater portion is a result of the inefficacious economic

---

[157] https://www.bbc.com/news/world-africa-27519044

program that only brought about shortages and worst case scenario, famine. These economies failed to produce the required amounts of food to feed and sustain a whole country.

But how does food shortage happen? For an average person living in the 21st century, this may be quite perplexing. Not perplexing in the sense that one is unfamiliar with the notion of famines, but quite perplexing in the sense that one fails to understand why such a phenomenon still exists. At a rudimentary level, we understand how a natural drought can lead to famines, we accept that when there's no rain, crops don't grow and we attribute most famines in the past to droughts. It is the case in particular countries like Egypt, China, Eritrea, Ethiopia, Siberia, India and those occupied by the Sahara desert; all these are plagued by periodic famines. We can *stomach* famines that result from drought; however, famines that result from inadequate (economic) food production are quite bewildering if not upsetting. One particular phenomenon is that of food shortages in the absence of droughts (we should also keep in mind that many countries have experienced long periods of drought without starving to death). How can a society be incapable of making enough food for all? To get to the bottom of this question, we must understand how a normal society produces food.

> *The Garden of Eden was a system for the production and distribution of goods and services, but it was not an economy, because everything was available in unlimited abundance. Without scarcity, there is no need to economize—and therefore no economics*[158]
>
> *- Thomas Sowell*

An economy is a system of economizing what is limited in supply; this may be in the form of labour, natural resources and capital. If one thinks of oxygen, one realizes that this does not

---

[158] Sowell, Thomas - Basic Economics pg10

form part of *the economy* as it's unlimited in supply. Economics is a system that redistributes the limited produce throughout the society, it also helps a society to determine which products and services are to be given priority; as Thomas Sowell wrote, it's a system that effectively deals with scarcity. The unrestrained Economy is a system that is able to utilize the self-interest of the entrepreneur for the greater benefit of the whole society by rewarding the producers that produce the products that prove to be most beneficial to the society. Ultimately, it is a system that simultaneously addresses scarcity while maximizing production.

The Organic Economic System
The producer operates under uncertainty, he or she does not have any assurance that their produce carries any utility (usefulness) or interest for the consumer, but they invest capital under this uncertainty nonetheless. Production heavily relies on an automated feedback mechanism and works to give feedback to the producers, this feedback conveys the interest and the utility of their produce.

> *In a changing economy, action always involves speculation. Investments may be good or bad, but they are always speculative. A radical change in conditions may render bad even investments commonly considered perfectly safe*[159]
> *- Ludwig von Mises*

This feedback comes in the form of consumption, the public consumes the production by spending what they themselves produce - their hard-earned money - on other products. It takes us back to the Acting Man; because the consumer has limited resources (money) to trade for the goods and services they desire, they will in turn '*pyramid*' their needs and acquire each product in accordance with the hierarchy status such a product holds within that pyramid. The consumers first buy what they need most at a particular time, but since the pyramid-order

---

[159] Ibid, Human Action   p551

changes frequently, it is only through their action of buying can a producer know which product is in high demand at each moment. When the consumer makes a purchase, he or she casts a vote for that product.

So the next time Susan opens up a business of manufacturing Hover boards, understand that she has no assurance that people will buy this device in droves, she merely speculates that they will. She may even borrow capital from financial institutions or raise money from investors based on this speculation. She will produce a few hundred Hover boards then put them up for sale, but she will only know of the usefulness of her ideas once the feedback in the form of public consumption starts coming in. High consumption will signal that she carries on producing the hover boards while a low consumption may be an indication that the world is not quite ready for her bold ideas.

The levels of consumption of each product also gives automatic feedback to the production function of the society, thus showing it which product is in demand and which product is not. The copy-cat[160] entrepreneurs get their cue from this very same feedback, thus enhancing their reputation as producers that always seem to mimic entrepreneurs. The producer that produces what is most needed will be in possession of goods and services in high demand. They will be able to perform the most transactions, the higher demand will enable the producers to charge higher prices and subsequently make the most profits. It is through this automated feedback mechanism can a society's production reach its full potential.

Centrally planned economies distort this feedback mechanism whenever they monopolize an industry, and any action towards the redistribution of income (wealth) quashes the incentive mechanism that drives individuals like Suzan to speculate; taking away the risk element inherent in entrepreneurship.

---

[160] No shame in being a copy-cat entrepreneur

Such a society has not come to grips with the limited nature of resources or what economists call scarcity. One can certainly economize what is already produced and redistribute it equally; however, this will only result in everybody having little of what is produced. A society prevents food shortages by producing the food before the food is needed; the society has to anticipate the demand. The element of speculation goes beyond the type of product made but also extends to quantity; this function explains why we would read stories of overproduction in the 1930s. As Ben Bernanke put it;

> *A main cause of the Great Depression was overproduction.*
> *Factories and farms were producing more goods than the*
> *people could afford to buy. As a result, prices fell, factories*
> *closed and workers were laid off. Prices for farm products also*
> *fell, as a result, farmers could not pay off bank loans and many*
> *lost their farms due to foreclosure.*
> *- By Ben S Bernanke on Essays on The Great Depression*

One cannot always determine what will be the most urgent product in need tomorrow as this relies on speculation; the producers will be speculating what will be needed in the future (i.e. planting crops that will produce fruits and vegetables that will be in demand in the near future). It is only through a profit-seeking model can a society maximise its potential in production; a collectivized effort towards production cannot achieve this. Any attempt at collectivising will lead to shortages which may occur simultaneously with the oversupply of other useless goods.

Localization of Failure
Whenever the ownership of the means of production is centralized (i.e. factories owned by the government); the speculative nature of the entrepreneur becomes centralized, and as a result, one person speculates. In a free market society, numerous entrepreneurs speculate on what is (or will be) in most demand, the entrepreneur who believes that she sees an

opportunity opens up a business with the belief that what she will produce or the services she will render, will be in high demand in the near future. If the entrepreneur is mistaken in her speculation, her business will not attract many customers as the demand for her products and services will not be as high as she had initially anticipated. It is quite possible that those wishing to consume her produce might not be willing to pay the prices charged by the producer. Although her business will fail, her failure will be localized, she alone will go out of business as her miscalculation will not affect the economy as a whole. It is not that the free Market system is free of failure, but that the failure of each speculator is localized, unlike with the centralized version where the miscalculation or *mis-speculation* impacts the whole society.

Where the means of production are centralized through ownership by the state, the effects of any miscalculation of speculation are felt by the whole society due to the fact that no other speculation within that field was made, all eggs are thrown into one basket and there's no competition. In South Africa, because electricity generation is the sole responsibility of Eskom[161], the South African public is saddled with constant power cuts. The electricity provider miscalculated the growth of the level of future consumption; it did not build enough power-generating plants. It failed to prepare for this demand resulting in the need to ration the little electricity produced amongst all South Africans today. If Eskom was a private entity, the effects of this malinvestment and miscalculation would have been localized, other competitors would have calculated and invested differently, with the one most accurate in speculation coming out on top. South Africa would have been extricated from these chronic menacing power cuts that plague her today.

---

[161] Electricity Supply Commission (ESCOM), the country's producer of electricity. – ESKOM in Afrikaans

The world is quite familiar with Food shortages and empty shelves in supermarkets, however, whenever this shortage comes in any other form, we often fail to see it for what it is, and electricity supply is a prime example. Countries like Nigeria, Zimbabwe and South Africa could produce the quantity required to keep the lights on, but as time went on, this capacity declined; now these countries have resorted to rationing (load shedding).

This is the reason why one would see an overproduction of certain goods in the USSR while there was a severe shortage of basic goods in other areas. Because the feedback mechanism was distorted, the central planners relied on calculation (modelling or guessing in other words) to try to determine what produce is most in demand or better yet, would be in high demand in the future. Collectivising the means of production leads to shortages and ultimately, economic collapse.

6. High Cost of Living

Collectivist governments that leaned toward agrarian society believed that they could produce enough food to feed the whole population. They too ran across the shortages that were prevalent in the USSR and the Ujamaa villages in Tanganyika and Mozambique. It is a pity that it was never evident to collectivists that when one looks at every country's geographical location, it is highly unlikely that one country can produce the diversity of food in stores as seen in free market economies. In my native country South Africa, it is cheaper to purchase chickens in mass from Brazil (and the USA) than it is to grow or farm them locally, this argument remains factual with regard to other foods. More money would be spent on chickens than necessary if we were forced to grow our own chickens rather than importing the cheaper ones from abroad; this increase in the cost of production would be relayed to the consumers; subsequently, South Africans would spend more in purchasing chickens. Recently, FairPlay South Africa called on the South African government to ban all imports of chickens.

While several countries have taken action against Brazilian chicken imports, Brazil remained the major source of chicken imported into South Africa. In 2018, South Africa imported a record 348 000t of poultry from Brazil, and 205 000t [from January] to September 2019. Much of this could potentially have come from producers associated with BRF SA[162].

However, Paul Matthew, the CEO of South Africa's Association of Meat Importers and Exporters (AMIE), confirmed that South Africa imported chicken from other countries because local production could not keep up with national demand.

The real reason why companies import goods is that it is cheaper to import them than to farm them locally. For political reasons that I for one fail to understand, this simple truth is somewhat unimportant if not controversial to many. Poultry is one of many examples of produce we import from other countries as a result of lower prices.

In an effort to ameliorate this production miscalculation, collectivist societies like the USSR would look to other free-market nations that relied on the automatic feedback mechanism of the free-market system. This was for the purpose of replicating the methods of production (and pricing) into their own economies. This of course meant that the collectivist was always a step behind developed countries in production; the free market nations would discover cheaper methods of production way before the collectivist nations did. It is for this reason that capitalist nations lower the cost of living (and improve living

---

[162] www.farmersweekly.co.za
https://www.farmersweekly.co.za/agri-news/south-africa/fairplay-calls-for-chicken-imports-from-brazil-to-be-banned/#:~:text=%E2%80%9CWhile%20a%20number%20of%20countries,from%20January%5D%20to%20September%202019.

standards) for their population compared to the cost of living and living standards in collectivist societies[163].

7. Stagnation

One common theme throughout all collectivist regimes, past and present, is that they do not produce wealth, the economy stagnates as the redistributive policies start to bear fruit. A large chunk of the years during the President Jacob Zuma presidency are commonly referred to as the "lost years" because the country, just like most African economies (i.e. Zimbabwe, The two Congos, Zambia, Nigeria, Cameroon etc.), experienced very little economic growth - the South African Economy stagnated. These countries are still faced with high levels of unemployment with a creditworthiness on the brink of junk status. At no point in history have we ever had a collectivist country that led the world in economic growth or innovation; the Soviet Union, undisputedly the most successful of all the communist experiments relegated itself to a position of merely mimicking the free world in terms of innovation.

Note on the Race to the Moon

It is true that the Soviets beat the Americans in the race to the moon, but the idea of space travel remained a western ideal and innovation. The problem with mimicry is that you tend to also mimic actions that have no intrinsic value. The space race was a vanity project that was of little use in terms of our day-to-day

---

[163] * This is why collectivist countries tend to be on the losing side whenever they go to war against more liberal nations, the liberal nations are often more innovative in their means of production of weapons and they are able to lower their cost of production, it was levels of production that tipped the scales in favour of the Allied Forces during the second World War. The Americans could churn out fighter aeroplanes at a much higher rate than the Germans due to her levels of production stemming from lowering the costs.

lives, that's why other Free world countries never bothered in entering the race to the moon. They were probably faced with the question they could not give a satisfactory answer to, "Say we get to the moon, then what" or better yet - "What is the importance of getting to the moon **first**?" These countries knew that one can take a lead in innovation despite being a latecomer to the party, the USA typifies this statement; it's one of the youngest western nations in history yet is most dominant in innovation and military strength today. As I said, the problem with mimicry is that you tend to also mimic actions that have no intrinsic value.

Back to Earth
In the central planning process, these governments are less committed to answering the question as to how will their countries achieve economic growth compared to their commitment in the fight to reduce inequality; as in how can they reduce the income or wealth of wealthy individuals. Their policies are that of expropriation, extraction and redistribution - be it overtly or via heavy taxation.

In March 2021, Ghanaian President Nana Akufo-Addo announced that Ghana would end the selling of raw materials (cocoa) to trade partners like Switzerland and other European nations. President Nana Akufo-Addo went on to state;

> *"Ghana is currently Switzerland's largest trading partner in sub-Saharan Africa, largely from the export of gold and cocoa to Switzerland and the import of chemical and pharmaceutical products...However, as I have stated on many occasions, Ghana no longer wants to be dependent on the production and export of raw materials, including cocoa beans. We intend to*

process more and more of our cocoa in our country with the aim of producing more chocolate ourselves[164]."

At face value, this sounds like a noble step in protecting Ghanaian farmers from the European exploitation that has plagued the continent for over a hundred years; however, our understanding of free markets and the typical side-effects of collectivist decrees should bring a moment of pause. The first mistake the president makes in this regard is to conclude that Ghana's cocoa beans and raw material industries are dependent on exportation to foreign countries. These industries can remain active without import and export; however, this would come at a higher price for the local consumers and producers - nevermind reducing employment.

The reason African cocoa bean producers sell produce to countries like Switzerland and the USA is because these buyers pay the highest price for these goods. It is the basic law of supply and demand; the seller sells to the highest bidder. It would be like concluding that Salif Keita is **dependent** on France after having learnt that a majority of his concerts are held in France*[165]. The very fact that the French are willing to pay the highest price for Salif Keita's music does not make him lose his independence, he is still free to take his music somewhere else, say his Mali local crowd; but he would just have to make peace with the fact that he may get less money for it.

The mere fact that Switzerland is prepared to pay the highest price for Ghanaian and Ivory Coast raw materials does not make Ghana and the Ivory Coast more dependent on

---

[164] https://honestmediablog.com/2021/03/22/ghana-no-longer-selling-cocoa-to-switzerland/
[165] I do not know for a fact if a majority of Salif Keita's concerts take place in France but merely stating this analogy to bring home my point

Switzerland, it **gives** them more independence. In fact, one would argue that Switzerland is the dependent one, but I guess Switzerland's understanding of markets will not cause them to lose much sleep over this fact. The OPEC countries (Organization of the Petroleum Exporting Countries) understood this power dynamic very well when they arbitrarily increased oil prices by 70%, thus triggering the 1970s oil crisis that brought about economic stagnation worldwide[166]. These countries were keenly aware of the fact that it was the western countries that were truly dependent on their oil, not the other way round. To insist that producers refrain from exporting raw materials is to insist that these producers lose money to alleviate a crisis that does not really exist (the dependence on Western-European countries such as Switzerland).

These decrees inherently harm the local citizens in the end as these producers will resort to cutting costs to maintain their profits. This cost-cutting usually comes in the form of labour cuts, retrenchments and a general decrease in investments; these are some of the actions inherent in collectivist thinking that eventually lead to economic stagnation.

When one looks at the history of collectivism, one can see that producing wealth was never its intention.

In Marxism, Karl Marx conceded that communism could only be built on capitalism. In another treatise, **"The Critique of Political Economy,"** Marx proclaimed that socialism could only come once capitalism had reached the limit of its productive possibilities, writing;

---

[166] Ibid - History of the Modern World – p 669

"No form of society declines before it has developed all the forces of production in accordance with its own stage of development."

The society experiences stagnation because it stops pursuing progress, thus proving the point that it's clearly a doctrine outlined with the aim to target the rich. Had the whole world followed such a prognosis, one can only imagine what we would have lost in terms of innovation and general technology. We'd still be travelling on horseback, steamships and trains. The creators of the personal computer, iPhone, cheap internet and the television set would have been reduced to mere cogs of stagnant primitive societies. Such governments hinder human progress and stifle the people's ability to create wealth for themselves and for the betterment of those around them.

Such a society kills innovation and prevents personal fulfilment since the state dictates any economic venture for the individual through central planning. As the good old saying went, *you don't see engineers and architects visiting Marxist countries for inspiration.* The individual is less inclined to pursue the risky venture of entrepreneurship because they might not get to enjoy the rewards or fruits of their labour. The adulation of Cuban hospitals and doctors is never buttressed by the traffic patterns; we hardly see people leaving free market societies for treatment in socialist countries. Statistics due to these inefficiencies are often manipulated even though the consequences are felt by the common man. A Collectivist country enters into survival mode, like the individual living hand-to-mouth on a minimum wage. These countries are preoccupied with balancing the books to keep the redistributive pyramid scheme from collapsing under its own weight. Collectivism is the reason Africa trailed the world in innovation. This statement does not condemn Africans but exonerates them from the racist murmurings that claim that the African is un-innovative as a result of his genetic disposition.

8. Happiness

Another casualty of collectivism is that of happiness. The fact that human beings find happiness under collectivist regimes does not disprove the notion that such societies hinder human happiness in general. We must remember that the human being is able to find moments of joy and laughter even under harrowing circumstances (i.e. prisons and concentration camps).

Happiness is quite a tricky subject to discuss, especially for adults. I believe that this difficulty is probably because as we grow, we gradually move away from happiness; or at least, the meaning of happiness. The bumps and bruises we experience along our journey to adulthood slowly chip away at our joyfulness and innocence analogous to the individual heading towards death by a thousand cuts - what the Chinese call lingchi. The scars we accumulate in this journey gradually move us away from our general happiness to such an extent that we even go through long periods of its absence to a point where we forget the feeling and meaning of happiness. If one were to ask an adult if they are happy, one finds that adults take longer to respond to this simple question than if the same question was posed to a child. I used to believe that children readily answered this question in the affirmative (yes) as a result of their misunderstanding of the word *happiness*; however, lately, I have come to the realization that it is us, the adults, who've lost touch with the meaning of happiness. It is evident in our hesitation when confronted with this simple question;

"What is happiness?"

I do not think it is possible to answer this question, as I do not believe happiness is necessarily a feeling but an occasion. The more accurate question is, **When is one happy?**

This is a far more accurate question because as humans, we carry memories (and extensive knowledge) of circumstances and behaviours that led to situations that make one unhappy. We often conjure up memories of events that brought us immense joy and a real sense of happiness. One might not remember how it felt to be happy but we certainly remember when we were happy. We also know what happiness **is not**, but rather than answering what happiness **is not**, I believe that exploring the circumstances that lead to happiness will be the best way to tackle the issue of happiness.

When is one happy?

As a child, one tends to believe that one will be most happy if one could get all the nicest things in life, i.e. sweets, more family time with one's parents, all the playtime in the world etc. However one would later discover that there were still moments of unhappiness even at the attainment of the good stuff such as those mentioned above. A child would eat all the sweets available to him, only to find herself feeling sick a few moments later. A child remembers moments during holiday trips interrupted by arguments that made them feel like returning home instantly, and finally, and this is from personal experience, one remembers moments where one was granted all the playtime in the world (typically the last day of the school term), as we played football for so long only to end up exhausted and frantically looking for water to drink. Basically, even when we got all that we wanted, the scourge of temporary unhappiness still reared its ugly head.

To our surprise, we've also witnessed famous people who seemed to have all that we could have wished for in life commit suicide. They seem to have concluded that their glorious lives, or as it appeared to the outside world - with all the money, women, adulation and fame - were not worth living. Out of respect for the dead, I will not give examples.

And to our further astonishment, we also come across people living lives of deprivation and absolute drudgery who yet come across as very happy individuals. The one thing we've come to learn from all these observations is that the attainment of material possession does not guarantee long-lasting happiness.

I have realized that man is happy not when he is in possession of earthly things, but when they feel like they are in control of their own lives; people are happy when their lives have meaning. As GK Chesterton put it;

> *"Meaninglessness does not come from being weary of pain. Meaninglessness comes from being weary of pleasure."*

Meaning is vital because it provides you with the will to see and live for tomorrow. Once an individual finds meaning in their lives, they take action in pursuit of fulfilling that meaning. The subject of Meaning has been thoroughly explored by many authors and philosophers including the likes of Freidrich Nietzsche or Viktor Frankl in his classic book titled "Man's Search For Meaning". But I, on the other hand, would also like to put more emphasis on the issue of control.

I believe that not having control of one's life is the route to unhappiness. One may find meaning in their lives but they need to have some control over their lives so they can fulfil that meaning; once they don't have control in their pursuits, they become terribly unhappy. As if the wind is taken out of their sails, they'll feel used by others in order to pursue other people's ends.

Animosity Toward Others
This partly explains the current animosity some individuals hold against their employers. Because their employers hold a certain level of control over their actions, that is their income and ultimately, their wealth. They behave (and feel) as if this lack of

control is arbitrarily taken away by their employers rather than accepting the cold hard truth that asserts that their remuneration is fair and probably justified. I briefly touched on this dynamic when exploring the Ghana-Switzerland cocoa relationship.

We see the same dynamics when studying the relationship between tenants and landlords. Although many may profess to have witnessed and experienced quite cordial tenant-landlord relationships, I think it's fair to say that many individuals hold some unwarranted animosity toward their landlords. I believe that this animosity also stems from a lack of control. Tenants accept that they need shelter but in some twisted sense, believe that their landlord is prohibiting them from attaining the kind of shelter they really deserve. This prohibition may come in the form of the landlord charging a 'higher' rent than necessary or that they are not adequately taking care of the property as they should. Although I accept these criticisms towards landlords may be valid in certain cases, my aim is to point out that the lack of control over one's shelter can raise animosity towards landlords.

As discussed in employment life, the very fact that the landlord exerts some control over a particular shelter perpetuates the false sense that the landlord is in fact taking away some control from the tenant. The tumultuous tenant-landlord relationship is definitely not helped by human history, especially the history of slavery and serfdom in particular which go a long way in discussing how landlords often collaborated with the state and autocratic rulers to subjugate the common peoples of the land. The Ethiopian peasant went into the 21st century under the yoke of serfdom perpetuated by 'landlords' in collaboration with the imperial state. Although the landlord profession may have a historical case to which they may need to answer to, the current tenant cannot claim to have suffered from these historical injustices. The reason for any animosity the tenant may have for their landlord stems from their loss of control over their provision of shelter.

One "institution" that also generates *quite a bit* of animosity is that of religion. Although I believe that a belief in God gives one the power to reclaim control over their lives (in the eyes of the religious), those rejecting God may do so for the opposite reason, arguing that a belief in God takes away control over their own lives. The very fact that religious doctrines come with certain expectations, commands and standards is the very fact that drives some individuals away from religion. Their "unbelief" is not from a lack of faith but sheer rejection of an entity that they believe takes away that element of control of their lives; basically, they would not follow God even if they met Him in their backyard.

The last group that I would like to discuss that constantly finds itself at the end of murderous animosity is the group of money lenders. Why is it that the group that borrows us money in times of need is the very same group that generates such sardonic animosity amongst many members of our society? Money lenders (e.g. traditional banks) provide many good services for societies and play a vital role in the building and development of any society. They purport to fund businesses and citizens wishing to attain more assets and embark on big projects, they purport to lend money to those wishing to grow themselves and fundamentally, those in need of their help (access any bank website and you will come across the "Need a loan?" question). I accept that money lenders do follow through in doing what they set out to do, however, it is the last statement that often lends them into trouble. When banks claim that they avail themselves to those in need of money, I believe that this claim is false. However, I understand why they would make this humbug anyway; as it is a good marketing strategy particularly because it resonates with the larger population in general. The fact that I would be making the same proclamations if I was in the money lender's position gives testament to my belief in the effectiveness of this marketing strategy, but nonetheless, it remains untrue.

Money lenders don't lend money to those in need of money, and I for one would not blame them for not doing so. One must accept that money problems generally derive from the employment of insufficient money-generating mechanisms (earning capacity) in one's life. This should not be a condemnation to anyone experiencing such circumstances as these are circumstances that can happen to the very best of us - and tend to be the most educational moments. It is only once the individual fixes these inefficiencies in their money-generating mechanism can they ultimately fix the money problems. Lenders intrinsically know that lending money to an individual with an insufficient money-generating mechanism will only result in further losses of money. It would be like boarding in passengers onto a sinking ship or pouring water into a bucket with a hole at its bottom.

Historically, many individuals in financial distress have approached money lenders only to find, to their astonishment, that these money lenders were not particularly willing to lend them any money, particularly because of their lack of money. As the great British-American comedian and author Bob Hope once said;

> *A bank is a place that will lend you money if you can prove that you don't need it.*

Many citizens have gone through similar experiences with money lenders and I think one can understand why this seemingly callous reception and attitudes by lenders often generated animosity. This refusal to help in a time of need is often seen as a man-made barrier to one's attempts to reclaim control of their lives. These individuals feel betrayed that these money lenders fail to live up to their promise of helping them in times of need.

In conclusion, it seems like in some twisted way, rather than showing gratitude, some humans tend to develop animosity toward those they need. They feel like their state of need is perpetuated by those very people that offer the services or products they need. In their minds, if their employer paid them fairly instead of 'exploiting' them, they would not need to work as much. Or, if the money lenders were more willing to assist, they would not be in such need of money.

Religion is another facet of life that gives the individual meaning and control in the sense that the religious wilfully gives himself to the Lord, the religious are able to take refuge in their teachings whenever they are faced with worldly hardships. When Horatio Spafford wrote "It Is Well with My Soul", he was ultimately using his faith to reclaim control over his life after having experienced the traumatic events of losing 4 daughters in a sea accident (and after having lost 1 son prior to that) - events that would have left many individuals broken and hopeless. As life throws tragic events, it would be easy to feel hapless like a stranded boat lost in the middle of the stormy seas; but faith gives the believer a channel to reclaim control over themselves rather than having life events exert control over their lives.

People might still have meaning in their lives but they don't live happy lives when they are no longer in control of their lives. Not having control over one's life takes away our happiness, this lack of control is the reason for the animosity we may hold over those that have control over us.

Collectivism takes this sense of control from the individual; because the central authority exerts control over the individual's life. Collectivism revolts against individual thought, it confiscates the individual and degrades the individual to the low status of the bolt or nut that forms part of a cold-hearted machine that pursues its own interests. Collectivism, at its very core, breeds unhappiness. As Winston Churchill once said;

Shortcomings of Collectivism

Socialism is a philosophy of failure, the creed of ignorance, and the gospel of envy, its inherent virtue is the equal sharing of misery.

The Progressives may argue that their progressivism is the route to happiness, but their neglect of means to such an end leads to the implementation of policies that bring great misery to the population as a whole.

When in the Pursuit of Happiness - the happiness should not merely lie in the destination, but in the journey as well. Those wishing to take the alternative route are completely regimented into the state's means, causing great discomfort to a point where even if the destination were to be achieved, it would not be worth the misery they endured during the journey.

In the pursuit of equal outcome, we are all prejudiced. The higher achiever is handicapped by the government while the receiver is robbed off any sense of worth and self-fulfilment; both parties are left unhappy, as guilt and resentment or animosity are the orders of the day.

To put it plainly, everybody wants to be fairly rewarded for the work that they've done, the concept of fairness is something Collectivists preach often, yet remain its greatest violators. From infancy, fairness is something the human being understands very well, a one-year-old child is able to detect unfairness before they can fully master speech. Distribution and portioning regardless of monetary production violates the notion of fairness, and this violation becomes the greatest producer of unhappiness among people in collectivist societies. As discussed in Maslow's hierarchy of needs, the individual is not free to pursue their most urgent need.

9. Labour Centric

Another reason why collectivism results in lower standards of living lies in Marx's belief that value is derived from labour. The notion that a product is valuable in proportion to the amount of labour exerted in the production of that product, regardless of innovation or development of expertise.

> **We know that the value of each commodity is determined by the quantity of labour expended on and materialised in it, by the working time necessary, under given social conditions, for its production[167].**

This notion buttressed the claim (and belief) that the factory workers are the true producers of wealth because they are the ones exerting the most labour in production. According to this theory, if a thousand men each spent a thousand hours producing 10 thousand sand castles made of waste matter, the sand castles would be of great value as a result of the labour employed.

This belief makes Collectivists lean toward a labour-centric government that puts labour above everything else. At face value, this seems noble, but when one looks at the effects of such a society, one realizes that this prohibits technological progress. As stated in one of the examples above, they are averse to mechanisation because they fear that it might lead to more unemployment. Karl Marx made the same argument when he wrote;

> **The instrument of labour, when it takes the form of a machine, immediately becomes a competitor of the workman himself. The self-expansion of capital by means of machinery is thenceforward directly proportional to the number of the**

---

[167] Marx, Karl – Das Kapital page 114

workpeople, whose means of livelihood have been destroyed by that machinery[168]

These governments renounce certain technological innovations that threaten the prevailing labour market. The fact that mechanisation leads to cheaper products for the general consumer is of little consequence to the minds of social planners as they do not have faith in the belief in technology's ability to create new industries despite replacing jobs that were carried out by man.

It was through mechanisation that the cost of the automobile was lowered to a point where the average middle-class home could afford transport for travel to and back from work. As the society moved from horseback, people could move from one area to the next much quicker; the availability of transport that could cover a distance of 100km within an hour meant that employees were no longer compelled to live closer to their workplaces. This lowered the demand for properties within the proximities of factories, consequently lowering the cost of housing for the working class and ultimately, lowering the cost of living. As the world embraced technology, the levels of unemployment decreased to a point where the market could accommodate the sudden influx of women who began to move away from the housewife role in the pursuit of career life from the 1940s onward.

These governments seek absolute control of the labour force; from teachers, doctors, and factory to mine workers. The government-run labour market (or business) suffers from inefficiency and struggles to compete in a *laissez-faire* environment. These struggles breed their adversity towards private schooling, private hospitals and private enterprise in general. The public clearly sees the contrast in the quality of services offered by privately run institutions compared to those

---

[168] Ibid page 258

run by government. This contrast serves as a constant reminder of the inferiority inherent in government-run institutions. That's why collectivists seek to monopolize industries because in the absence of private industry - competition; there's nothing to upstage the product and services offered by the government.

Eskom is keenly aware of this fact, despite its mediocre service delivery that comes with daily rationing; some citizens fail to envision better services because they've never lived in a society where one was free to purchase electricity from a private enterprise. When the Soviets monopolized the production of automobiles, it took the public quite a long time to realize the inherent inferiority of the Lada.

One must also acknowledge the fact that if governments were to leave the supply of education and healthcare to private institutions, a large chunk of the society would be unable to access such services due to unaffordability. A return to this autarkic society would leave those without means hapless and at the mercy of people's charity; thus making them vulnerable to exploitation - so I am not arguing against the existence of government-run institutions, but arguing against government monopoly. It was for these reasons that governments felt the need to offer such services to people who could not afford the privately run institutions. However, by aiming to take over the provision of education and healthcare, governments journeyed on a path of conflicting ideals; the ideal to provide services was in conflict with the ideal of providing employment. As we've witnessed in the hierarchy of needs, one can in fact pursue two or more ideals at a particular time so long as the ideals don't come into conflict with each other; but when conflict arises, one has to choose one ideal over the other. Governments offering free education and healthcare seem virtuous, but those familiar with the anatomy of the state know that such a noble cause can never achieve its goals.

Shortcomings of Collectivism

The first reason why it will not meet its ends has to do with the conflict of ideals. When the government opens education schools, it also gets to provide employment according to its standards; at this point, the two ideals are in harmony. But there comes a time when these ideals come into conflict with each other. For instance, think of a scenario where a teacher's teaching methods fail to produce adequately educated learners (i.e. the whole class fails the grade). The government school is suddenly faced with two options, that is - does it keep the teacher's services or not. The government school will have to sacrifice one ideal in order to maintain the other - quality education or provision of employment.

Now for a private school, the decision is a *no-brainer*, because their ideal is quality education - any hindrance to the attainment of this ideal will be removed, and this will mean terminating the employment of the teacher if necessary. But a look at government-run institutions helps one realize that they behave quite differently whenever they are faced with a similar situation - they lean towards retaining the employment of the underperforming teacher. All government institutions have this quality in common; their proximity to the labour unions makes them averse to terminating the employment of underperforming staff. The general public is even aware of this fact; it's witnessed by how we commonly associate government employment with long-term employment (longevity). But this retaining of underperforming staff results in a deterioration of the quality of services. And over time, we witness that the government institution's standards gradually deteriorate, becoming worse off compared to the privately owned institutions.

The government-run schools eventually choose the ideal of providing employment over the ideal of providing the quality education offered by private schools. The institution becomes an employment factory rather than a services factory and the general reluctance to reopen public schools post-lockdown is a testament to this sentiment. The institution evolves into a wealth redistribution factory paying exuberant salaries to some individuals who could never warrant such a salary in the private sector.

These institutions become labour centric. It is not that government-run institutions are devoid of smart, hardworking individuals; it's that they do not rid themselves of unproductive employees. So one should not misconstrue this analysis and conclude that all government employees are incompetent or unproductive, instead, we should realize that for as long as those highly skilled and competent individuals continue to operate in an institution that is averse to getting rid of bad apples, these apples will inadvertently infect the good apples; this infection will come in the form of not competency but general morale. The very fact that teachers working in government schools take their own children to private schools whenever they are able to afford it proves that they are aware of the government school's inferiority.

The second reason why it will not meet its ends is that the state is not designed to operate in a way necessary to meet this end; that is to provide a quality education similar to that offered by private schools to the poorer masses. As discussed above, the reason the private sector is able to operate more efficiently is due to the fact that it does not localize its effort. Many different entrepreneurs open schools (speculate)[169] at varying locations, offering varying types of syllabi through varying teaching methods and charging varying prices for their services. Schools that engage in malinvestment or poor performance end up closing down as a result of losing clients; thus suffering the consequences of their malinvestment - however, the government does not localize its effort. Secondly, because the government does not operate in the profit and loss domain, it has muted the feedback mechanism that would assist it in operating efficiently.

---

[169] Speculation as explained in point number 5

That's why all failures of government-run schools are attributed to a lack of funding. Because the schools cannot fail, they are unable to utilize resources to the maximum or to put it differently, they are not incentivized nor compelled to economize. In the end, government-run schools continue to suffer from a misallocation of resources because misallocation of resources is not punished. In South Africa, the decision to move towards the distribution of tablets to all students was quickly abandoned by most private schools due to the fact that most parents were simply not willing to purchase the tablet offered by the schools at the stated prices. However, government schools remain resolute in implementing the same initiative and will not be able to evaluate the resourcefulness of such a move because the feedback that was available to the private sector will be absent in the government sector.

History shows that this analysis is not limited to education; it shows that wherever government tries to emulate private institutions, the consequences are the same. In South Africa, we are stuck with Eskom (and the national airline) and our politicians oppose any forms of privatization or move to allow private companies to enter the market unrestrained by government-imposed limitations because they fear that this will result in the reduction of the over-bloated staff. It's not what is good for the country as a whole that matters, but the will of the workers and their unions.

How to Fix This
The government's wish to provide services to those without means remains noble, but the ways in which it tries to achieve this end will always fail. Rather than trying to emulate the private sector, governments should assist the poorer population by providing them with what prevents them from accessing the services offered by the private sector, which is money. But this would not be money in the form of cash or a cheque but in the form of vouchers. If the population was given vouchers, the free

market feedback mechanism would be in effect and the parents would be able to remove the children from underperforming schools, thus incentivizing these schools and employees to improve their service delivery overall. This would also reduce the government's burden to build schools as the private sector would take up a bigger stake in education as a result of being incentivized by the existence of vouchers. In this context, resource misallocation in existing government-run schools would be punished, forcing underperforming schools to economize, and it would force these bad schools and educational departments to reduce wasteful expenditure; subsequently lowering costs and improving the quality of services. The society would have been *decollectivized* as each citizen would be empowered as an individual and the institutions would move from a more labour-centric view to a customer-centric view.

10. Foreign Investment

One needs skill and capital to produce goods (and services); it is a common occurrence (especially in developing countries) for a country to have valuable resources underneath its belly but not have the capital or the skill to extract those resources. When Venezuela discovered the large amounts of oil that lay deep underground, its jubilation soon dissipated when they came to the realization that extracting the oil would come at costs exceeding the revenue they would receive at the prevailing oil price. It was only after the oil price began to rise that they began to extract the oil for export. To alleviate this predicament, nations have resorted to foreign investment; international corporations are given *mining rights* to come into the country and extract raw materials to refine them abroad. In the 2019 Economic Development in Africa Report, the United Nations Conference on Trade and Development said the following;

> **There is a possible dichotomy concerning Africa's participation in the cocoa value chain. On the one hand, most**

> cocoa-producing countries are integrated through the supply
> of raw materials and semi-processed intermediates (forward
> participation) embodying limited value added and are
> directed mainly to developed markets. On the other hand, a
> few manufacturing hubs – for example, Egypt and South
> Africa – supply final chocolate products for their domestic
> and sub-regional markets, but predominantly source their
> intermediate inputs (backward participation) from outside
> the continent[170]

As a result, most African countries consume little of what they
produce; in fact, most cocoa farm workers go for long periods of
time, if ever, without eating chocolate, the final product of the
cocoa beans they work all day. CNN's Richard Quest (and the
CNN Freedom Project) visited one of these farms where they
made one of the long-serving farm workers taste chocolate for
the very first time[171].

Countries benefit from foreign investments because this brings
in foreign capital that can be planted into production for the
purpose of producing goods and services that will work to the
benefit of the country and its population. Even the controversial
gold or coal mines brought capital and skill that was not present
in these countries. The inhabitants of the City of Johannesburg
benefit from the infrastructure due to foreign investors who
brought in foreign capital with the aim of extracting the vast
amounts of gold that was buried deep underground. This
investment brought employment to people from all over South
Africa; including the people that wished to move away from the
rigid monotonous agrarian lifestyle in the out-skirting villages.
This is not to exonerate the pillaging, hardships and abuses
experienced by the native population but to highlight the
benefits of foreign investment and the kind of boon it can bring

---

[170] https://unctad.org/press-material/facts-figures-
0#:~:text=For%20the%2020%20products%20in,refined%3B%20diamonds%3B%20and%20cars.
[171] https://edition.cnn.com/videos/world/2014/02/25/cfp-cocoa-nomics-clip-4.cnn
  https://edition.cnn.com/2014/02/13/world/africa/cocoa-nomics-does-chocolate-grow-on-
trees/index.html

to primitive or struggling societies. The continuation of foreign investment is largely dependent on trust, not trust in the people but trust in the government's commitment to human rights, law and order. Investors need to believe that government will respect their property rights and the assurance that the fruits of their investments will not be confiscated by the leaders. But as I've stated earlier in this chapter, collectivist governments are in essence lawless; they are lawless because there is no creed they hold sacred apart from that of absolute power and control. Any law or constitution that limits this power is easily amended and the malleability of laws erodes any confidence any foreign investor might have in such a society.

The Zimbabwean president, Emmerson Mnangagwa, may attempt to re-assure the world of Zimbabwe's readiness for foreign investment, but as long as the leadership continues to display authoritarian tendencies that undermine property rights, the country will not be able to garner the levels of trust required to attract much needed foreign investment.

11. Poverty

Collectivism is the most efficient political ideology in the sense that it always meets a common end - abject poverty. The collectivist movements that take over industries do not just leave the economy and technological innovation stagnant, but impoverish everybody in the end. Such governments deal poorly with natural disasters; be it in the form of famines or other natural disasters such as large-scale earthquakes. Kwame Nkrumah's Ghana adopted Marxism only to see the country bankrupt by the early 1970s. Sékou Touré's Guinea adopted Marxism only to suffer the same fate, with deadly riots in 1977 resulting in the death of 3 governors[172]. Collectivism impoverished Tanzania, Algeria, Mozambique, Mali, Ghana, Ethiopia, Mauritania, Somalia, and Benin; and consumed all the wealth these countries had before the collectivist state was implemented.

The fact that collectivist governments do not produce wealth is a non sequitur because the production of wealth is not their aim, their main aim is to;
      1. Take from the wealthy and redistribute to the needy
      2. Prevent anybody from getting wealthier

It was common teaching amongst African figures like Julius Nyerere, who proclaimed that seeking to attain wealth was behaviour not acceptable for the socialist movement.

One should take note that this analysis is only applicable to the collectivist movements that took over the means of production. In the previous chapter I discussed the National Socialists (Fascists) and how they managed to allow the market to operate freely so long as the enterprise's operations never contradicted the vision of the state. One cannot dispute how Adolf Hitler managed to lift the German state from a state of hardship and economic depression to a point where the country grew so strong militarily that it had to take the partnership of 3 first world nations to bring it down to its knees.
These governments do not just redistribute wealth and prevent anyone from becoming wealthy, but have policies that lead to the destruction of everything that was built. Mauritania, Mozambique and Tanzania are still recovering from the utter destruction caused by their Socialist policies.

---

[172] Ibid Guy Arnold p 483

12. Big Government

"Socialism requires that government becomes your god"
- Rafael Cruz

One understands that if they wish to see everything going on all around them at once, they would need to have very big eyes; or like George Orwell's 1984 – have big brother watching you everywhere. To hear everything said, you would need big ears and to evaluate the consequences of each decision you make, you would need the ability to see way ahead into the future, something that is indeed out of anyone's capabilities. In this micro-management approach to governing, it is no surprise that the size of government inadvertently increases exponentially in size. A planned, top-down society; from the economy, education to healthcare, necessitates the bloating of the size of the government. A big government society produces selfish, passive, hedonistic individuals that are preoccupied with the attainment of benefits they can get from government rather than giving quality service. A big government propagates an environment riddled with regulations and red tape, giving immense power to rent-seeking bureaucrats. You find that those put in charge of implementing policies succumb to the temptations of money and resort to corruption for self-enrichment.

Corruption

The more power the government has over the citizen is directly correlated to the politician's likelihood of getting away with corrupt activities. As we edge closer to a society where the watchers are expected to watch over themselves, we are confronted with the dilemma that plagued Roman/Greek societies long ago; ***Quis Custodiet Ipsos Custodes*** *(Who Watches the Watchmen)*

13. Thought policing and freedom

> *"The tragedy of collectivist thought is that while it starts out to make reason supreme, it ends by destroying reason because it misconceived the process on which the growth of reason depends"* - *By FA Hayek*

Any regimentation of society tends to induce less friction when the collectivist policies have the full backing of all the members of society. But because collectivism is inherently destructive, it can never sustain the support of the public and any opprobrium directed towards such policies will invoke the government's repression, thus awakening the population to this regimentation. Collectivism is based on fear and the sustaining of beliefs in untruths; untruths like the notion that poverty is a result of capitalism, exploitation and colonialism and the ridiculous notion that profit is the creation of labour.

Collectivists could counter this criticism through debate in defence of the merits and superiority over other ideologies, but if they sense that they will not be able to prevail in such debates (due to the intellectual bankruptcy of the ideology), they opt for the silencing of opposing ideas and dissent instead. That's why collectivists; be it in the form of communism, etatism, fascism, tribalism or theocracies; always suppress free thinking.

'Truth is treason in the empire of lies[173].' – Dr Ron Paul

One is a free thinker when they are exposed to all ideas, proselytes and ideological advocates; but free thinking is curbed when a set of ideas are held too sacred for reproach. To upkeep the faith in the collectivist doctrine, the ideology will have to operate in a vacuous environment free of criticism; the population must not be allowed to question nor proselytize against their ideology. The public must not be allowed to think freely.

---

[173] Paul, Ron - The Revolution : A Manifesto Preface page x

One would believe that since Marxists often tend to be from an intellectual background, their foundations would render them open to dissent or debate with regard to the validity of their claims, but as in *The Inquisition*[174]; they silence, prosecute or murder those that hold different views. Law enforcement departments (secret police) are established to police dissenting thoughts, from the Stasi in GDR, the Cheka in USSR to various misinformation boards set up by governments. The collectivist's predilection for social justice rather than mere justice leaves them susceptible to irrationality, thus corrupting their reasoning.

It's the policies, stupid!
What cannot be disputed is the fact that all attempts at building collectivist societies have resulted in failure. In **Why Nations Fail,** authors Daron Acemoglu and James A Robinson described a peculiar situation at the US and Mexican border. There's a city called *The City of Nogales* which is cut in half by a fence. Nogales-Arizona in the Santa Cruz County lies to the north of the fence and Nogales-Sonora lies to the South. The US Nogales had an average household income of $30,000 per annum compared to the Mexican Nogales household with an income of $10,000 per annum.

The Mexican Nogales residents have shorter life expectancy than that of their northerly neighbours. Amongst other things, this is due to poor health care and high infant mortality rates. Basically, everything in Nogales-Sonora is worse off in comparison with Nogales-Arizona; from road management, crime, electricity supply, corruption and bribery to sewage systems. Though the City of Nogales residents share a common history, ancestry and traditional beliefs, the disparities witnessed

---

[174] A group within the Catholic Church tasked to combat heresy

in Nogales showcase the impact government policies can have on a society's fortunes and living standards. Another obvious example is the two Koreas in the far eastern region of the world.

Chapter 7: Lure of Collectivism

Now that we've clearly outlined postcolonial Africa's relationship with Marxism, it is important to also deal with the attraction of Marxism and collectivism in general. For what seemed to be the end of Marxism in 1989, the 2016 US presidential elections showcased the youth's acceptance and admiration of Marxism for the entire world to see.

When Senator Bernie Sanders ran on a socialist platform based on socialist policies, this garnered great support from the youth and professors all over American universities. The highly-favoured candidate and opponent, Secretary of State, Hillary Clinton even lost a few states in the primaries to her surprise socialist opponent that the Democratic Party felt the need to press its thumb on the scale in favour of Mrs Clinton for her to become the eventual Democratic Party nominee.

 The South African electorate also witnessed a rise (the SACP would argue that it's a comeback) of Socialism/Marxism in the form of the EFF (Economic Freedom Fighters); who've advocated for the state ownership of mines, Airlines and various parastatal institutions. South Africa's youth seemed to be also very much captivated by the policies and fiery, combative perorations espoused by the EFF.

The revival of Marxism in academic and social circles has left many wondering; why after all these years, all these deaths, murders, labour camps, famines, failed governments and devalued-or-dead currencies - do we still have so many people advocating for these collectivist policies? How can a system that has not produced one good government still have many people, including the educated and wealthy class, believing that such policies offer a better way forward compared to the free market system that has led to modernity and the current levels of prosperity?

The validity of this question proves that there is a certain and perhaps persistent attraction to Collectivism; the ideology itself. It proves that certain human beings are susceptible to Collectivism because of their very nature and way of thinking; that it takes a certain kind of person to become a Collectivist. We need to understand this kind of person to understand why Collectivism is attractive and their eyes. I will offer 10 personality types that we should be wary of in order to guard against any move or encroachment toward collectivism in all its guises.

The 10 Personality Types

1. The Green-eyed Personality Type

You have to understand that the Marxist, a collectivist; is a covetous human being. After years of religious teachings, it has been socially accepted that being jealous of those richer than you is socially unacceptable, it is condemned in the Judaeo-Christian faiths (Abrahamic religions) and is often regarded as a feeling that a human being should suppress and renounce. Dubbed the "green-eyed monster" in Shakespeare's plays Othello and The Merchant of Venice[175]; it is a sin that has been rightly rejected but has never "gone away".

Rather than subduing this emotion prevalent in every human being, some members of the philosophical and intellectual classes of our society have found means to mask jealousy so they can act on it. Instead of openly admitting that they want the rich man's wealth for the sake of it, through the art of emotional manipulation and mental gymnastics - they've theorized rationales that advocate the claim that an individual is wealthy because they have taken more than what they deserved from the rest of society. They argue that their wealth is a result of theft from the true producers and generators of

---

[175] Shakespeare, William - Othello Act 3, Scene 3

profit, the working class. A point Karl Marx alluded to in *Das Kapital*, where he argued that rather than the owner keeping the money after paying off expenses, he (they were often he's) ought to take out what he has invested prior to production, pay expenses, then distribute what is left amongst the workers as they deserved an equal share[176]. He argued that by not doing so was an act of theft from the workers.

People realised that in a civilised society, one could not just approach the wealthy man to forcefully take his possessions, even if one had the political power (and backing) to do so; this would of course be seen for what it exactly is - robbery. Hence they resorted to covering up this expropriation in the name of various crusades such as the fight for equity, equality or social justice; proclaiming that taking from the wealthy and giving to the poor is an overall act for the betterment (and good) of society – the victim becomes the perpetrator and the thief becomes the righteous benevolent party. Marxists believed that tolerating unrestrained capitalism was in fact tolerating the on-going theft, exploitation and insatiable greed of the wealthy class. It is in this demonization of the wealthy that the covetous individuals can act on their envy - this is in fact the whole theme of the Marxist doctrine. It is a Trojan horse that covers up the same evil emotions that drove the Philistines to fill Isaac's wells with sand once they felt that he was becoming 'too rich' and powerful[177] for their liking.

2. The Naïve Personality Type (Useful Idiot)
Another characteristic prevalent in the adherents of collectivism is naivety; others may call these members the

---

[176] Marx, Karl – Das Kapital
(The 10lbs of cotton analogy in Chapter 7 makes this argument - *The capitalist paid to the labourer a value of 3 shillings, and the labourer gave him back an exact equivalent in the value of 3 shillings, added by him to the cotton: he gave him value for value)*

[177] Genesis 26:15 - Now the Philistines had stopped up all the wells which his father's servants had dug in the days of Abraham his father, and they had filled them with earth. And Abimelech said to Isaac, "Go away from us, for you are much mightier than we. NKJV

suckers in the game. They are not motivated by envy because they are not Marxists; however, their adherence is a consequence of the fact that they are incredibly naive. These are the individuals that mean well, their support of Marxist policies come from a good place because they genuinely believe that redistribution of wealth would indeed eradicate poverty. They are naive because they genuinely believe in the rationales and crusades that cover up the true motivations of the envious group; they truly believe that the Trojan horse is a gift. Those afflicted may be well-educated (they often are) or uneducated with a majority generally in their youth. Humanities professors, sociologists and to my surprise, economists; also tend to fall within this group. The naïve; or useful idiots as the KGB*[178] called them) would even vote to increase their own taxes, protest in the street and write blogs and newspaper columns condemning capitalism.

The naïve have done more to advance the collectivist cause more than the covetous group, thus making naivety vastly more dangerous to the well-being of society when compared to the actions of those motivated by nefarious agendas. They remind me of a man called Adam Wayne, one of the fictional characters in G.K Chesterton's *The Napoleon of Notting Hill*. In accordance with the custom of randomly selecting the King of England, one clerk named Auberon Quin is chosen to be the next king. To amuse himself, as 'he cared for nothing but a joke'; he establishes ridiculous rules and practices that made a mockery of the general decorum and aristocracy in the city of London. People saw this for what it is and were generally annoyed by the king's antics except for one man by the name of Adam Wayne; who with a deadly combination of assiduousness, competence and naivety, managed to coerce the whole population into adopting the comical decrees passed by their King. We need to understand that a lot of

---

[178] The main security agency for the Soviet Union, equivalent to the CIA

suffering in this world is a consequence of actions by people that 'mean well'.

3. Believes in the Incorruptibility of Man

Another form of naiveté is found in the individual who fails to acknowledge that human nature was the reason all communist governments failed in the past; that all Collectivist governments without exception, suffered from debilitating corruption due to the centralizing of more power to the state. They fail to acknowledge the fact that taking care of an individual through a welfare program may have the unintended consequence of making them less productive (as witnessed in societies with welfare for those younger than retirement age). The people tend to be less entrepreneurial when they believe that their returns will be, through heavy taxation, redistributed amongst everybody else (including the non-risk takers). They fail to acknowledge that a society is less innovative when risk-taking (entrepreneurship) is unrewarded. Despite its reliance on terror, the Soviet Union was generally less innovative than free-market countries. One can certainly force people to labour on tirelessly through coercion and terror, but one cannot force people to be innovative; one certainly cannot force people to speculate or take risks necessary for innovation.

This group fails to acknowledge that some people just work harder than others. They also fail to accept that working for the greater good of society is not a sufficient incentive to stimulate production and innovation. One simply cannot ignore the fact that Human nature is not altruistic, that most people are just concerned with taking care of themselves and their families. The overall refusal to accept that human nature is incompatible with collectivism is a characteristic that leaves one susceptible to all collectivist ideologies. This naiveté stems from a general ignorance of human nature and the history of the world.

4. Believes People are Basically Good

Believing that people are *intrinsically good* leaves one susceptible to Collectivism. In his now infamous speech *Why socialism makes people selfish,* Dennis Prager made me aware of the fact that there's a group of people - adults mind you - that genuinely believe that "people are basically good". I had always been of the opposite mindset and therefore assumed that other people held the same belief. I was surprised to learn that this was not the case as I started exploring the matter a bit further in my social circle.

I've also started noticing it amongst social workers and analysts whenever they were discussing violent crime and other general social issues plaguing society. This group believes in the *Tabula rasa*, a theory that individuals are born with a blank slate mental firmware, a sponge-like brain free of any built-in mindset and predilections. The notion that an individual is a blank hard drive that is gradually populated by their surroundings, absorbing various insights and stimuli that works to shape their mindset by the time they reach adulthood. One sees this in how modern society deals with criminality, its averseness to the death penalty and the soft-handed approach in dealing with the more wicked members of society. We are taught how and why society, through poverty, is to blame for the criminal's absolute depravity.

This group believes that with the right education, emotions like greed, selfishness, dishonesty, individualism and the general yearning or longing-for freedom can be uprooted from the consciousness of society. Ultimately, it's a belief that birthed the "You'll own nothing and you'll be happy" platitude.

5. The Armchair Intellectual

Another type of personality susceptible to collectivism is the Thinker, the individual that looks at issues only in the macro while overlooking the micro. The individual that believes social problems can be resolved with a macro solution. This is your tree vs forest person. They look at laws that will benefit the majority and are not concerned about the minority; the advocate of social justice over justice. Advocates for collective farms to the detriment of one's freedom to choose; the typical forest person that will find a home in Marxism because Marxism also views issues in the macro over the micro. This is the tyrant that has come to the frightening conclusion that one has to break a few eggs to make an omelette.

6. The Adult-Child

There are individuals who would rather delegate the responsibility of making a living and ultimately feeding themselves to a larger entity. They yearn for this setup and are prepared to proceed in delegating eking out a living even if it comes at the expense of their Liberty. They see no value in liberty because they don't have any grasp of the notion of Liberty; as a result, they easily surrender their liberty in exchange for government hand-outs. Like many things of intrinsic value, liberty is not an easily tangible concept; one only gets to appreciate it once it is lost. They are like Esau who traded his birthright for a plate of food. One sees this in the woman's suffrage, most women realised their bondage once they were introduced to other women from different societies, who enjoyed certain privileges that they had lived without. The individual who has little value for freedom is the type of person who is easily lured by Collectivism.

7. Revolting against Need

A potential collectivist, the Marxist in particular, is one that has failed to accept the general tribulations and difficulties of life (i.e. the existence of poverty, loss, inequality, rejection, defeat, pain and meritocracy). They believe that human suffering results from a lack of societal central planning, limited government and the coordination of society. These are the tragic individuals struggling to come to terms with the very existence of need, arguing that human suffering is propagated by the capitalist system that requires all members to earn some money just to live for another day. They are troubled by the fact that the responsibilities (burdens) that come with adulthood can only be fulfilled through individualized actions; as a result, they seek to collectivize such responsibilities in order to ameliorate such burdens.

8. Prisoners of Guilt

The 8th personality that can lead one into advocating for collectivism is guilt. Throughout history, groups in societies have subjugated other (weaker) groups through slavery, serfdom, colonisation, autocracy and other various forms of discrimination; leaving these subjugated groups impoverished and prejudiced. These unjust acts are correctly classified as crimes against humanity. These atrocities have left the descendants of the subjugators with mass amounts of wealth and many unearned privileges. The awareness of this unearned privilege has the unintended consequence of generating the levels of compunction that often drives them into opting for policies and ideologies that promise to uplift the historically disadvantaged groups. This is a phenomenon greatly discussed in Shelby Steel's book *White Guilt,* where he outlines how some descendants carry certain levels of guilt that makes them feel like they need to equalise the injustices of the past. They find refuge in egalitarian doctrines in collectivist societies. In their minds, Collectivism offers these individuals a channel to uplift the historically disadvantaged.

9. The Germanic Analyst

A free market society aims to give all its members equal opportunity, but this may not always be possible because we are not born under the same set of circumstances. This society allows for class movement (where the poor become rich) where even those with no education becoming more prosperous than the intellectual elite; contradicting the utopian world of the intellectual and his vision of how things ought to be.

From childhood, we were taught that the accruement of knowledge (good grades etc.) would put us in the upper echelons of society; so to see a plumber or artisanal entrepreneur with half the knowledge of the book-smart intellectual lead a more affluent life symbolises a broken societal order in the eyes of the intellectuals and social academics.

In one of his masterpieces titled *Intellectuals and Society*, Thomas Sowell took a closer look at the relationship between intellectuals and the whole society. He defined the intellectual as *an occupational category, people whose occupations deal primarily with ideas—writers, academics, and the like*. In essence, the intellectual is the individual that espouses ideas that cannot be readily tested because they are not subject to scientific falsification. Another reason why collectivism finds many supporters amongst the intellectual elite is that a collectivist (communist) society puts intellectuals at the upper echelons of society; it appoints them as the central planners, they are the bureaucratic leaders of the collective farms drawing road maps for the whole populace to follow. Collectivism also gives the intellectual (i.e. epidemiologist) ample opportunity to test social theories and computer-generated models on actual human beings. As a result, it is no surprise that collectivist doctrines were advocated by intellectuals in the comfort of their classrooms

10. The Compassionate

The last kind of person worth discussing is the individual whose thinking tends to be clouded by emotion more than rational thinking. Their moral compass is their emotions, how something makes them feel. People became so keenly aware of this fact that it led to the growth of many axioms that speak to this fact; i.e. Maya Angelou's *People will forget what you said, people will forget what you did, but people will never forget how you made them feel.* It is the human being completely void of reasoning and considers any idea they find upsetting as acts of violence. All human beings were at some point in time more emotional than rational thinkers but some outgrew this way of thinking as they were exposed to the realities of life; sadly - some never outgrew this thinking. Winston Churchill alluded to this truth when he stated;

> *"If a man is not a socialist by the time he is 20, he has no heart. If he has not a conservative by the time he is 40, he has no brain"*

My first genuine encounter with compassion happened when I and other members of my family managed to catch a thief red-handed with goods he had stolen from our house in the early hours of the morning. I distinctly remember how his shameless pleadings nearly convinced us not to press charges despite knowing that he had repeatedly invaded many families (houses) before ours[179]. The fact that I frequently played soccer with him in my childhood did not make my decision to support his prosecution easy, but I had to proceed out of principle in the best interest of the whole community. It was in that moment I experienced the internal struggle of compassion vs principles. At that moment I learnt that in particular instances one has to be cruel to be kind and that being kind may in fact be cruel

---

[179] An interesting side note for the slightly older generation- his first name was Dennis

Those that do not outgrow this way of thinking are individuals that are easily lured by Collectivism. Outlining the 10 personality types lured by Collectivism is certainly necessary to understand African Collectivism; however, we still need to also understand why Africa in general is attracted to Collectivism. As discussed in chapter 4, pre-colonial African societies were fragmented into groups of Tribes under kingdoms and chiefdoms. These kingdoms and chiefdoms consisted of social orders and norms that would not differ much from Marxist societies. In tribal societies, the availability of food was the responsibility of the ruler. Yes, each family eked out its own living through subsistence farming, however, the ruler had to ensure fertile land was available (conquered if needs be) and that every man had food to eat. A tribal society has no alienable rights as all rights are granted by the ruler. It is a society that does not recognise individualism and expects every member to act in service and for the greater good of the tribe. All members are associated by group identity and the society is organised in accordance with the will of the ruler (Central planner). This society puts intellectuals (advisors) at the top of society. In the modern state, a political party, leader or doctrine may have replaced the tribal leader's position, but the dynamics in the ruler-citizen relationship remain unchanged.

After the decolonization of Africa, there's been a longing amongst some Africans and their leaders to return to the pre-colonial society. So although the longing is prevalent, they've come to a realisation that a direct return to such a life is not feasible since the world has modernised technologically and socioeconomically; as a result, they looked for a social system that would uphold the tribal values while accommodating the modern world. Marxism, once again fit this criterion.

The Hiddenness of Capitalism
The virtues of the free market/capitalism are not immediately apparent, these values need to be preached and taught in all

corners of society. They might be readily apparent to clearer thinkers, but living in a fast-paced world where contradictory values are promoted in abundance, large sections of societies never get the time to sit back to reflect on these fundamental issues. In an interview with Hamza Yusuf from Zaytuna College, the late British philosopher Roger Scruton encapsulated this dynamic when he explained how the average (unthinking person) is born a conservative (on the right) until they start thinking. This 'thinking' person then gradually moves to the left side of the ideological spectrum. However, he added that once that individual thinks a little bit further, this individual will move back to the right side of the ideological spectrum again[180]. I think this view also correctly explains the difficulty of readily grasping the virtues of individualism and the free market system. All these personalities or characteristics listed above are present worldwide but what gives Africa an extra challenge in its fight against the attraction of Collectivism is that Collectivism holds many similarities with pre-colonial societies of Africa.

One very good documented case study in Africa's transition from colonialism is the case in point of Julius Nyerere and African Socialism in the Tanganyika region. The notion of Ujamaa was a clearly laid out concept that was put into practice in the Tanganyika region. This documentation, today gives us the opportunity to reflect on that society and to understand the intentions of most newly elected African leaders post colonialism.

When one looks at Ujamaa (Brotherhood) within the realm of African Socialism, one is redirected to the Tanzania of the 1960s and 70s. My reason for focusing on Julius Nyerere's reign is because his Villagization project was one of the most earnest and determined attempt toward the atavistic restoration of the

---

[180] Roger Scruton: Why Intellectuals are Mostly Left
https://youtube.com/watch?v=FYo4KMhUx9c&feature=share

perceived African society that we lost. When Julius Nyerere took office, he sought to develop a society based on the spirit of Ujamaa.

Nyerere believed that socialism was not just a political ideology but (like all Marxists believe) an essential part of everyday life. He famously stated that socialism was a state of mind and that with the right education, anyone could be a socialist. In his essay titled *Ujamaa - The basis of African socialism*, he wrote

> *"In the individual - as in society, it [UJAMA] is an attitude of mind which distinguishes the socialist from the non-socialist. It has nothing to do with possession or non-possession of wealth. Destitute people can be potential capitalists - exploiters of their fellow human beings. A millionaire can equally be a socialist, he may only value his wealth because it can be used in the service of his fellow men. But the man who uses wealth for the purpose of dominating any of his fellows is a capitalist. So is the man who would if he could[181]"*

These beliefs help explain how one could want a society built on altruism and socialism. Although the society did not ban wealth outright, it made the generation of wealth quite difficult as it did not see millionaires in a positive light.

The wealthy continued to be castigated as parasites in Collectivist societies. In the very same essay, Julius Nyerere continued;

> *"Even when you have an exceptionally intelligent and hardworking millionaire, the difference between his intelligence, his enterprise, his hard work, and those of other members of society, cannot possibly be proportionate to the difference between their 'rewards'. There must be something wrong in a society where one man, however hard-working or clever he may*

---

[181] www.juliusnyerere.org
https://www.juliusnyerere.org/resources/view/ujamaa_-_the_basis_of_african_socialism_julius_k._nyerere

be, can acquire as great a 'reward' as a thousand of his fellows can acquire between them[182]."

The Ujamaa society was a society in which the possession or pursuit of wealth was frowned upon and the bearers of wealth were perceived to be greedy, immoral and generally *unsocialist.*

"Apart from the anti-social effects of the accumulation of personal wealth, the very desire to accumulate it must be interpreted as a vote of 'no confidence' in the social system."

This was a society in which the individual was expected to not worry about their tomorrow but put all faith in the community and its ability to fend for everybody within the society. From wives, children, and widows to the elderly; each individual was expected to have complete faith in the distributive state's ability to take care of their tomorrows. Despite the fact that land ownership was banned, one was only given the right to use the land for subsistence; more evidence supporting my claim that Marxist societies had a lot in common with pre-colonial African societies. This also explains the current atavism, the longing amongst Africans and the leaders to return to the pre-colonialism social order.

You'll fully understand this longing once you remember that modernisation for Africa was a painful experience. Lands were expropriated as people were forcefully uprooted from their historic lands; lives were indentured if not killed and whole languages were forever wiped out of existence[183] as a result of this colonization. Modernisation for Africans came hand in hand with mass exploitation, enslavement, violation of rights and dispossession of land and dignity. Lost languages remain a sore topic for many of us as it symbolizes a break (severing) of the modern African from his past.

---

[182] Ibid (www.juliusnyerere.org)
[183] When Germany colonized the Tanganyika region, the founded extermination of many ethnic languages and centralized ethnic languages into Swahili (as they only permitted Swahili)

For most Africans, African socialism seems to offer the best way to recapture the past while accommodating the quickly modernizing developing world. In general, we must accept that there will always be a certain attraction to Collectivism. It will take continuous dialogue and exposure of all the failed collectivist governments and policies in order to *educate and convince* the common African man (and woman) of the virtues of liberty and responsibility and obligation to defend our indefeasible God-given rights, never surrendering these rights to any central planning authority.

Chapter 8: Current plight of Africa

One must also note that some of the social ailments previously discussed are not exclusive to Africa; however one cannot dispute their concentration to one continent (and prevalence in every African country without exception). Contrary to popular opinion, it has now become evident that Collectivism did not die in the late '80s upon the dissolution of the USSR; however discredited, like the Trojan horse it simply put on a mask and continued making a moral case for equality as our countries continued to implement redistributive policies in the name of fighting inequality. Welfare, for instance, serves the purpose of taking care of the elderly population but inadvertently opens the pathway for the pursuit of redistributive policies; where the government is given more responsibility (power) over certain sectors of society i.e. health care, education, power generation etc. The second unintended consequence is an increase in the size of government; making it very lucrative for opportunistic individuals to get into government for financial gain.

Africa experiences common challenges as those experienced in some South American and East European countries. At this point, it is clear that the current plight of Africa is a result of poor governance, (it is the case in every African country) regardless of varying levels in terms of wealth and GDP. The lack of a first-world nation in Africa is a result of poor governance and poor economic policies.

Whenever one is involved in discussions concerning the current state of Africa, one of the culprits that always enter the conversation is corruption. Any situation that allows (or necessitates) any member of the human species to overlook the allocation of financial resources and governmental contracts worth loads of money fertilizes the ground for corruption; As the saying goes, Power corrupts and absolute power corrupts absolutely. What First world countries have done to combat

218

corruption is to set up processes, procedures and well-trained law enforcement to make corruption a more risky activity. Processes, procedures and law enforcement work in tandem with each other and corruption can only thrive if one of these features is subverted. Ultimately, the fight against corruption stems from good governance; as a result, to fight corruption in Africa, we need to have good governance in place.

The biggest acts of corruption in every country are always carried out with the assistance and sometimes instruction of the leaders. In my previous interactions with state institutions, I have come to realize that they do have very concrete checks-and-balances accounting procedures that guard against fraud and the looting of funds. I have come to realize that one can only accomplish any looting with the assistance of a higher-ranking official who can order lower-ranking officials to sign off invoices for houses and bridges that were never built. In the South African context, the "capturing" of South Africa was done with the consent of the then-sitting President Jacob Zuma. Angola experienced its own case of corruption and put this into perspective when former president José Eduardo dos Santos's government, within a two-year span, awarded Isabel dos Santos - his daughter, four lucrative contracts worth over US $22 billion[184]. The DRC also went through its episode of kleptocracy when former president Mobutu Sese Seko abused his office to amass mass amounts of wealth through the takeover of the Congolese economy. There are countless examples around the continent. Overall, we realise that one feature of mass corruption is that it generally occurs with the consent of the leaders. The leader's consent serves to protect the corrupt individual from prosecution because the leader can influence prosecuting authorities to simply not bring cases to court – and these leaders plant biddable judges as an extra measure just in case some cases sneak into the courtrooms.

---

[184] https://www.makaangola.org/2018/07/isabel-dos-santos-the-fall-of-africas-richest-woman/

Another cancerous impact of corruption from the head of government is that it *metastasizes* by trickling down to the general members of society; from the president, minister, local councillor right down to the local policeman and average citizen – a government riddled with corruption destroys society as a whole. The stripping of assets and money from state-run entities affects the productivity of these entities. As I write this, South Africa is going through a string of inquiries (i.e. The Zondo Commission) that are unearthing corrupt activities that are at such a large scale that the country is going through a collective sense of despondence, anger and frustration.

A South African mutual bank called VBS (Venda Building Society) recently declared bankruptcy as a result of mismanagement; officials granted risky loans to politically connected individuals at very low interest rates. In the spirit of supporting black businesses - people and municipalities were encouraged to utilize VBS as their main banking services provider and urged to deposit their life savings and investments into this bank. Municipalities were *guilted* into moving their funds into VBS, thus suffering greatly when the bank finally collapsed in 2018. As the Daily Maverick reported;

> *The unionists were outspoken against the decision by the Vhembe District Municipality to invest more than R300-million of public funds in the VBS Mutual Bank. The municipality has since lost the money after more than R2-billion was stolen from the bank, leading to its collapse in 2018.*[185].

The failure to (successfully) prosecute anyone in the VBS saga sets a very bad precedent because other banks might be tempted to adopt the same reckless lending tactics after

---

[185] (www.dailymaverick.co.za) https://www.dailymaverick.co.za/article/2021-08-21-vbs-scandal-they-took-the-very-little-we-had-and-bought-fancy-items/
https://www.iol.co.za/pretoria-news/news/vbs-mutual-bank-accused-danny-msiza-tipped-to-be-next-limpopo-anc-secretary-5f0624d5-cc59-42e5-b08d-0ce81b2c6039

witnessing that no one in the VBS scandal was brought to Justice[186].

The Zondo Commission which also served to look into Eskom subsequently revealed how the previous South African President, Jacob Zuma, colluded with a foreign business family to have Eskom's assets stripped and sold off at discounted prices to politically linked companies. Contracts that were not financially beneficial (to the power utility) were offered to companies linked to the same infamous Gupta family. Corruption erodes trust and produces utter dysfunction. Eskom admitted to having paid out R1.6-billion worth of "consultation fees" to McKinsey and Trillian Capital Partners, a multinational consultation company allegedly linked with the Gupta family[187].

Another reason why our current efforts to combat corruption remain futile is that our bad leaders always capture crime-fighting institutions before they commence on their path to self-enrichment. As mentioned above, it's a simple matter of charges not being brought to court. South Africa had a high crime-fighting unit (**The Scorpions**, or the Directorate of Special Operations) disbanded in 2009, its biggest crime was being "in conflict" with the head of the South African Police Service Jackie Selebi, former presidents Thabo Mbeki and Jacob Zuma. The fact that a majority of African presidents appoint the head of a prosecution authority is another highlight of why fighting corruption with bad leaders is futile.

Corruption does not just erode State-run entities but kills small businesses and breeds an environment inconducive to entrepreneurship. Stealing from Gresham's Law, which in

---

[186] As I write this, numerous individuals have been charged however, the NPA is yet to attain a successful conviction.
[187] https://www.gupta-leaks.com/salim-essa/how-mckinsey-and-trillian-ripped-r1-6bn-from-eskom-and-planned-to-take-r7-8bn-more/
https://amabhungane.org/stories/the-mckinsey-dossier-part-1-how-mckinsey-and-trillian-ripped-r1-6bn-from-eskom/
https://mg.co.za/news/2021-01-13-zondo-commission-testimony-billions-wasted-at-eskom/

economics argues that "bad money will always drive good money out of circulation"; one may conclude that bad businesses (those that engage in corruption) will always drive out good businesses. Bad businesses can get more business contracts via corrupt means and they can lobby for laws that act as barriers to keep out emerging smaller businesses. It was no surprise that corporations such as *KPMG, McKinsey & Trillian Capital Partners, Bell Pottinger* and *Bossasa* were implicated in the corruption scandal that engulfed South Africa in the last decade.

Corruption also increases organized crime because it is in essence organized crime. Mandy Weiner, through her fantastic book, *Ministry Of Crime*, documented the nexus between organised crime figures, corrupt police officials and powerful politicians in detail. Corruption is a problem, but we need to realise that in order to defeat it, we don't just need to have an ethical good leader at the helm; we also need to find a way of severing the link between prosecuting authorities and leaders. South Africa has made provisions for private prosecution[188] to ameliorate this situation; however, private prosecution is dependent on the state declaring that it will not prosecute - *nolle prosequi*. The problem with this caveat is that this declaration often comes so late that parties that end up taking on these private prosecution cases are in effect working with *cold cases*; a type of case more difficult to prevail in as compared to normal cases.

The collectivist's predilection for a redistributive government inches them toward a big government. The government has to be big because it has to overlook and direct many industries through regulations. The government increases its operational costs and bureaucracy, presenting more avenues for corrupt officials to enrich themselves. Collectivist leaders disrupt the

---

[188] South African Criminal Procedure Act 5 of 1977

free market, leaving many impoverished with few opportunities to better their lives

What about poverty
Another ailment plaguing the continent is the scourge of poverty. All countries have some levels of poverty, but what differs is the level of poverty across all nations when all other things are considered equal. Basically, when nations talk of poverty, they are not talking about the same levels (or extents) of poverty. A poor man in Chad, Nigeria or Malawi is worse off compared to a poor man in Britain, Italy or the USA even if the individuals are of equal standing within their relative countries. The poorest man in Britain/ Australia/ Brazil will enjoy certain privileges the middle-class man in Nigeria[189] can only dream of.

The free basic education offered in African countries pales in comparison with the education the poor receive in countries outside of Africa. I can make the same case with regard to healthcare or water and electricity supply. It is no surprise that most countries in Africa struggled to contain the Ebola pandemic (or various other epidemics) that other countries managed to eradicate or treat with little difficulty within their countries. Despite some improvement in the last 20 years, the average life expectancy of a man in Africa, as of 2018 is 9 years younger (10 years with regards to women) than the life expectancy worldwide[190]. This is supported by Statista, a German company specializing in market and consumer data analysis. This gap increases when compared to 1st world countries. The wealthiest countries in Africa struggle to supply electricity to the masses without constant power outages; a phenomenon spreading worldwide. Typical examples would be daily outages in Nigeria or the already-mentioned South African power utility resorting to "load shedding" just to keep it afloat.

---

[189] Malawi, Egypt, South Africa etc.
[190] https://www.statista.com/statistics/274511

The poverty levels in Africa have also affected education. In 2017, UNESCO revealed that the global literacy rate for all people aged 15 and above is 86%. The rate varies throughout the world, with developed nations having a rate of 99% (2013); Oceania having 71.3%; South and West Asia having 70.2% (2015) and sub-Saharan Africa at 64.0% (2015). Seventy-five percent of the world's 781 million illiterate adults are found in South Asia, West Asia and sub-Saharan Africa and women represent almost two-thirds of all illiterate adults globally[191]. Government education in most African countries is so poor that a child graduating from its senior grade tends to be as literate as a primary school student at a private institution. A poorly educated individual has very little opportunity to better their lives.

Another sign of poverty is the state of structural development as discussed in the opening chapter. African countries suffer from poor road management (that's if a road is built at all) with colonial buildings still towering over cities 30 years later. If it wasn't for the Chinese expansion in Africa, this statistic would be worse. Power grabs, civil wars and countless coup *d'etats* have left the continent ravaged, riddled with land mines and perilous to explore. Corruption and poor structural development encompassed with poor education hinder us from making the most of our natural resources, as some African countries are unable to extract and process or export natural resources without foreign intervention.

The rest of the world has experienced similar levels of poverty before, but due to good governance at one point, alleviated these levels thus marching on to economic prosperity. One does not have to look any further than the cases of post-War Germany,

---

[191] http://gem-report-2017.unesco.org/wp-content/uploads/2017/10/2017-GEM-Report-Statistical-Tables.pdf
   https://unesdoc.unesco.org/ark:/48223/pf0000261971

India, China, the United States, Russia or Brazil. Poor governance in some countries worsens the scourge of poverty.

In the previous chapter, I highlighted why and how Collectivism produces dictatorships; and how Africa suffers from poor governance due to dictatorships. Authoritarianism maintained its ubiquitous status throughout the last 60 years with South Africa offering its unique contribution through an arguably worse form of authoritarianism when the bible-thumping National Party introduced and remained committed to the apartheid policy. These governments localised their country's resources into the hands of the few upper classes. When the colonialist (and authoritarian) governments were removed from power, they tended to be replaced by other authoritarian governments. This observation is constant throughout the continent; from Zaire with regards to Mobuto and Lumumba, Ethiopia with regards to Haile Selassie I and Mengistu Mariam, Libya with regards to Gaddafi, Tanzania, Algeria and Zimbabwe etc.

These collectivist governments were counterintuitive to the spirit of individual Liberty thus quelling the innovation spirit of its population. A free market environment produces wealth and fosters innovation; the wealth produced reduces poverty and incentivizes production and creativity. If a man is certain to keep his harvest, he will be more inclined to plant a seed. A free market environment reduces power struggles as people are afforded other avenues to climb up the socioeconomic ladder because one does not have to go through government employment to attain wealth and financial freedom. The countless number of African leaders who refused to relinquish power even amid high unpopularity shows that these leaders (and their cronies) knew that a loss of control over a high office was equivalent to the loss of prosperity and the various amenities that came with the high office. These leaders knew that the environment they created was not one in which they would prosper without the power to wield governmental structures for their benefit. Joseph Kabila for instance, did not believe that the DRC could give him a life of economic opportunities and equal rights if he were not in power while Tony Blair and Barrack Obama had no such fears. Tony Blair and Barrack Obama knew that they lived in countries with free market economies (to a certain extent) and as a result were not terrified of life after presidency.

In the opening chapter, one of the fundamental questions was why, after 50 years of failed governments, Africans keep electing poor leaders. Is it because these leaders change once they are in power or is it because we as the electorate failed to vet the candidates while they were pursuing our votes? I would suggest that it is the latter with a few exceptions such as power grabs via *coup d'etats*. We need to understand that Marxists or collectivists can remain Collectivist even after abandoning the Marxist approach to the economy. Collectivism, like a religion, does not just deal with economic issues, but shapes your worldview and directs your moral compass. It has a set of values that it imposes on society, it is (in the words of American journalist Garet Garrett); *"furnished with all the properties proper to a church, such as a revelation of its own, a rigid doctrine, a symbolic language, a propaganda, a priestcraft, and a demonology"*.

Many African countries were forced to relax certain aspects of their Collectivist policies due to the economic hardship, famine and sometimes - total economic collapse that sparked the unmitigated ire of the whole populace. As we entered the 90s, the USSR had collapsed, inadvertently cutting off the supply chain of fellow Marxist regimes. The remaining alternatives were to approach the IMF or the western countries for assistance; however, they were not prepared to assist a country with a collectivist approach to its economy – like all banks, the IMF was not willing to lend any money to any nation with a bad money-generating mechanism. And so with Marxism utterly discredited, socialist countries in peril had a choice; prove that they have abandoned their collectivist approach to receive aid or continue facing economic hardship and risk an uprising from the disenfranchised citizens. Those thinking with their stomachs found it to be an easy choice. Tanzania abandoned certain aspects of Marxism after Nyerere left office, and so did Mozambique under Joaquim Chissano. Algeria followed suit under the leadership of Chadli Benjedid, Guinea under the leadership of Conte, Benin under Kerekou and Ghana under Jerry Rawlings are just a few examples that come to mind.

Today most African countries are still governed by leaders who idealize Collectivism, leaders whom the teachings of Karl Marx still shape their worldview through and through. As stated before, Collectivism makes its case on moral grounds and just like all religions; it makes a case that cannot be disproven. This is exactly what the great Karl Popper discovered right before he formulated his **Falsification Principle.** In this principle, he concluded that every scientific claim should hold some fact that if proven wrong, should render the whole theory false. This makes the claim scientific, just like Newton's law of motion, gravity or the simple notion that all swans are white. All these claims subject themselves to testing and give a clear route in which they can be falsified. A levitating cow will disprove the law of gravity just like the discovery of black swans disproved the notion that all swans are white.[192]

Below is an excerpt that will do more justice to the paper than my summation;

1. It is easy to obtain confirmations, or verifications, for nearly every theory — if we look for confirmations.

2. Confirmations should count only if they are the result of risky predictions; that is to say, if, unenlightened by the theory in question, we should have expected an event which was incompatible with the theory — an event which would have refuted the theory.

---

[192] Taleb, Nassim N. – The Black Swan

3. Every "good" scientific theory is a prohibition: it forbids certain things to happen. The more a theory forbids, the better it is.

4. A theory which is not refutable by any conceivable event is non-scientific. Irrefutability is not a virtue of a theory (as people often think) but a vice.

5. Every genuine test of a theory is an attempt to falsify it, or to refute it. Testability is falsifiability; but there are degrees of testability: some theories are more testable, more exposed to refutation, than others; they take, as it were, greater risks.

6. Confirming evidence should not count except when it is the result of a genuine test of the theory; and this means that it can be presented as a serious but unsuccessful attempt to falsify the theory. (I now speak in such cases of "corroborating evidence.")

7. Some genuinely testable theories, when found to be false, are still upheld by their admirers — for example by introducing ad hoc some auxiliary assumption, or by reinterpreting the theory ad hoc in such a way that it escapes refutation. Such a procedure is always possible, but it rescues the theory from refutation only at the price of destroying, or at least lowering, its scientific status. (I later described such a rescuing operation as a "conventionalist twist" or a "conventionalist stratagem.")

One can sum up all this by saying that the criterion of the scientific status of a theory is its falsifiability, or refutability, or testability.

I may perhaps exemplify this with the help of the various theories so far mentioned. Einstein's theory of gravitation clearly satisfied the criterion of falsifiability. Even if our measuring instruments at the time did not allow us to pronounce on the results of the tests with complete assurance, there was clearly a possibility of refuting the theory.

    Astrology did not pass the test.

Astrologers were greatly impressed, and misled, by what they believed to be confirming evidence — so much so that they were quite unimpressed by any unfavourable evidence. Moreover, by making their interpretations and prophesies sufficiently vague they were able to explain away anything that might have been a refutation of the theory had the theory and the prophesies been more precise. In order to escape falsification they destroyed the testability of their theory. It is a typical soothsayer's trick to predict things so vaguely that the predictions can hardly fail: that they become irrefutable[193].

This theory gives us a clear indication and argues that an economic collapse won't necessarily convince a Marxist that the whole theory is "false", just like a huge drop in the average climate will not convince the environmentalists that their *warnings* might be hyperbolic if not unfounded. It is worth mentioning that some collectivists that ruled us were legitimately elected into office and I will offer two reasons as to why we keep electing such poor leaders into office time and time again.

The first reason is a lack of understanding of the teachings of the liberation movement and spirit; the liberation spirit that awakens one to the fact that each person is an individual with individual rights; Rights that are not granted by any government, leader or king but by God (or some externality for the non-believers). A few examples of these alienable rights are:

1. The right to life – the right not to be murdered.

2. Right to access the comprehensive fruits of their labour. Despite Marxists arguing that the "fruits of labour" are the profits of the factory; truth is that the fruit of the Labour of the factory worker is his or her salary. The worker's toil from day to day is rewarded by a salary/wage regardless of whether the factory makes a profit or not.

---

[193] Popper, Karl R. - Conjectures and Refutations p37

3. Right to property ownership - you have a right to keep property that you've purchased or currently own. We have witnessed '*propertyless*' individuals bastardize this creed by arguing that since ownership of property is a right, the surrounding community should work to provide them with such property; however, this right serves to protect the ownership of property in the same way the "right to access the comprehensive fruits of their labour" serves to protect the earnings of individuals. Property has proven to be a robust form of saving and investing; it protects you from inflation, the government's unmitigated printing of fiat money and other forms of currency devaluation.

4. Freedom of Movement - i.e. the right to migrate in pursuit of a better life – The large-scale concentration camp called North Korea violates this right by prohibiting its people from leaving the country.

5. Freedom of expression (speech) – that one is free to express oneself. This is one of the rights that are limited by other rights. For example, one cannot incite violence towards another group. Incite in the sense of motivating one group to act against another group.

6. All men are equal before the law

7. To be free from Government coercion. – i.e. One's life should not be expropriated to serve the ends of the ruling body, state or entity

8. This is not a right but an obligation – The legal field calls this 'corresponding obligation', which teaches that each right confers an obligation or limitation on other members of society (e.g. The right to own a car limits others from using it without your permission).

As previously mentioned, another reason why Africans keep electing poor leaders is due to tribalism. Sometimes loyalty to anything makes one suspend their previously held convictions and it is no different when it comes to electing a leader who happens to be from the same tribe. Tribalism can be ethnic or racial, kith or kin. For instance, a white individual that is not willing to vote for a party that shares their values because its majority in terms of membership consists of individuals from a different group or the black man continuing to vote for a party that continues to govern poorly just because the alternative party overwhelmingly has a majority of members of a different tribe. Zimbabweans kept electing former president Robert Mugabe for many years regardless of his atrocities and human rights violations just because he happened to be of the same tribe as the majority of Zimbabweans (the Shona-speaking tribe). I have also delved into how tribalism culminated in the Rwandan genocide following the supposed "killing" of President Juvénal Habyarimana.

Since Collectivism continues to speak to the emotional being, we need to preach libertarian values amongst ourselves so we can instil a sense of liberty across all corners of our society. Our continent is rich with resources that continue to generate immense wealth for the outside world and it is blessed with a large population that has so much potential in having a greater impact on the economic world stage. But if we continue to elect poor leaders, we will still see governments that produce little prosperity as they continue to plough countries into more debt, bringing regression that keeps sections of our fellow countrymen in dire straits of poverty.

Chapter 9: The Virtues of Decentralization

It is very common for a group to hold certain virtues and axioms regarding certain subjects in certain areas of life, yet still fail to transmit those virtues and values to the following generation - their offspring. This normally stems from an inability or failure to make the case for their values. We explored countries that have benefitted from the free market system yet are currently going through an onslaught of a collectivist wave that is threatening to destroy everything that they've built. We are better at explaining why the opponent's opinion is bad if not nonsensical than we are at proselytizing the advantages and virtues of the current positions we hold. If one listens to a collectivist debating an individualist, one notices that each participant spends more time highlighting the shortcomings of the other side's position than proselytizing the benefits of their own position. Unfortunately, it is a shortfall even this author could not avoid.

The Defence of Values

The problem with this approach is that it always leaves room open for defeated ideas to sneak back from the dead like Lazarus waking up from his eternal sleep. In the USA, Marxism was defeated, socialism was a dirty word and every American; from the long haul truck driver, and coal miner to the executive in Wall Street; all accepted the fact that they lived in a prosperous country as a result of the free market system (capitalism). I use the US as an example because the United States was one country even the staunchest Marxist would have conceded that the people's revolution was unlikely to take place. The US elections were races between the conservative and the liberal, with each side holding opposite views on drug policies, marriage, conscription, war and abortion yet both were still in agreement with regard to the virtues of capitalism and the immorality of the socialist state.

However, as we learnt in the 2016 USA presidential elections, widespread uniformity (or consensus) is not a signal of the absolute defeat of the opposing idea. This is because as time goes on, this uniformity inadvertently starts to breed a certain level of ignorance. To fully grasp this point, the reader needs to fully understand the difference between ignorance and stupidity. One is ignorant as a result of lacking information while one is considered to be stupid when they are unable to comprehend the information even if it is laid out before their very eyes.

As these truths become axiomatic, the later generations adopt the values of previous generations as a matter of fact while losing the ability to defend such values. Such is the paradoxical nature of axioms, the more axiomatic they become, the more disconnected people are from the reasoning as to why they are 'true'.

The uniformity allows them the privilege of carrying on with their daily lives never having to defend their values because these values never face organized opposition. Well, that was the case until recently. The phoenix-like rise of socialism in the 21st century caught many off guard and completely unable to defend their current society; with those enjoying lives of prosperity shamed into self –flagellation in an effort to repent for having benefited from the fruits of the capitalist society they inherited.

The Marxist never has to be wary of this problem because his childlike ideology is tailor-made for individuals (personality types) such as those discussed in the previous chapter. The collectivist also carries an inherent advantage in the sense that he can lose the debate a thousand times, the liberal society always affords him the opportunity to debate another day. However, this is not the case when the tables are turned around because when the collectivist wins the day and gains a foothold within the political sphere of that society, he does not offer the defeated the same courtesy to fight another day - the collectivist resorts to shaming, vilifying and in extreme cases jailing opposition; he silences anyone preaching against his ideology.

For as long as we never proselytize in favour of decentralization, as FA Hayek put it[194], we will be like the conservative that advocates for the status quo, nothing but a mere handbrake as the leftist drags him to the other side of the ideological spectrum. After having made the case against our current state of affairs (and our marriage to collectivism), my work would be incomplete if I were to not take time to delineate the virtues of a decentralized society.

The whole chapter is not meant to focus on the collectivist mindset and the collectivist form of governance but to accentuate the virtues of the decentralized state; an open market decentralized society.

1. On Poverty – again

Since the biggest problem facing Africa is poverty, it's fairly obvious that to eliminate abject poverty, the solution would lie within the countries that have walked this path before us. I have stated that a free market system has offered the best solution in

---

[194] Hayek, FA – The Constitution of Liberty – Why I am Not a Conservative (PostScript)

eradicating poverty, and so it follows suit that we delve deeper into why such a system was able to accomplish such a feat.

What causes #poverty? Nothing. It's the original state, the default and starting point. The real question is, What causes #prosperity?
Prof @Per Bylund (@PerBylund Twitter)

This fact, that people are less poor today due to free market policies is not disputed. This has become such an axiom that one picks this up even when listening to the Collectivist's critique of socialism, one notices that the talk has shifted from "look at the poor people everywhere", to "look at the inequality gap"; or to more recently….. *"where's the equity"* - this being the disparities in the demographics of those occupying high positions of wealth and success.

The critique has evolved from "Capitalism is bad, look at the poor" to "Capitalism is bad because it concentrates 90% of the wealth to the top 1% of people on the planet". To criticize a system for not making us all wealthy to equal extents is quite unreasonable if not nonsensical. It is no longer in dispute that the decentralized (even partially free) market system has lifted millions from poverty. Because capitalism has done a great job of eradicating poverty where ever it's implemented, the opponents that wish to still get rid of the free market system regardless of this fact now argue that a move toward a collectivized centrally planned society will finally eradicate the last vestiges of the ailments that still plague society today. Remnants like "Inequity" and poverty. In essence, they argue that even though socialism could not begin to eradicate poverty at its zenith, it's the best solution to eradicate what is left of it. But if one were to look at it from the other end, why would capitalism be inadequate at eradicating less (small) poverty if it competently eradicated abject (Big) poverty?

This view only serves to highlight the collectivist's myopic view and misunderstanding as to why the free market system eradicates poverty in the first place. Detailing exactly how Capitalism eradicates poverty will be a good starting point in extolling the virtues of decentralization.

How does Capitalism defeat poverty?
We take it as a given that capitalism eradicates poverty but we do not often take the time to ask ourselves how exactly does it achieve this? Regardless of race, gender, religion or creed, we've noticed that the free market system enables those who adopt it to experience new levels of prosperity. The one feature that is largely prominent in a collectivized society is its labour-centric view of the economy; the society is organized in order to generate jobs for the people. However, when a society shifts toward decentralization; the society's view shifts from "jobs" to production.

The simple fact of the matter is that **'Production lessens poverty'**, it's quite *extraordinary* that this banal fact warrants mentioning; but if one listens to politicians excoriating the current "levels of inequality" (or poverty), the solutions put down don't evolve around production. As I discussed in the happiness paragraph, poverty stems from a lack of production, or as Per Bylund perfectly explained it "It's the original state, the default and starting point" - a state before man starts to produce.

The real problem of poverty is not a problem of "distribution" but of production. The poor are poor not because something is being withheld from them but because, for whatever reason, they are not producing enough[195] - Henry Hazlitt

Just like the poor man, society is poor as a result of an insufficient money-generating mechanism, and this insufficient money-generating is an element of production. The beauty of production lies in the fact that all societies have that quality within and can discover that latent quality when each society affords itself the opportunity to embark on such a journey in perfecting that ability.

Let us go back to Amaju from chapter 6. In the free market, Amaju faces uneasiness; we called this 'need'. He quickly realizes that he needs to alleviate this uneasiness, and the best way to achieve this lies in the resources at his disposal; he knows that some resources that may not be in his possession lie in other people's hands. He realizes that in order to attain goods currently not in his possession, he will either have to produce the resources he needs. Alternatively, he can produce resources his fellow countrymen need so he can enter into a transaction with them. All alternatives available to Amaju all point to the fact that his future prosperity lies in **production**, he has to discover what his fellow countrymen need. If they like apples, he plants *them apples*. Amaju's countrymen also wake up to the same realization; subsequently, they all wake up to a society that aims to produce goods at the service of each other – making each man a producer and consumer.

In a very small village, this rudimentary explanation of production is all that would be required to explain how this leads to prosperity; however, as a society grows bigger, the

---

[195] Sowell, Thomas – Basic Economics page 261 5th Edition

question "what others need" grows in its complexity, the production feature moves from a spectre of economic calculation to a spectre of speculation.

Speculation is Key

Because production takes time, those in production learn that it is often futile to try and discover what consumers need at that particular time because consumers' preferences keep changing from time to time - preferences are fluid. In fact, consumers don't even know what they want, as Steve Jobs once said; ***"People don't know what they want until you show it to them"***.

Henry Ford also made a similar observation when he said that if he had asked people what they wanted, they'd have asked for faster horses.

Even if Amaju were to wake up this morning with the realization that there's a high demand for button-less (keyless) smartphones, he may not be in a position to take advantage of this newfound knowledge because of the time it would take to develop a button-less smartphone and have it ready for the market. He also realizes that those most prosperous in the current market somehow had the foresight to "predict" that there would be a demand for keyless smartphones before these kinds of phones were ever made. Since Amaju is fully cognizant of the fact that people cannot see into the future, his current streak of epiphanies continues when he again realizes and reaches the logical conclusion that those that had a product readymade and available for the sudden need that arose must have speculated that such a need or demand would arise.

The free market is largely a market of speculation, those that speculate and hit the sweet spot will reap the fruits of their speculation before the rest of us wake up to the existence of the new demand. Although they will get richer before the rest of us follow suit, we should not hold animosity toward such individuals but see (through our green envious eyes) and accept that their speculation has afforded millions of us additional channels to grow our prosperity; it has afforded us more ways to pick ourselves up from the levels of poverty we may be experiencing. Consequently, we will get wealthy, but those that got there first will be wealthier. Inequality is an inherent feature of the free market system that cannot be eradicated because it is a **by-product** of another feature that enables the free market to flourish. That other feature is localized speculation.

In the late 1990s, The Dot-com era saw those that invested in a technology called "The Internet" grow their wealth quite significantly (e.g. Peter Thiel, Elon Musk of Paypal). They were one of the speculators that *'got there first'*, but their speculation (one could replace the word "speculation" with "risk") and success was a signal to the whole society that maybe there's great potential to this technology than we had initially anticipated. A basic understanding of the word speculation should lead one to the basic conclusion that this involves risk. When one speculates, they do not necessarily gamble but fastidiously operate under a cloud of uncertainty fully accepting that their actions carry a high likelihood of failure.

Bitcoin could be another form of speculation that has the potential of obliterating the status quo with regard to governments and its monopolization of fiat currencies. Those currently participating in this speculation will reap great rewards if it turns out to be successful. One can clearly see that the whole society benefits more than any of these individuals who initially speculated due to the fact that the greater society follows a path cleared by the speculators - a particular advantage these risk-takers did not always enjoy. Just like soldiers on the front line, the speculators bear the brunt of things in the face of defeat and are first to the spoils in the event of victory. To believe that a system should allow us to all get rich at-once shows a total lack of the basic understanding of how wealth is generated or generally how life works.

> *Inequality is a feature of the free market system that cannot be eradicated because it is a by-product of another feature that enables the free market to flourish - Inequality is a by-product of Speculation (Risk)*

A free market system is able to eradicate poverty because it, as the name suggests, offers liberty. It is through this liberty that the people are given room to speculate. A regimented society offers its citizens little room to manoeuvre because each act of speculation requires the approval of a central authority - a governing body that has its eyes firmly in the past. The Central Planner's love of certainty causes them to eschew speculation whenever possible. Poverty is eradicated when a government promotes a free market system that allows people to speculate and is at peace with the fact that there will be some people who will become richer than others just as there will be those who will start businesses and fail.

Because Capitalism encourages man to produce goods and services that best serve his fellow man; man (and woman) in general benefits from this state of affairs because he now lives in a society that is constantly searching for means and solutions to alleviate any uneasiness that may hamper his happiness. Since this uneasiness largely stems from impoverishment, the society's collective effort towards the alleviation of uneasiness has the intended result of reducing the levels of poverty. I gather that this **collective effort** is something even our collectivist friends can gladly sign up to.

2. On Liberty

Another virtue of the decentralized society is the levels of liberty it offers to its citizens. Liberty is a difficult virtue to defend because one only appreciates it once it's lost; and when one thinks of the difficulties involved whenever a people strive to regain liberty, one realizes that a loss of liberty is often far more catastrophic than one would have initially imagined – there's little hope that North Koreans and Iranians will ever regain the liberty they lost in the 1940's and 70's.

Why Liberty Matters

Before one delves deeper into the loss of liberty, a good start is in exploring why liberty matters in the first place. Liberty is the avenue through which one exercises freedom. When I talk of liberty, I am simply referring to, amongst several trivial things, 2 main freedoms; the individual's freedom to act and the individual's freedom to property. These freedoms are solely limited by the freedoms equally intrinsic to other individuals; i.e. I may be free to act so long as my actions do not violate another person's liberty. Say I am starving, I am free to embark on any actions that will yield fruits that enable me to alleviate my hunger so long as they do not violate someone else's property or ownership; I am free to embark on actions that earn me money for food but may not steal another person's money or food.

Liberty is thus essential as it affords individuals the opportunity to take actions that they deem necessary to alleviate the uneasiness they may be experiencing. Without Liberty, the individual's actions are severely constrained as the options that should be available to them in a free market society are curtailed. People are restrained from exercising options that would help them make their lives better. A slave is restricted from bettering his or her circumstances as a result of the expropriation of his or her labour.

"You legitimately own a property if you are free to dispose of that property any way you see fit"

Right to property is another facet of liberty that, although easy to ignore, leads to dire consequences for the population the moment it is inhibited or eradicated. When one talks of property, one not only refers to something one can touch, feel, see, produce or destroy, but also includes intangible things such as intellectual property and promises (contracts). In the same case as the liberty to act, the liberty to own property is limited by the freedoms of other individuals.

A case in point is one of slavery; the pro-slavery advocates would often cite 'their liberty' to own property as a defence against the emancipation movement that was gaining momentum in the 17th and 18th centuries. The slave masters were correct in asserting their right to ownership of property; however, they were mistaken in believing that in terms of natural law – a human being can be categorized as property. They believed that the government forcing them to free the slaves off their chains violated their basic right to own property; they believed that their government should defend that ownership, not have it expropriated. Their argument falls apart when they include the human being under the carapace of property.

From the slave master's perspective, one could understand their indignation of having to relinquish something (or in this tragic case...someone) they have bought or invested in, especially since the prevailing law and market conditions allowed for such a transaction to take place. But such is the nature of abolishing anything, just like a pyramid scheme, when the whole thing collapses, the last round of "investors" carry the biggest losses.

Slavery forces us to confront quite an interesting question; can someone own a human being? Or to put it in a slightly more interesting (and leading) way, why can one own a dog but cannot own a human being? Well, the answer goes back to Liberty; the liberty to own property. This property includes the human being's body, a slave cannot be said to have the liberty of property if his whole being belongs to somebody else. You legitimately own a property if you are free to dispose of that property the way you see fit. Slavery thus becomes illegitimate and illiberal because it violates the human being's Liberty to property - in this case, that property being the slave's whole self as well as his labour. Labour is property and is protected by the same basic alienable human rights that protect other forms of property. That's why a wage earner ought to receive remuneration after a hard day's work. Labour, be it physical or mental, is how individuals derive an income. The expropriation of the slave's income was indeed a violation of their property and liberty. The slave master's right to property ends where the slave's right to own property begins.

This leads me to another interesting question, can a human being sell himself; or put differently, say Amaju from my neighbourhood approaches me with an offer I could not refuse? He offers to become my slave doing various chores around the farm (for the rest of his life) in exchange for an immediate payment of R1 million. Could I own him if I were to get his full and unbridled consent? After all, Amaju owns the property of self and he has the liberty to embark on endeavours he deems fit. So, could I find myself in the possession of a slave called Amaju after this transaction? Well, as paradoxical as it may seem, the answer is NO!

At a first glance, Amaju's inability to sell his property, the property of self, may seem like a violation of **his** liberty, but that would be because the interpretation of this situation is incorrect. He cannot sell his autonomy to me because he can always evoke it at any moment he wishes to. Firstly, although the word slave may have been used, Amaju could not be a slave due to having received R1 million for his "slavery". Secondly, I would have deluded myself if I led myself into believing that by consenting to Amaju becoming my slave; he sold me his property of self. By combing through this transaction, I quickly come to realize that I simply "bought" Amaju's services and just decided to pay for these services in advance. This fact becomes more emphasized one morning when I wake up having reached the conclusion that I no longer have any use for Amaju. But instead of simply releasing Amaju from my care, I decide to euthanize him (after all, I own the man), and my false sense of believing that I own Amaju prohibits me from seeing the criminality (nevermind sheer barbarity) of my actions. Cognizant of his impending death, Amaju frantically jumps to his feet and points out that the transaction was R1 million in return for not his life or self, but his work i.e. his services; and he quite frankly asserts that the terms of the transaction are directly hinged on services. Additionally, he points out that I bought the services and if I were no longer in need or desire of his services, it is I who wishes to terminate the terms of the transaction, furthermore, he reminds me of my Liberty to walk away from making use of his services*[196].

I slowly come to the realisation that Amaju never really sold himself, my use of Amaju has always been constrained to the terms that he agreed to. The fact that I never had ownership of Amaju is proven by the fact that I could not make use of Amaju in any way I see fit, (one morning, I saw it fit to kill Amaju but could not do it….legally). We see that even on the smallest scale, Liberty protects the individual – even from himself; and intrinsically, this is why Liberty matters. It offers the individual an opportunity to live freely even in cases where one *sells* himself to slavery (as allegorized in the transaction with Amaju)

The Virtue of Property
Property is a facet of liberty more difficult to defend because when one speaks of property, one thinks of a nice house and vehicle. And our world is in a sad state where millions don't own property, so they are not as enthusiastic about its protection. Property serves a vital role in society because it has two main functions.

---

[196] [Side note; Under objective law, Amaju has the liberty to employ someone to end his life, but my elaborations of this view lay beyond the scope of this book]

1. Property enables us to enter into transactions i.e. money to buy stuff or use our houses, diamond earrings, watches and our bodies for bartering. As mentioned in the free market discussion, transactions enable us to grow our wealth by producing goods that people want. In another rudimentary explanation, the goods are my property and the money I'm after is in the consumer's wallet. I trade my property (my produce) in return for her property (her money) and we are able to enter into this transaction as a result of ownership of property. In this transaction, I may become wealthier as a result of attaining more of what I need and the consumer becomes wealthier as a result of attaining more of what she needs.

"Property makes us wealthier"

2. Another function of Property is that gives us an avenue to store value; the more property we accrue, the wealthier we become. Another way property makes us wealthier is through a significant increase in its perceived value. When discussing Maslow's hierarchy of needs, I stated that the hierarchy of needs forms a pyramid in order of importance, I added that the hierarchy varies for each individual and that it keeps on changing with time.

"The individual's needs are hierarchal and are satisfied in order of importance. Once a need is satisfied, man acts to satisfy the next level of need."

In essence, I may be in the possession of goods that may not be in as high a demand as they will be next year. Consumers may not be willing to pay a higher price for my produce today as a result of these goods not occupying a high status in most people's pyramid of needs. However, like Joseph and the

Pharaoh, I come to learn of an imminent food shortage or drought so I hold on to those goods until such a shortage comes into effect. Now that there's a shortage, my goods gain a higher status in the consumer's hierarchy of needs, rendering consumers more willing to pay a higher price for my produce than what they would have paid before the drought. Like Egypt in biblical times, my storing of property opens up the avenue of increasing my wealth which is derived from selling my produce at a higher price than I would have previously. A society that protects private property ownership is reciprocally protecting its future because it incentivizes its producers to store and invest for the future; thus mitigating the effects of droughts, famines and various shortages should they arise. The earlier discussion on Speculation adds emphasis to this point; investors buy into projects when the share price is low and are able to charge higher prices for these shares when the demand increases. It is also through ownership of property that one can store property in surplus for a "rainy day" when a need for that property suddenly arises. Man resorted to cured meat, pickling and various other methods of food preservation in an effort to store surplus food for a rainy day. The ownership of labour also affords us ways of increasing the value or quality of our labour through the attainment of experience and skills. Liberty is the freedom to act and the freedom to own property.

Harbours Heresy

The Enlightenment Era in the 17th and 18th centuries is largely considered to be one of the Ages that saw humanity take large strides toward the world we live in today. It's an age that produced the likes of Isaac Newton and his book titled *"The Mathematical Principles of Natural Philosophy"*, it's an age that gave us Adam Smith's *Wealth of Nations* and *...gifted* humanity a man called Jean-Jacques Rousseau and *The Social Contract.* It was during this period that the debate on the separation of church and state was settled and it was also during this period that one of the 2 powerful modern nations, the United States of America, was born.

The examples are quite numerous; however, my reason for bringing up the age of enlightenment is to accentuate the point that although these events were heretical in their infancy, they were made possible by a political environment that accommodated heresy in the name of Liberty. This period proves that one of the virtues of Liberty is that it allows a people to question prevailing dogmas and *'settled sciences'*. This has been well documented in the scientific field, or to be more precise, scientific discoveries. When one looks at scientific discoveries, one notices that these discoveries came from sources within the minority camp of the scientific field rather than of the majority; sources that had to withstand public persecution and condemnation coming from the social and governing elite with the full backing of the majority within the same field. These were individuals questioning the collective. As George Bernard Shaw stated;

"All great truths begin as blasphemies"

For instance, Hungarian physician and obstetrician, (a doctor specializing in childbirth and women's reproductive system), Ignaz Semmelweis was literally ridiculed all the way to the asylum when he tried to convince his colleagues that washing their hands before performing any medical procedures could significantly reduce the post op deaths (mortality rate) of the women in his birthing ward. In those days, it was common practice for doctors to transition from operating on cadavers to live human beings without adequately washing their hands; resulting in numerous deaths as some patients developed puerperal fever - one of the bacterial infections following childbirth or miscarriages. Dr Ignaz Semmelweis penned his findings in his book *"Etiology, Concept and Prophylaxis of Childbed Fever";* but this work together with an actual significant drop in deaths, did little to change the prevailing opinions of the general medical community. This unconventional wisdom was so left-field that even the Pest University maternity clinic, where Semmelweis operated from, returned to its old ways once the doctor left. This was despite the hospital having witnessed the decline in mortality rate first-hand. Even though Dr Semmelweis' science was correct and is widely accepted today, he sadly did not live to see the widespread implementation of his discovery, which could explain the melancholic depression he suffered in his lifetime.

Dogma – the belief in theory over one's eyes.

Some medical practitioners were not as lucky as Dr Semmelweis, considering the fact that he was not thrown in prison or guillotined as many scientists were in the past centuries. Tim Noakes, a South African scientist and professor in the *Division of Exercise Science and Sports Medicine* at the University of Cape Town, is a more recent example of individuals persecuted for their heterodox opinions and public declamations. He was hauled before a tribunal committee when The Health Professionals Council of South Africa (HSPCA) accused him of "unprofessional conduct" for giving "unconventional" advice to a breastfeeding mother and for advocating for the "low-carb, high-fat diet". In numerous "trials", the professor had to defend himself against the prevailing orthodox practices despite having documented extensive research supporting his claims.

Science is Heretic

Author Frank Sulloway wrote a whole book titled *Born To Rebel*, documenting similar examples throughout history. He goes through a few discoveries and theories that were at one point heretical positions that were only prevalent in the minority and in contravention of the majority's views. Theories like Nicolaus Copernicus' Copernican revolution which introduced a theory that went against the prevailing scientific opinions within the astronomy community; the community which had a geocentric view of the sun revolving around the stationery planet Earth.

The book also explores the receptions of Charles Darwin's Origin of Species, germ theory, Continental drift and William Harvey with regards to blood circulation; it explains how these were at the receiving end of hostile receptions from the prevailing scientific elite that felt threatened by this immerging minority view.

I am not suggesting that views in the minority are always on the correct side, but merely listing these examples to show that there are instances where heterodox views that countered prevailing orthodox proved to be correct in the end. It is to show that a lot of scientific breakthroughs came from minority circles and ultimately, I list these examples to prove how the scientific field benefits from liberty and individual actions. Individuals need liberty to question and explore without fear of persecution.

Slowly They Inch

When one looks at history, one quickly learns that totalitarian regimes hardly come into power overnight; they often begin as promising movements led by promising leaders gradually evolving into despotic presidents building regimes that rip citizens off their civil liberties. Fortunately for us, totalitarianism is so incompatible with liberty that the very first step any leadership takes toward totalitarianism is the curbing of liberty; to paraphrase professor Gad Saad - *"slowly they inch"*.

Tyranny, though highly scalable (sadly), always starts at a small scale; it always starts at the individual level. The Nazis started with the Jew, the Bolsheviks went after the kulak, Said Barre terrorized the Isaaq and Idi Amin went after the Asian. The point is these tyrannical actions always take place at a lower level before they are scaled to the national level, or for those ambitious enough, an international level. Today's maltreatment of the individual is a window to tomorrow's maltreatment of the collective.

This is one of the main reasons why a populace needs to have a keen understanding of liberty so that they can sense it once their government inches towards curbing liberty. Because liberty is a worldview, those who don't hold liberty as a value have no guardrails that protect them against totalitarianism or any government encroaching on their liberty. This lack of awareness is one reason it may be important to offer people a tangible symbol of liberty that serves as an alarm bell for people whenever their liberty is threatened.

The Virtues of Decentralization

"Liberty is a value" – Dennis Prager

For Americans, the Second Amendment to the United States Constitution may serve as this symbol. I think we can all accept that an armed citizenry may not be strong enough to defend itself against the modern state army (or past states for that matter) but whether one agrees with it or not, there's no denying that the right to bear arms can act as a symbol of liberty that serves to notify the population whenever a government inches towards their liberties. The federalists were keenly aware of the fact that a despotic leadership at some point moves toward disarming the population. They were fully cognizant of the fact that even those who lack any fundamental understanding of liberty can sense an encroachment against their liberty when they are given a tangible notion that symbolizes liberty. For the American, the 2nd amendment symbolizes liberty.

Abortion may be another symbol for the woman's 'emancipation' movement. The fact that the prohibition on abortion was seen as one of the fundamental elements in a repressive society, access to free abortions became a symbol of the woman's emancipation. Freedom of the Press may act as a symbol for the British who are historically renowned for their veneration of free speech and the newspaper's freedom to report whatever issue they see as a matter of public interest. Whether one agrees with these symbols or not, I think these examples prove that having a tangible facet of life may improve a people's sensibility to liberty or in this case, the loss of it. The people may not be keenly aware of what liberty is, but having something tangible symbolizing that liberty serves as an alarm bell in the face of an encroaching tyrannical government.

3. The Individual vs The Collective

The virtue of a free market society (and decentralization) is that it fosters a better environment for the individual. As I have documented, it eradicates poverty, it prevents tyranny and it protects the individual's liberty. Fundamentally, it breeds an environment better suited for the individual.

But what if we are faced with a policy that achieves a greater good collectively but comes at the detriment of individual liberty? For instance, what if a very charismatic politician proposed a policy that forced individuals to participate in a Ponzi scheme; say a government feeding scheme. After all, surely everybody being covered by this scheme serves a greater good; nobody goes without services offered by this scheme when in need. The proponents of this scheme may go on to say; *"So what if some individuals have to be coerced, it's not like the collective good brought on by the scheme is worse than the bad brought on by this government's coercion"*. When individualism is pitted against collectivism, why should individualism prevail? They'll continue; *What is so sacred about this individual that he or she should not be coerced (sacrificed) for the collective good? In purely mathematical terms, why must 1 prevail over 100 as even pure mathematics asserts that 100 is more than 1?*

Well, my above assertion that tyranny always starts at the individual level partly explains why individualism should always prevail. But I think that it is necessary to emphasize this point.

The Society
There are two ways in which one can attain an individual's commitment to serving the collectivist's ends.

You can incentivise him to offer you his commitment to serve. This, however, requires you to offer him something in return. The individual's option to offer entails an option to withhold. The individual, let's call him Musa, is keenly aware of the fact that he owes you nothing for his commitment and that if you wish to get his commitment, you will have to offer him something in return; and that something must be of certain value justifying the commitment. But there is another option that would enable you to rob Musa off this agency.

The second option would be to convince Musa that he is obligated to serve the group; or even better, you convince Musa's fellow citizens that he is obligated to serve the group. But how would you achieve this mafia-like tactic? Well, you sit him down and "remind" him of his surroundings and "educate" him about this construction called Society. You remind him that he is part of this Society, like a fish is to the ocean. The fish may not be aware of the ocean in the same way the human being may not be aware of Society, but this lack of awareness would surely not discount the ocean's existence. You go on to convince Musa that this Society is an independent sovereign entity that possesses independent rights. It is a wholly separate entity that has an independent will and operates independently towards the achievement of that will. You argue that since human beings are part of this Society, human beings are somewhat subordinate to this "Society". That the individual is expected to do everything within their power to ensure that this "Society" achieves its will.

If "society's" will is egalitarianism, then man, as argued by Jean-Jacques Rousseau's *Social Contract,* is expected to make personal sacrifices in honour of the collective will.

One notices that this skewed representation of "Society" does not offer Musa an option to opt-out of this servitude. But how is this representation of society skewed?

It is skewed in the sense that society cannot have an independent goal because it cannot have an independent ideal. There was never a man called 'Society'*[197], so there was never a *Society vs Individual* dichotomy; only individuals vs individuals, with one side having a majority over the other. Society - the Collective - is an amalgamation of individuals that may wish to pursue the same actions but for various reasons and are willing to go to various extents in achieving those goals, as Mises said;

Action is always action of individual men.

The aim behind the personification of Society is to establish avenues in order to expropriate the individual off his autonomy. It is to absolve the expropriators from any obligation to compensate the individuals on the receiving end of the expropriation. "For the good of the Society" means for the benefit of a band of individuals.

Now let's go back to the above-mentioned proposed policy which supposedly aims to achieve a greater good collectively. When the charismatic politician argues that it's for the greater collective good, he is essentially arguing that a greater number of individuals will benefit from this policy at the expense of the smaller number of individuals. The smaller number of

---

[197] Okay, maybe one guy on the other side of town.

individuals is forced to serve the greater number of individuals, hence the talk of sacrifice. That is the supposed "greater good"; remember tyranny always starts at a small scale. But as John Stuart Mill so eloquently said;

> *If all mankind minus one were of one opinion, and only one person were of the contrary opinion, mankind would be no more justified in silencing that one person, than he, if he had the power, would be justified in silencing mankind.*

Note on (South) Africa's Land Issue

In South Africa, I believe that the African National Congress (ANC) is not moving quickly enough in resolving the land issue. The apartheid government confiscated land from black South Africans and gave it to the minority ruling class; this meant that less than 10% of the populace was in the ownership of 87% of the land. The ANC had proposed to compensate those that had their land expropriated by the apartheid government; to their credit, some have been compensated, but sadly, they are in the minority. Post-apartheid, the numbers haven't moved much and a lot of black South Africans still have little economic opportunity due to the fact that a majority inherited little from their parents who had no land or means to pass on to them.

The newly democratically elected South African government passed *The Restitution of Land Rights Act (No. 22 of 1994),* this act was to remedy the damage caused by policies that forcibly moved people from their homes between 1913 and 1994. As stated in its preamble, the purpose of this act is to;

> *To provide for the restitution of rights in land to persons or communities dispossessed of such rights after 19 June 1913 as a result of past racially discriminatory laws or practices; to establish a Commission on Restitution of Land Rights and a*

Land Claims Court; and to provide for matters connected therewith.

The National Party's grand Apartheid Homelands policy is one of these inhumane policies addressed by this act. A policy which led to more than 3 million people being forcibly moved from the lands, some of these people had owned and lived in these lands for generations.

In claims that are valid, instances where an individual or a community lodge a claim in accordance with the act, the Land Claims Court may compensate the claimant(s) in three ways;
>   i. Hand over the land you were due to have restored to you
>   ii. Issue alternative land or
>   iii. Monetary compensation

South Africa's Land Claim issue is another domain that pits collectivism against individualism. This is accomplished by the 2 ways in which claimants are compensated. In 99% of the cases where land is restored (or alternative land is issued), this land is issued to a collective in a form of a tribe, a communal society or a particular dynasty. The collective elation gradually subsides once each member wakes up to the fact that the land may be theirs collectively but not really theirs in any individual sense - i.e. it cannot be used to pursue personal ends. As we know by now, you only own property if you can use, sell or rent it out for money, all three prerequisites must be present.

But in this context, the claimants soon learn that the communal land portioned to them cannot be sold. They learn that the use of that land has to be approved by the communal "stakeholders". They realize, as showcased in George Orwell's *Animal Farm*, that the best lands are reserved for the inner circle of the

257

communal leadership. They also realize, to their credit, that it would be unwise to make any long-term investments on such lands because the 'stakeholders' might decide to designate those lands for other uses once the investments start to yield fruit.

Then the words of a very charismatic author come back to mind; *"You legitimately own a property if you are free to dispose of that property any way you see fit"*, these words help them realize that they were not GIVEN back any land in the true meaning of the word.

It's for this reason that I always advocate for monetary compensation in this Land Issue debate. By offering monetary compensation, the government manages to perfectly balance the delicate issue of property rights (and the freedom to own property) while still addressing the cries of many families that had lands inhumanely expropriated from them in the past. The monetary compensation is the truest form of compensation because one is free to use that property (money) in any way they see fit. It affords the recipient an opportunity to purchase true property, a property they can invest in, upgrade and sell for profit or leverage it against other bonds and bank loans (surety, contracts etc.).

Because of this delay, today we see that frustrations are boiling over, and we are seeing a reprisal of Marxist movements gaining ground on this very issue; calling for the expropriation and nationalization of land, land ownership that will be centralized into the hands of the government for equal redistribution. Our neighbours and scholars of history will be quite familiar with the consequences such actions produce, but our collective mindset (and frustrations) leaves us open to such a message. I am quite disillusioned by the South African government's slow pace in addressing the land issue as the delay in settling land claims is starting to generate agitation, especially among individuals who are certain that their claims are valid. Newly elected into his presidency, President Ramaphosa faced newly invigorated calls to pass the Amendment of Section 25 of the Constitution, to pave the way for Land Expropriation without compensation. Such calls were validated by claimants that had valid claims but were yet to be awarded any kind of compensation. This is an issue that should have been addressed more than a decade ago during the first 2 administrations.

Jomo Kenyatta was confronted with this same issue when he was elected into office as the first black Kenyan President. Under British colonial rule, Kenyans lost vast amounts of land they had owned for decades as a result of British land expropriation, a phenomenon all Africans are all too familiar with. As Historian Paul Johnson wrote;

> *"..the White Highlands was cleared of its Kikuyu inhabitants to make way for white farmers. In the 1930s, there were in Kenya 53,000 square miles of African reserves, 16,700 reserved for Europeans and 99,000 of crown lands[198]."*

In times of war

Then what happens in a time of war, should individualism take precedence over collectivism? This is another question people often ask, pitting Collectivism against Individualism. To help answer this question, we'll need to understand the choices available to each individual in a country that's fighting a war. Say my country is under attack but I choose to not enlist for

---

[198] Johnson, Paul – History of the Modern World page 159

combat citing my right to do so; in essence, citing my individualism. Should my individualism prevail over the collective calls shouting that I *man-up* to defend my country?

Now whether I join the defence effort or not, I am fully cognizant of the fact that the outcome of that war will affect me directly. I am fully aware of the fact that if my country suffers defeat, my community will be invaded by foreign peoples moving in to enforce their foreign wills. My home will be destroyed; my relatives' homes will be destroyed and my country, community and family life will be transformed. So what would be the reason for my refusal to participate in the war effort despite knowing what is at stake?

One reason would be that I am secretly (or openly) in favour of my country's defeat. I am aware that my refusal to participate weakens my country's war effort; maybe I am that German citizen that secretly rooted for the Allied forces.

But what would explain my actions If I were rooting for my country to win. Then clearly I would be hoping to reap the benefits of what comes with victory without having put any effort in it. As I said, I am always fully cognizant of the fact that the outcome of that war will affect me directly. So in a victory, I get to share the spoils without having taken any risks that come with the military defence effort. I would have merely "relied" on other individuals' risk-taking, hoping to enjoy the liberties that come with victory without having fought for them. When you conscript a man to defend his home, you are preventing him from leeching on the works and sacrifices of other men who fight to defend his home. He cannot be allowed to be in a situation where he benefits from other people's efforts if he does not offer any effort himself.

The Virtues of Decentralization

I purposefully framed my analogy in the form of a country defending itself from an invasion by another country because I believe that it is the only kind of war that can justify conscription. It is the only time collectivism may take precedence over individualism because it is a state of abnormality. I nonetheless remain conflicted by this conclusion as I have read of many instances where leaders ordered young men to fight wars that offered little hope of survival nevermind victory.

This reasoning is erroneously followed in societies that wage war on other nations. These nations - often dictatorships, conscript millions of men into military campaigns that aim to achieve goals wholly unrelated to them i.e. Invading Iraq in search of weapons of mass destruction. This explains why authoritarians always keep their societies in a continuous state of war, a state of victimhood that assists in convincing (and justifying) the populace to buy into the prevailing collectivism. What makes this conscription so grotesque is that in this conscription, you are conscripting one individual to fight for another individual's interests, not his or her own.

This still goes back to the individual; the reason why Individualism prevails over collectivism is because collectivism is never really collectivism. These acts are never synchronized with one another, even in "collectivism", one individual coerces another individual. To paraphrase Ludwig von Mises, *"Collective Action is always actions of individual men"*

The encompassing virtue of Decentralization is that it protects the individual, this is crucial because one can only act against the collective by first acting against individuals. Therefore, decentralization protects against despotism because it unmasks despotism in its infancy.

Decentralization leaves avenues open for discovery as each individual is granted avenues to explore ways in which he can produce. As already established, one maximizes production for themselves by helping others the most. As a result, each individual is constantly searching for ways to best produce for their fellow human beings. This is how the continent of Africa will turn the tide toward prosperity – this is why collectivism matters.

Conclusion

Collectivism has given us freedom from colonization; it has also given us endless poor governments, civil wars, coups d'etats and juntas. We should not wish to revert to colonialism but adopt the liberal values (in the classic sense) that brought the outside world out of the very same malaise we are currently suffering today.

Steve Biko

I've always wondered why the apartheid government took such a heavy-handed approach when confronting Steve Biko, and finally got to my answer once I read about the man's work. With the Black consciousness movement, he advocated for change in one's thinking, teaching the average black man to see the white man truly as his equal. This is trivial in today's world but was quite radical in the 1970's apartheid where there were many well-meaning, kind-hearted black people that genuinely believed that the white man held a certain superiority. Steve Biko was affecting minds because he understood that long-lasting change starts with a mindset. Once the mind sees things through a different lens, it starts reacting differently. Biko said

> **"Black Consciousness is an attitude of the mind and a way of life, the most positive call to emanate from the black world for a long time."**

And from this quote I will conclude;

> **"Liberty is an attitude of the mind and a way of life, the most positive call to emanate from Africa for a long time."**

Thank you for reading my book.

Resources

Books

Alsény René Gomez,	- La Guinée peut-elle être change (Can Guinea be changed?)
Johnson, Paul	- History of the Modern World
Valery Besong	- Coup d'etats in Africa: The Emergence, Prevalence &
Eradication	
Frederik W de Klerk	- The Last Trek

Guy Arnold,	- Africa, A Modern History
Ludwig von Mises,	- Socialism
Ran Abramitzky	- Mystery of the Kibbutz into daily life within this society
Karl Marx	- *Critique of Hegel's Philosophy of Right* essay
Thomas More	- Utopia

GH Sabine	- A History Of Political Theory 3rd edition
William Doyle	- The French Revolution
Paul Johnson	- Intellectuals
Jean-Jaque Rousseau	- The Social Contract (Christopher Betts)
Roger Scruton	- Fools, Frauds and Firebrands

Collin Haydon and William Doyle– Robespierre
JM Thompson	- Robespierre
David Priestland	- The Red Flag

Karl Marx & Freidrich Engels - The Communist Manifesto, (Intro by Stedman Jones) Penguin Edition

Robert L. Heilbroner,	- The Worldly Philosophers
Ludwig von Mises	- Theory and History
Ludwig von Mises	- Marxism Unmasked
Karl Marx	- Das Kapital Volume 1
Karl R Popper,	- The Open Society and Its Enemies
Vladimir Lenin,	- State and Revolution

Karl Marx & Freidrich Engels - A Critique of The German Ideology

Paul Johnson	- History Of Christianity
Thomas Sowell	- Wealth, Poverty and Politics
Thomas Packenham	- The Scramble for Africa
Kahin McTurnan	- The Afro Asia Conference

Frantz Fanon	- Toward the African Revolution
Malcolm Gladwell	- Outliers
Gilbert K. Chesterton,	- Orthodoxy

John Bowker	- Beliefs That Changed The world
Stephan Feuchtwang,	- Handbook on Religion in China
Giovanni. Gentilè	- Che cosa e il fascismo? Discorse e polemichi, Florence.
J.B Druck,	- Weiß´sche Buchdruckerei - Das Programm der NSDAP
Isabel V. Hull	- Absolute Destruction; page

Christi vd Westhuizen - White Power
Ludwig von Mises   - Human Action
FAA-H-8083-9A, Aviation Instructor's Handbook
Erusmas, B ; Strydom, Johan, Kloppers, Sharon - Introduction to Business Management

Thomas Sowell   - Basic Economics
William Shakespeare - Othello
Karl R. Popper   - Conjectures and Refutations
Ron Paul   -The Revolution; A Manifesto

Websites

www.fragilestatesindex.org
www.bbc.com
www.wigandiggersfestival.org
www.culturematters.org.uk
www.courses.lumenlearning.com
www.nytimes.com
www.ethics.utoronto.ca
www.nrzam.org.uk
www.alphahistory.com
www.cnn.com
www.gem-report-2017.unesco.org
www.unctad.org
www.facebook.com
www.dailymaverick.co.za
www.dsausa.org
www.gupta-leaks.com
www.makaangola.org
www.sciencespo.fr
www.statista.com
www.vox.com
www.farmersweekly.co.za
www.sahistory.org.za

www.allafrica.com
www.worldbank.org
www.marxists.org
www.britannica.com
www.bugandawatch.com
www.africanactivist.msu.edu
www.skybrary.aero
www.historyza.blogspot.com
www.atrocitieswatch.org
www.encyclopedia.ushmm.org
www.honestmediablog.com
www.unesdoc.unesco.org
www.bbc.com
www.juliusnyerere.org
www.encyclopedia.com
www.iol.co.za
www.peoplesworld.org
www.simplypsychology.org
www.theguardian.com
www.youtube.com
www.zimfieldguide.com

Papers and Reports

Lagos Plan of Action – Point number 5
Life below Zero season 5 episode 4
Julius Nyerere's- "Ujamaa—the Basis of African Socialism